Maangchi's
Real Korean Cooking

Maangchi's
Real Korean Cooking

Authentic Dishes for the Home Cook

Maangchi

with Lauren Chattman

Photographs by Maangchi

A RUX MARTIN BOOK
Houghton Mifflin Harcourt
Boston • New York

For information about permission to reproduce selections from this book, write to trade.
permissions@hmhco.com or to Permissions, Houghton Mifflin Harcourt Publishing
Company, 3 Park Avenue, 19th Floor, New York, New York 10016.

www.hmhco.com

Library of Congress Cataloging-in-Publication Data
Maangchi.
  Maangchi's real Korean cooking : authentic dishes for the home cook / Maangchi with
Lauren Chattman ; photographs by Maangchi.
      pages cm
  ISBN 978-0-544-12989-4 (hardcover) — ISBN 978-0-544-46575-6 (ebook)
1. Cooking, Korean. I. Chattman, Lauren. II. Title.
  TX724.5.K65M33 2015
  641.59519 — dc23

Book design by Hirsheimer & Hamilton

Printed in China
SCP 10 9
4500657051

**To David,
for always being there**

ACKNOWLEDGMENTS

Writing and photographing this book has been a huge job and a long journey, huger and longer than I expected. It would not have been possible without the support and limitless help of my husband, David. Since I started sharing my recipes via videos and my website, he's always been there to guide me to the next step.

I also can't thank my website readers and viewers enough for trusting me and my recipes. They've always been passionate cooks and tireless recipe testers, and when I hear about their successes in the kitchen, I feel so proud.

I also want to thank the wonderful professional book people who saw this through from start to finish: Janis Donnaud, my agent, for believing in me from the very beginning; Lauren Chattman, for being a talented writing partner; Rux Martin, my editor, for her guidance and encouragement; Jacqueline Beach, for her fast work on last-minute changes; Christopher Hirsheimer and Melissa Hamilton, for their skillful photo editing and magnificent design; Paul Brissman, for the cover photo; and Roy Finamore, for his tough editing and persistent questions that sometimes made me laugh. I'm very lucky to have had the chance to work with the best of the best.

My mom encouraged me throughout the long process of writing this book, and she was always worried about my health if I worked too hard. Thanks for everything, Mom!

All the recipes in this book were made for or inspired by my children, Chan and Hwanhee. Everything I do, I do with them in mind, and sharing my food with them makes me happier than anything else in the world. Cooking for them is everything to me. If the recipes are in this book, it's because they said they were delicious.

CONTENTS

Facing page: clockwise from top left, Cold Noodle Soup (page 58); Korean Fried Chicken (page 220); Green Chili Peppers Seasoned with Soybean Paste (page 132); Cooked and Seasoned Soybean Sprouts (page 140); Dried Persimmons (page 15); Crispy Pork with Sweet-and-Sour Sauce (page 234); Fernbrake with Garlic and Soy (page 146); Napa Cabbage Kimchi (page 114).

INTRODUCTION

Hi, everybody!

For those of you who aren't already my old friends, let me introduce myself. I'm not a professional chef. I didn't go to culinary school. I've never owned or worked in a restaurant. But as long as I can remember, I've been fascinated by food—eating it, of course, but also by how it was made, and how I could make it myself at home.

I was born in Imsil in North Jeolla Province and raised in Yeosu, South Korea, which is on the southernmost tip of South Jeolla, the southernmost province of the peninsula. Korea is a nation of food lovers. In daily life, delicious food is a given, to be devoured with gusto, and so it goes without saying that no party, no vacation, no occasion happens without something special being prepared. South Jeolla Province has a reputation for its wonderful food, and the people of Yeosu have the ability to make any type of fish that comes from surrounding waters taste incredible. Their dishes may be spicy or not, raw or fermented, and stewed, braised, or roasted over charcoal. My father owned and ran a fish auction business, and fishermen came from all over to sell their fish there. In gratitude, they often left my family samples of their best catch. We weren't rich by a long shot, but we always had great seafood.

From an early age, I was interested in what my mom, grandmother, and aunts were cooking and would quietly determine who made the best version of each dish. I also watched the women in the marketplace who were known for certain special dishes and paid close attention to how they made them.

I was a very social kid and a real organizer. I would schedule lunches with my friends, telling each one which dish or ingredient to bring to school that day. When we put everything together, we'd have a meal all the other kids would envy—a real feast of bibimbap, the one-dish rice meal full of tasty components like sunny-side-up eggs, hot pepper paste, cooked soybean sprouts, sesame oil, and various other colorful vegetables.

I was sent off to high school in Seoul, where my family thought I would get a better education. Moving to the big city on my own was thrilling, and it gave me a chance to cook more. The friends I made in school were all foodies. Whenever we had free time on a weekend, we would cook something at one of our houses.

One of my favorite things has always been sharing my knowledge, so after finishing high school, I went to teachers college in Seoul and got a certificate in social studies. University life convinced me that I wanted to be a college professor, and so I got a master's degree in education. I became a teaching assistant and then a research assistant and a part-time professor, but before I could start my career in

Facing page: clockwise from top left, L.A. YouTube studio; shooting in the Netherlands with a fan; a fishmarket in Mexico; eating noodles with black bean paste in L.A.; taking photos in my N.Y. kitchen.

earnest, I got married. My husband was a university professor as well, and when he got a posting in the city of Gwangju, in South Jeolla Province, we moved south, and I put my dream of being a full professor on hold to build our family.

I had a son and then a daughter, and my passion for cooking turned toward my little family. I poured everything I had into making the best food I could for them. While the children were still young, my husband got the chance to study for his PhD in Columbia, Missouri. I was apprehensive about moving to the United States, but I knew it would be good for the children to learn English at a young age, and it would be good for my husband's career, so off we went.

expat korean cooking

Missouri was an eye-opener for me. Part of it was living in America, of course, but part of it was the Korean expat community I found there. The small group of people had come from all over the country, and we helped and encouraged each other— and shared delicious home-cooked Korean meals at epic potluck parties. Every woman brought her best dishes, and as we ate them, we discussed how they were made. As a result, I learned about many regional recipes that I would never have tasted if I hadn't left Korea.

When my husband finished his degree, our family moved back to Korea. But after my children grew up, my husband and I divorced, and I returned to North America to start over in Toronto. I did all kinds of things to make a living: I was a cashier in my neighborhood grocery store, a movie extra, a translator, and an interpreter, and I also taught English grammar to Korean immigrants and students. It was difficult to be so far from my daughter, who was in college in Korea, and my son, who was working in Silicon Valley, but I was trying so many new things that it was always interesting, and I was grateful that I could make a living and be independent.

No matter what I was doing, food was always on my mind. Watching customers buy sandwiches at lunchtime gave me the idea to sell gimbap (rice rolled up in sea-weed paper, a bit like sushi) and Korean fried chicken in the store. I made a batch of my killer Korean fried chicken with peanuts and brought it in to convince the manager that it would be a top seller. The other cashiers raved about it, but it turned out that the most important judge, the manager, had a peanut allergy, so he couldn't even taste it!

maangchi is born

I eventually landed a good job as a family counselor at a nonprofit organization, help-ing Koreans adjust to life in the West. I also developed a new hobby: playing online computer games. I found that I could turn on the computer every night and make friends in Singapore, Los Angeles, and Montreal as I ran around in a virtual world, fighting bad guys. We had camaraderie, mayhem, a sense of accomplishment—

even fashion. My character was a tough, sexy fighter with purple hair and a big hammer. I led the team to battle and knocked the biggest enemies down. For a name, I chose *Maangchi*, "hammer" in Korean: a cool name for a tough girl.

Right around this time, YouTube was rapidly gaining popularity. It was my computer-savvy son who suggested to me that I make videos about cooking Korean food and upload them there. There were already a few Korean cooking videos on YouTube, but I knew I could do better, and there was a video function on my digital camera. It sounded like fun!

At first, though, I was afraid to show my face. My son suggested that I could just show my hands at work, and I thought about that for a few weeks. Then I decided that if I was going to do it, I would *really* do it. I'd show my face, and everyone would know who I was.

In April 2007 I filmed myself cooking ojingeo-bokkeum, a sweet and spicy stir-fried squid dish. I edited it the next day. I added a Morrissey song for background, which might have been too loud. The camera wasn't always in focus, and the smoke detector went off. But I thought the video was great, and my recipe, of course, was totally delicious. I chose Maangchi as my account username, uploaded the video to the website, watched it there, and went to bed.

"For a name, I chose Maangchi, 'hammer' in Korean: a cool name for a tough girl."

A few days later I found that people had started posting comments. They had questions about ingredients. They wanted to know what kind of hot pepper flakes and soy sauce I used, and where they could buy them. They also gave me a lot of encouragement. But mostly they wanted to know when my next video was coming. I filmed and edited one for doenjang-jjigae—a fermented bean paste stew with shrimp, tofu, and vegetables—and uploaded it about ten days later. And ever since then, I've been posting Korean cooking videos regularly to YouTube, which has brought together all my lifelong passions: cooking, teaching, meeting new people, and learning about different cultures. Inundated with comments, e-mails, and questions, I no longer had time for video games. My good friend Dave—now my husband—helped me create my own website, www.maangchi.com, and I put up my videos there, as well as recipes and information and photos of hard-to-find Korean ingredients. The site became a forum where everyone could talk to each other and chime in with their own answers to other readers' questions about Korean cooking. Eventually my site grew so popular that I was able to leave my job, move to New York City, and become Maangchi full-time.

maangchi and friends

The readers of my website live all over the world. Many have wandered into a Korean restaurant, been stunned by tastes they have never tried before, and want to re-create them at home. Some have traveled to Korea, loved the food, and want to learn how to prepare it at home. Others are second-generation Koreans who grew up with their mothers' authentic Korean food but never learned how to make it. Some are Korean adoptees who left their homes when they were very little. Some married into Korean families or adopted Korean children.

Their reasons for wanting to learn how to cook Korean food are incredibly varied, but they all come with tons of questions: Can I make my own hot pepper paste? How long does kimchi last in the fridge? What is jjajangmyeon? What dishes can I make if I'm a vegetarian? A Muslim? Can I make my own rice flour with rice? What's a good substitute for fish sauce?

These questions were understandable. Few Korean recipes had been adapted for English speakers. The descriptions on restaurant menus can be confusing and often the waitstaff doesn't speak English. It's hard for Westerners to navigate a Korean grocery store if there even is one nearby—because English translations on packages are often inaccurate. Sometimes when I posted a recipe, I turned out to be the first person on the Internet to mention the dish's English name, let alone explain how to make it.

"Cook your way through this book, and you will discover the wonderful variety that exists in traditional Korean cuisine."

However, my job "translating" Korean cuisine for a Western audience is made much easier by the versatility and diversity of my nation's cooking. Because of the country's geography, Koreans have always had a variety of ingredients to choose from and have been resourceful and creative with substitutions (see page 10). The country was isolated for long periods of time, so imported foodstuffs were few and "eating local" has been a way of life for centuries. Moreover, we've been practicing some of America's favorite ways of cooking—marinating, skewering, and grilling or barbecuing meat—since the beginning of recorded time. In addition, Buddhist influence gave rise to many vegetarian dishes.

Cook your way through this book, and you will discover the wonderful variety that exists in traditional Korean cuisine. There is lots of seafood, the result of a country bounded on three sides by water. We love beef and pork, but our cooking has always featured plenty of vegetarian food, a legacy of our history as mountain foragers and Buddhists. Koreans are famous for their spicy dishes, but we also cook lots of mild ones. We love casual street food, but we are also proud of our refined and beautiful Royal Court cuisine. Always we are mindful of the connection between food and good health. Long before scientists discovered the healthfulness of fermented foods, we were consuming kimchi by the gallon. Recipes like Seaweed Soup (page 89) and Ginseng Candy (page 293) are prized for their rejuvenating properties as well as their flavor.

Kimchi and rice are always on the table. But these foundational elements, far from being monotonous, are served in amazingly different ways. Various kimchis add complexity to soups and stews, lend brininess to cold noodle dishes, are used in savory appetizer pancakes, and round out the endless variety of side dishes that can be part of a meal. Rice dishes, too, change character, from a soothing break- fast (Sesame Seed Porridge, page 75) to a dessert (Panfried Sweet Rice Cakes with Edible Flowers, page 286) to an invigorating and malty beverage (Rice Punch). The crunchy cooked rice at the bottom of the pot (nurungji) is one of our prized snacks.

From the beginning, I knew I had countless recipes to share—I could continue for years and never finish. My goal has been to make this the essential cookbook for anyone who wants to learn how to cook real Korean food. As you cook my Korean food, your refrigerator will fill up with containers of all sorts of good things— substantial side dishes, hot pepper paste, fermented bean paste, kimchi made with cabbage, radishes, or cucumbers—all waiting to be used for flavorful breakfasts, lunches, or dinners.

Note: The Korean words in this book have been romanized using the rules of the Revised Romanization of Korean in accordance with the Korean Food Foundation's *Korean Food Guide in English* (2003). Hyphens have been added to assist in pro- nunciation. (All syllables are equally accented.) You should be able to use this book to order anything you want at a Korean restaurant or need at a grocery store.

the essential korean pantry

Whenever I travel, I always pack the following ingredients. With just these few basic supplies, you'll be able to make many of the recipes in this book:

Fermented soybean paste (doenjang)

Fish sauce (aekjeot)

Korean hot pepper flakes (gochu-garu)

Korean hot red pepper paste (gochujang)

Short-grain white rice (mep-ssal)

Soy sauce (jin-ganjang)

Toasted sesame oil (cham-gi-reum)

THE KOREAN MEAL

An authentic Korean meal is prepared and presented differently from a Western one (although you can certainly use the recipes in this book to make a Western-style meal). To begin with, all the dishes (except for dessert) are placed on the table at the same time.

rice: the foundation

With just a few exceptions (meals based around certain noodle dishes, porridge, dumplings, or rice cake soup), most Korean meals are built around a bowl of rice. Rice is more than a main dish. In fact, the Korean word for rice, *bap*, is also used to mean "meal."

kimchi, soup or stew (sometimes both), and sauce

At a traditional Korean meal, the rice is served with three other basic components: kimchi, soup or stew, and a small bowl of soy sauce. These three components are so essential that they're considered requirements rather than separate dishes, although these days most Koreans omit the sauce, for simplicity's sake.

A great deal of variety and diversity is possible with this simple arrangement. Kimchi is fermented, so the same batch will taste different over time. And there are many kinds, so there's a lot of choice. The same is true of soup and stew, with many variations on basic recipes. The most popular Korean soup, fermented soybean paste soup, is made with different vegetables depending on the season, so the flavor and texture is always different.

banchan

The rest of the meal consists of *banchan*, often translated as "side dishes." These might include a fresh, cooked, or fermented vegetable dish; a pancake; braised seafood or grilled or panfried fish or meat; fermented seafood; raw fish with a sauce; and a stir-fried fish dish.

Traditionally, banchan are served in groups of three, five, seven, nine, or twelve, with three for the simplest meal and twelve a meal for a king. A traditional three-dish meal (sam cheop bansang) consists of rice, kimchi, and soup served with three banchan and a small bowl of soy sauce—so it's really a seven-dish meal. (However, these days, busy cooks might not prepare any side dishes at all and simply stick to a quick meal of rice, kimchi, and soup or stew.)

the five elements

According to ancient Chinese philosophy adopted by Koreans, five elements govern everything in the cosmos: wood, fire, earth, metal, and water. How these elements work together can explain almost everything, from the way the planets move to why you have a stomachache to the results of a presidential election to what you should have for dinner tonight.

In cooking, the five elements correspond with sour, bitter, sweet, spicy, and salty tastes. These tastes, in turn, are associated with five colors: blue/green, red, yellow, white, and black.

COLOR	ELEMENT	TASTE
blue/green	wood	sour
red	fire	bitter
yellow	earth	sweet
white	metal	spicy/pungent
black	water	salty

Traditionally a meal is assembled based on how the different tastes and colors contrast and harmonize with each other, and this must be done with skill for the meal to be deemed a success.

yin and yang

Another fundamental Chinese principle that has had a strong influence on the Korean mind and way of cooking is that of yin and yang (in Korean, *um* and *yang*), the idea that two great opposing but interconnected forces govern everything in the universe and must always be in harmonious balance.

Your body has a yin-and-yang balance, which you need to carefully maintain to stay in good health. One way to do this is through food. If your body is high in yang, you may crave food that is yin to balance it. Individual dishes also need to be balanced internally and in relation to other dishes in the meal. For example, Pork Wraps (page 238) are made with pork, which is a yin food, and served with salted fermented shrimp, which is yang.

achieving harmony and balance

No Korean housewife tastes her dishes and thinks, "This needs more wood." Or counts the banchan she's serving to make sure they're enough to match the occasion and the importance of her guests. Or works feverishly to add more yang to a dish. But nonetheless, these ancient philosophies have had an undeniably lasting influence on the colors, textures, and tastes of Korean foods.

Ideally, yin and yang should be balanced and all five elements should be present and in balance too. There are no absolute rules, but all elements of the meal should complement each other. If your dinner table is filled with colorful dishes made with different ingredients, levels of spiciness, temperatures, and cooking methods, the meal can be considered in harmony. For ideas for harmonious meals, see the Menus for Korean Meals on page 295.

seasons, the weather, and health

Seasonality, the weather, and good health also guide Korean cooks. We consider seasonal eating healthier because it is harmonious with nature. While it's true that in the modern world we can get pretty much any ingredient we want at any time of year, it's still true that some ingredients are better at certain times than at others: Napa cabbage harvested in late fall, for instance, will make the best kimchi.

The weather is also a factor in planning a meal. If it's raining out, we might make something like Hand-Torn Noodle Soup (page 66) to cheer us up and make us feel cozy on a damp day.

Regard for health has always influenced Korean cooking, since traditional Korean medical practice doesn't separate food from medicine. Mealtime is a chance to maintain and improve our well-being. The choice of dishes often reflects particular medical conditions and needs of the diners. Someone who just got out of the hospital and can't digest normal food easily can start with porridge for a meal. If you are exhausted from the summer heat and your appetite is poor, how about Cold Cucumber Soup (page 136) with rice? I eat a piece of Ginseng Candy (page 293) every day, not only to satisfy my sweet tooth, but also to boost my immune system.

eating the meal

The traditional Korean table is low to the ground, and diners sit on cushions on the floor. Historically, most houses had a subfloor heating system (*ondol*), making the floor the warmest part of the house. Today, though, many families and restaurants use Western-style tables.

The banchan are shared by everyone at the table, but diners get their own individual bowls of rice and soup. Your bowl of rice is set in front of you and your soup to the right of that. A spoon and chopsticks sit to the right of your soup, with the spoon next to the soup and the chopsticks on the outside.

The spoon is for eating the rice, soup, and any other liquid. It's considered rude to lift, hold, or drink out of your soup bowl, as is done in some cultures, and Koreans never pick up the rice bowl to eat out of it. The chopsticks are used to pick what you want out of the banchan bowls and to eat everything else. Korean chopsticks are made of metal, and it takes practice to learn how to use them, because they're thinner, heavier, and smoother than wooden chopsticks. But once you get used to them, you'll see how agile they are.

It's rude to use the chopsticks to pick through the banchan for choice pieces. Pluck out the morsel you want—preferably just enough to eat in one bite—with determination and purpose. If the food that you've taken is too big to be eaten in one bite, put what's left on a small individual plate.

I know that some non-Koreans are uncomfortable eating banchan that may have been touched by someone else's chopsticks. If this is likely to be the case with my guests, I put out serving spoons and separate chopsticks for the banchan dishes, to keep everyone at ease.

"It's rude to use the chopsticks to pick through the banchan for choice pieces. "

With all the dishes on the table, no one should start eating until the oldest person at the table has begun. Then you can have a bit of each side dish in turn, mixing and matching them to create your own idea of harmony and balance. Have a bite of rice, then some crispy kimchi, then a beautiful pollock pancake, tender white fish in an egg-based batter. Then, you may want something to moisten your palate—how about a spoonful of beef radish soup? Then after you go back to warm rice, you might like something spicy and rich, such as spicy stir-fried pork. Every bite is enhanced by the contrasting flavors of the one before it and the next.

Koreans don't usually serve water at meals, feeling that soup or stew provides enough liquid. Alcohol is sometimes served during the meal, and scorched rice tea or barley tea is often served afterward. In the winter, tea is served warm; in the summer, it is cold.

Many modern Koreans serve desserts of seasonal fruits like strawberries, grapes, melons, apples, persimmons, and pears after the meal. For special occasions, dishes like rice punch, dried persimmon punch, pear punch, or sweetened rice with dried fruits and nuts (see the Dessert chapter) are served.

how to use this book

A great strategy for preparing delicious meals in a snap, one employed by Korean housewives all over the world, is to lean on *mitbanchan*, side dishes prepared in advance in big batches. This way, assuming you will be cooking rice and have kimchi on hand (you will, right?), you can quickly mix and match a few of the mitbanchan you have in the fridge to make a delicious, nutritious meal. If you make a big batch of Spicy Beef and Vegetable Soup (page 96), Seaweed Soup (page 89), or Soybean Sprout Soup (page 93), for example, you can eat it over the course of a couple of days.

Another strategy is to use the weekend to practice new recipes until you are confident enough to whip them up on a weekday after work. My website is always busiest on Saturdays, Sundays, and Mondays, when my readers are hard at work trying new things and reporting back to the community.

Some of the recipes in this book can be put together in minutes, but I encourage you to go all the way and make the longer recipes too, like kimchi and the "jangs," fermented sauces and pastes (such as gochujang, doenjang, and ganjang). Not only will these dishes give you a real sense of accomplishment, but they will provide nourishment and pleasure for weeks or even months. They are the heart of Korean cuisine.

substitutions at a glance

A few Korean ingredients—hot red pepper flakes and toasted sesame oil come to mind—have no substitutes. If you want to make many of the recipes in this book, you will have to seek them out.

But in other cases, if you are willing to sacrifice authenticity for convenience (and who isn't, at one time or another?), there are many ways to substitute one ingredient for another with delicious results. Over the years, many of my readers have written to me about their successful substitutions: spaghetti for jjajangmyeon noodles, regular big purple eggplant for Korean eggplant, and so forth. If you want to try something different, go for it. And let me know how it turns out.

Many of my recipes include suggestions for substitutions when appropriate. Here is a general list for reference:

Asian chives: scallions
Azuki beans (red beans): dried mung beans
Beltfish: fresh mackerel
Chrysanthemum greens: mint or basil
Crab sticks: cooked shrimp, crabmeat, or carrots (for color)
Dried jujubes: dried cranberries
Enoki mushrooms: oyster mushrooms cut into thin strips
Fernbrake: fiddlehead ferns
Jjajangmyeon noodles: spaghetti

Korean eggplant: purple eggplant
Korean green and red chili peppers: jalapeños, serranos, or other 3- to 4-inch-long red or green chili peppers
Korean (Asian) pear: Bosc or Anjou pear
Korean soup soy sauce: fish sauce
Korean mustard seed powder: regular mustard powder
Korean radish: daikon
Rice syrup: corn syrup
Soybean sprouts: mung bean sprouts
Water dropwort: watercress

INGREDIENTS FOR KOREAN COOKING

Many recipes in this book can be made with ingredients found in any supermarket. But cooking authentic Korean food does require some special ingredients, which can easily be found in Korean or Asian grocery stores and online (see page 301). To help you with your shopping, I have included the Korean names for all of these ingredients here.

ASIAN CHIVES (Buchu): Sometimes called garlic chives or Chinese chives, these tender shoots with a garlicky kick add flavor and color to many dishes. If you can't find them, substitute scallions.

ASIAN PEAR (Bae): Also called Korean pear, this round fruit has thin, golden-brown skin and sweet flesh similar to that of the Bosc. It's crisper and juicier than other pears and should be peeled before using. It is often available at supermarkets. If you can't find it, use Bosc or Anjou pears (which are smaller, so you'll need more of them) instead.

AZUKI/ADZUKI BEANS (Pat): These red beans are grown throughout Asia. Koreans often use the dried beans in sweet or sweet-and-savory dishes, such as Red Bean Porridge with Rice Cake Balls (page 77). Dried azuki beans are available in many supermarkets, natural foods stores, and Korean grocery stores.

BARLEY MALT POWDER (Yeotgireum-garu): An essential ingredient for homemade Korean Hot Pepper Paste (page 258) and for Rice Punch (page 284), this powder supplies sweetness and malt flavor. It is available at Korean grocery stores.

BELTFISH (Galchi): This long, slender fish resembles an eel but has delicate, sweet white flesh. Look for beltfish in Asian fish markets or at the fish counter or freezer case of Korean grocery stores. Mackerel is a good substitute.

BLACK BEAN PASTE (Chunjang): Black, salty, and slightly sweet, this paste is used in the sauce for Noodles with Black Bean Paste (page 62). It is made with a mixture of soybeans, flour, and caramel that is fermented. You can buy it at Korean grocery stores. After opening, store it in the refrigerator for up to 3 months.

BLACK SWEET RICE (Heukmi-chapssal): Due to the presence of healthy compounds called flavonoids that are also found in large quantities in blueberries, black sweet rice, also called black glutinous rice, is actually dark purple. Adding just a tablespoon or two to white or brown rice will give it a pretty lavender color and a mildly nutty flavor; see Multigrain Rice, page 38. You can find it at Korean grocery stores as well as many supermarkets.

BROWN RICE SYRUP (Ssal-yeot): A sweet and sticky liquid sweetener, rice syrup is similar to corn syrup but is made with rice. It has a slightly nutty flavor. It's available in some supermarkets and natural foods stores, and in Korean grocery stores. If you can't find it, use corn syrup instead.

BROWN SWEET RICE (Hyeonmi-chapssal): This whole-grain rice with a sticky texture (it has more starch than regular short-grain brown rice) can be cooked with white rice and barley for a typical Korean multigrain rice blend. Look for it in Korean grocery stores.

BURDOCK ROOT (Ueong-ppuri): Raw burdock root is very hard, but when this root vegetable is braised, it has an herbal flavor and a crisp, chewy texture. When shopping for it, choose roots with a smooth surface and no blemishes. Look for it in Korean, Chinese, or Japanese grocery stores. Lotus root can be substituted because the typical method of braising these vegetables is similar.

CANNED CHESTNUTS (Bam-tongjorim): Cooked chestnuts packed in syrup are used in Korean sweets, such as Sweetened Rice with Dried Fruits and Nuts (page 288). Canned chestnuts are available at Korean and gourmet markets.

CHRYSANTHEMUM GREENS (Ssuk-gat): Sometimes called edible chrysanthemum or chop suey greens, chrysanthemum greens have a refreshing herbal flavor and are delicious raw or lightly cooked, as in Seafood Stew (page 102). They are available at Korean, Chinese, and Japanese grocery stores and at some farmers' markets. You can substitute a few sprigs of fresh basil or mint (which are more powerfully flavored than chrysanthemum) if necessary.

CRAB STICKS (Ge-massal): Crab sticks are a processed seafood product made of pulverized white fish and starch, shaped to resemble crabmeat. They add a vivid red color and mild fish flavor to gimbap (seaweed rice rolls; see page 44) and many other popular dishes. Look for them in the fish section of the supermarket, wrapped in airtight plastic packages. After opening, they will keep in the fridge for up to 2 weeks; you can also freeze them.

CYLINDER-SHAPED RICE CAKES (Tteokbokki-yong-tteok): Rice cakes, made with short-grain rice flour, steamed and pounded into a sticky mass and formed into cylinders or other shapes, are one of Korea's most popular street snacks; see Spicy Rice Cakes (page 212). Freshly made rice cakes and refrigerated packaged rice cakes are sold at Korean markets.

DRIED ANCHOVIES (Mareun-myeolchi): Dried anchovies, sorted by size and sold in packages, plastic bags, or boxes, are available at Korean grocery stores. Smaller anchovies are toasted with soy sauce and hot pepper paste and eaten whole as a side dish; larger anchovies are used to flavor stocks and soups. The tiny bones contain a lot of calcium and are really good for you. Store in a zipper-lock bag or airtight container in the freezer. Before using larger anchovies, remove the heads and guts (the black innards).

DRIED BELLFLOWER ROOT (Doraji): These roots are widely used in Korean cuisine and also for medicinal purposes. They look similar to ginseng root and taste bitter, with a strong ginseng-like smell. Dried bellflower roots are sold in packages in Korean grocery stores. Avoid spindly brownish roots; thick white ones are best.

DRIED FILEFISH (Juipo): Dried filefish fillets are sold in airtight packages in Korean grocery stores. With its chewy, jerky-like texture, dried filefish is a popular choice for lunch boxes. When cooked and seasoned in a sweet, spicy sauce, it becomes a delectable banchan for the table.

DRIED JUJUBES (Daechu): Jujubes, sometimes called Chinese dates or Korean dates, are the edible berry-like fruit of a tree native to southern Asia. Dried jujubes are red and crinkly with a sweet-tart flavor that is somewhat like that of raisins. Look for them at Korean or other Asian markets. Keep them in the freezer in an airtight container or zipper-lock bag.

DRIED KELP (Dasima): Called *kombu* in Japan, dried kelp is a nutritious sea vegetable used in many Korean dishes, such as Crunchy Rice-Flour-Coated Kelp Snack (page 202), and Anchovy-Kelp Stock (page 86). Store it in a cool, dry place in an airtight container or zipper-lock bag.

DRIED KOREAN BLACK BEANS (Geomeun-kong): Smaller and rounder than ordinary black beans, these are black soybeans. They are used in dishes like Braised Black Beans (page 153) and sometimes added to multigrain rice mixtures. Look for them with the other dried beans and soybeans at Korean grocery stores.

DRIED PEELED SPLIT MUNG BEANS (Geopi-nokdu): These split yellow beans, which are the size of lentils, have had their outer skins removed. They are the base for delicious Mung Bean Pancakes (page 186). Look for them in the dried beans and grains section of Korean grocery stores, natural foods stores, and large supermarkets.

DRIED PERSIMMONS (Got-gam): Dried persimmons are sweet and chewy. In Korea, the fresh fruit is harvested in the fall, tied with string, and hung to air-dry. A whitish bloom on their surface indicates that they are dry and sweet. Look for them in Korean, Japanese, or Chinese markets. They will keep in the freezer for a few months.

DRIED SEAWEED (Mareun-miyeok): This dried brown seaweed, also known as wakame, has many uses in Korean cooking; see Seaweed Soup (page 89) and Seaweed Salad (page 134). When rehydrated, it expands greatly in volume. Look for it along with other dried seaweed at Korean and Japanese grocery stores or natural foods stores.

DRIED SEAWEED PAPER (Gim): Also called nori or laver, these sheets are made by shredding and drying seaweed in a process similar to making paper. Koreans use seaweed sheets to roll up gimbap (page 44). Crisped over an open flame and then crushed into small pieces, the seaweed is good as a garnish for Mixed Rice with Raw Fish (page 52) and Mung Bean Jelly with Vegetables and Beef (page 228). Keep it in the freezer for up to 6 months.

DRIED SHIITAKE MUSHROOMS (Mareun pyogo-beoseot): When shiitake mushrooms are dried, their flavor is intensified and they become pleasantly chewy. They add umami and great texture to many banchan and soups. You can find them at larger supermarkets or Korean grocery stores.

DRIED SWEET POTATO STEMS (Mallin-goguma-julgi): In Korea, sweet potatoes are harvested in the fall, including their long, sweet, succulent stems. The fresh stems are used in soups, stews, and side dishes. Fresh stems are rarely available in the United States, but dried stems can be found at Korean grocery stores. They will keep for several months in an airtight container in a cool, dry spot.

DRIED YELLOW SOYBEANS (Meju-kong): Dried yellow soybeans are widely used in Korean cuisine. They are the main ingredient for Fermented Soybean Paste (page 253)

and Extra-Strong Fermented Soybean Paste (page 256), and a good substitute for dried black soybeans in the recipe for Braised Black Beans (page 153). Look for them at Korean or Chinese grocery stores.

DRIED WHOLE SQUID (Mareun ojingeo): Dried whole squid are packaged individually or by the dozen in plastic packages. The dried has a much more intense flavor than the fresh. Look for it with other dried fish at Korean grocery stores. It can be kept in the freezer in a zipper-lock bag for up to 3 months.

EDIBLE FLOWERS (Sik-yong-kkot): Edible flowers add beauty to many Korean desserts. Buy organic flowers from a farmers' market, so you know they haven't been sprayed with pesticides, and always check that they are edible (many flowers are not) before using in cooking.

ENOKI MUSHROOMS (Paengi-beoseot): These 4- to 5-inch-long thin mushrooms are used in many Asian dishes. Look for firm, white specimens (avoid slippery or discolored ones) at supermarkets or any Asian market.

EXTRA-STRONG FERMENTED SOYBEAN PASTE (Cheonggukjang): If you don't want to make your own (see page 256), you can buy this paste, which has a powerful aroma, in Korean markets. It is used in Extra-Strong Fermented Soybean Paste Stew (page 99). It will keep in the refrigerator for up to 1 month or in the freezer for up to 3 months.

FERMENTED SKATE (Hong-eo): Fermented skate is a delicacy that is sold sliced and skinned in the fish or frozen section of Korean grocery stores.

FERMENTED SOYBEAN FLOUR (Meju-garu): This flour is an essential ingredient in Korean Hot Pepper Paste (page 258). Look for it in the beans and grains section, usually next to barley malt powder, in Korean grocery stores.

FERMENTED SOYBEAN PASTE (Doenjang): Doenjang is a classic fermented seasoning used in soups and stews;

vegetable, meat, and seafood dishes; and dipping sauces. The paste can be used as is, tossed with vegetables or combined with garlic, sesame oil, and Korean hot pepper paste to make the dipping sauce; see Soybean Paste Dipping Sauce (page 272). It is most commonly used to flavor the broth for Soybean Paste Stew with Dried Anchovies (page 108). Today most Koreans use commercially made soybean paste, available in any Korean grocery store, but it is possible to prepare it at home the old-fashioned way; see page 253.

FERNBRAKE (Gosari): Fernbrake is a wild green gathered in the springtime in the mountains in Korea and eaten fresh. It is also blanched and dried to be used out of season. Dried fernbrake is available in Korean grocery stores. Store it in an airtight container or zipper-lock bag in a cool, dark spot. Fiddleheads, with their papery outer coating removed and blanched in boiling water, are a good substitute for the fresh green.

FISH CAKES (Eomuk): Fish cakes are a processed fish product made with ground fish, squid, or shrimp, and potato starch, flour, and sugar. It is used for the sweet, chewy Stir-Fried Fish Cakes with Soy Sauce (page 170). It's also often added to spicy rice cakes, a popular Korean street food (page 212). Look for it in the refrigerated and frozen sections of Korean grocery stores. After opening, it can be refrigerated in an airtight container for up to 1 week or frozen for up to 3 months.

FISH SAUCE (Aekjeot): Good fish sauce is savory, salty, and even a little bit sweet, with a deep, aged flavor. It's an essential ingredient for kimchi, and I use it in place of homemade soup soy sauce in many of my recipes. I prefer the 3 Crabs brand of fish sauce, produced by Viet Huong; it's not made in Korea, but it is sold in Korean grocery stores here because it's very popular among Korean immigrants.

FRESH GINSENG ROOT (Susam): The fleshy root of a slow-growing perennial plant, ginseng is one of the world's oldest and most popular herbal medicines. Koreans value ginseng for its health-giving properties and use it to make tea and candy. Find it in the refrigerated section of Korean grocery stores. It can be refrigerated for up to 2 weeks.

FROZEN OYSTERS (Naengdong-gul): If you don't have access to high-quality fresh oysters, you can use frozen oysters imported from Korea and sold at Korean markets. They are safe to eat raw.

FROZEN POLLOCK ROE (Naengdong-myeong-ran): Pollock roe, used in Spicy Pollock Roe Stew (page 105), can be difficult to find in American fish markets. Any frozen or fresh roe can be substituted.

GLUTINOUS RICE (Chap-ssal): Sometimes called sweet rice, this rice is actually not sweet at all, nor does it contain gluten, as many people think. It's much stickier and chewier (i.e., glutinous) than regular short-grain rice. Store in a cool, dry spot in an airtight container. Look for it with other rices at Korean grocery stores and other Asian markets and some supermarkets.

GLUTINOUS RICE FLOUR (Chap-ssal-garu): Glutinous rice flour is made from glutinous rice and, since it's not made from wheat, contains no gluten. It is known as *mochiko* in Japan and often labeled as such by American producers, such as Blue Star in California. Store in a zipper-lock bag or an airtight container in a cool, dry spot or the freezer. Glutinous rice flour can be found in Korean, Japanese, and Chinese grocery stores.

KOREAN BREAD CRUMBS (Ppang-garu): These large, flaky, crunchy bread crumbs are similar to Japanese panko. Buy them at a Korean market or substitute panko.

Korean chili peppers

GREEN KOREAN CHILI PEPPERS (Cheong-gochu): These 3- to 4-inch-long thin peppers have a sweet and spicy flavor. Koreans don't usually remove the seeds before chopping them. Buy green chili peppers in Korean grocery stores, or substitute serranos or jalapeños.

RED KOREAN CHILI PEPPERS (Hong-gochu): Korean red chili peppers, green chili peppers that have ripened, are slightly tangy and sweeter and a little less spicy than green ones. They are used in Chili Pepper Pancakes (page 194) and also as a garnish for many banchan. For garnish purposes, you can substitute chopped or shredded red bell pepper.

SHISHITO PEPPERS (Kkwari-gochu): These mild-to-hot peppers are 2 to 3 inches long and have thin, ridged skins. In Korean cuisine, they're steamed, stir-fried, boiled, or sautéed and seasoned. If you can't find them, you can substitute any small, mild green pepper such as piquillo.

KOREAN CURRY POWDER (Ka-re-garu): This blend of curry spices is different from Indian curry powders. It's used in Korean-Style Curry Rice (page 42). Seek it out in a Korean grocery store.

KOREAN EGGPLANT (Gaji): Thin, light purple Korean eggplants are more tender and less bitter than regular eggplant, with a softer, more airy texture. Look for them in Korean, Chinese, and Japanese markets or, if you're lucky, at your local farmers' market. Small regular eggplants can be substituted.

KOREAN HOT PEPPER FLAKES (Gochu-garu): These pepper flakes can be either mild or hot. For some dishes, I use the less spicy flakes so I can add more and make the dish redder. It helps to know a little Korean when you shop for these at Korean grocery stores: Mae-woon gochu-garu is very hot and spicy; deol-mae-woon gochu-garu is milder. Try to buy the flakes that are from sun-dried peppers (tae-yang-cho). After opening, store the pepper flakes in an airtight container in the freezer. Regular crushed pepper flakes are too coarse, not red enough, and are made of too many varieties of peppers to be useful in Korean cooking.

KOREAN HOT PEPPER PASTE (Gochujang): This staple adds fire and some sweetness to innumerable dishes. Today most Korean home cooks buy commercial hot pepper paste at the grocery store, but you can make your own in the traditional way; see page 258. After opening it, keep the paste in the refrigerator.

KOREAN HOT PEPPER POWDER (Gochujang-yong-gochu-garu): From the same peppers as Korean hot pepper flakes, this finely ground powder is mostly used to make a hot pepper paste (see page 258). Buy it at a Korean grocery store and store it in the freezer. Cayenne pepper is not a good substitute.

KOREAN MUSTARD SEED POWDER (Gyeoja-garu): Ground Korean mustard seeds have a bright yellow color that I love. The powder has a flavor similar to regular English powdered mustard, which you can substitute in Mustard and Garlic Sauce (page 275).

KOREAN RADISH (Mu): Korean radishes are somewhat similar to daikon radishes, but they are shorter, stouter, and firmer. They are pale green at the top, and the flesh is sweet, juicy, and crisp, especially in peak season in late fall. Look for the radishes at Korean grocery stores, and choose ones with a smooth surface and firm flesh. If they're unavailable, substitute daikon.

Maangchi and Friends

Elizabeth: *Since I don't know Korean, your site has helped translate things for me. Last week I went to the Korean grocery store with my list. The worker in the produce section looked in my basket and said, "Ah! Bibimbap," and then helped me find the last item. My family loved it and wants me to make it again.*

Maangchi: *That's wonderful! Even though you don't understand Korean, you should have no problem finding ingredients. It's funny that the worker at the grocery store knew what you were making simply by looking in your basket.*

KOREAN SOUP SOY SAUCE (Guk-ganjang, Joseon-ganjang): Korean soup soy sauce is stronger and saltier than regular soy sauce. Soup soy sauce can be found in Korean grocery stores, but I've never found a commercially made soup soy sauce that satisfies me. If I don't have homemade soup soy sauce on hand (see page 264), I use 3 Crabs fish sauce rather than commercial soup soy sauce.

L.A.–STYLE BEEF SHORT RIBS (L.A. Galbi, sometimes mistakenly spelled kalbi): L.A.–style beef short ribs are cut across the bone so each piece is a long, thin strip with 3 or 4 bone sections in it. These are also known as "flanken" cut, though flanken short ribs are usually cut ½ to 1 inch thick, while L.A.–style should be ⅛ to ¼ inch thick. You can buy precut short ribs at Korean grocery stores, or ask your butcher to cut them to your specifications.

LOTUS ROOTS (Yeon-geun): Lotus roots, technically rhizomes, come from an aquatic plant and have a distinctive pattern of holes (a bit like Swiss cheese) when sliced, a crisp texture, and a sweet flavor. Buy them fresh in the produce section at Korean grocery stores or Chinese markets; they can also be found sliced in the refrigerated section of some markets. Lotus root is delicious braised.

MANDU SKINS (Mandu-pi): These little round wheat flour wrappers are filled with savory combinations of vegetables, seafood, and meat and steamed, fried, or boiled in soup. You can find the wrappers in the freezer section of Korean grocery stores, usually near the rice flour and rice cakes. The English on the package may read "dumpling wrappers." They come 50 to a package and are very cheap. Take home a few extra packages and freeze them for later use. Defrost the packages overnight in the refrigerator before using.

MUNG BEAN SPROUTS (Sukjunamul): Mung bean sprouts can be found in most supermarkets or at farmers' markets. Refrigerate them and use within a couple of days. Wash just before using.

MUNG BEAN STARCH (Cheongpomuk-garu): Sometimes incorrectly labeled as mung bean flour, this is fine-grained starch extracted from mung beans. It is used to make Mung Bean Jelly (page 228). Find it at Korean markets, near the potato and cornstarch powders.

noodles

JJAJANGMYEON NOODLES (Jjajangmyeon-yong-guksu): These wheat noodles, used for Noodles with Black Bean Paste (page 62), are sold frozen in Korean grocery stores. Thaw if using immediately or store them in the freezer in a zipper-lock bag; let them thaw slightly on the countertop before using. Frozen noodles will keep for up to 3 months.

NAENGMYEON NOODLES (Naengmyeon-yong-guksu): These dried brown noodles are made from buckwheat and sweet potato starch and wheat flour. They are used for Cold Spicy, Chewy Noodles (page 60) and Cold Noodle Soup (page 58). Buy them in Korean grocery stores.

SWEET POTATO STARCH NOODLES (Dangmyeon): These dried noodles are similar to glass noodles, also called cellophane noodles or Chinese vermicelli, which can be substituted. They are made from sweet potato starch and are nearly transparent after they've been cooked. Look for them in Korean grocery stores.

THIN WHEAT FLOUR NOODLES (Somyeon): These very thin wheat noodles are used in both hot and cold dishes. Keep them in the pantry. Look for them in Korean, Japanese, and Chinese grocery stores.

YANGJANGPI NOODLES (Yangjangpi): These clear noodles made of mung bean starch come in large sheets that must be torn into manageable pieces after cooking. Look for them in Korean grocery stores.

PACKAGED FRIED TOFU (Yubu): This prefried tofu is crispy on the outside and spongy and chewy on the inside. I use it in the Basic Noodle Soup in Anchovy Broth (page 64) as well as in the vegetarian versions of Mixed Rice with Raw Fish (page 52) and Seaweed Rice Rolls (page 44). Look for it in the frozen section of Korean or Japanese grocery stores. After opening, store it in the freezer for up to 3 months.

PERILLA LEAVES (Kkaennip): Perilla is a member of the mint family, and it is easy to grow in your garden or in pots. It's self-seeding and, once planted, it grows rampant. Perilla seeds are available online. Fresh perilla leaves are available at Korean grocery stores. Their season is at its peak from May to July, but leaves from plants raised in greenhouses are available year-round. Perilla leaves are used in Perilla Leaf Pancakes (page 196) and are added to seafood stews, where they impart a minty flavor.

PERILLA SEED POWDER (Deulkkae-garu): Perilla seeds are ground and used as seasoning for soups, stews, and dried vegetable dishes like Braised Dried Sweet Potato Stems (page 142), adding a nutty, rich, herbal flavor. Look for perilla seed powder in the spice section of Korean grocery stores.

PINE NUTS (Jat): Pine nuts are used to garnish many dishes and desserts, and for Creamy Pine Nut Sauce (page 275). Mediterranean pine nuts are fine, but I prefer the smaller and more flavorful Asian pine nuts sold at Korean grocery stores.

SALTED FERMENTED SHRIMP (Saeujeot): A variety of salted and fermented seafood (*jeotgal*) is used in Korean cuisine, and salted fermented shrimp is a common and versatile ingredient. It is used as a seasoning in dishes like Sautéed Zucchini and Shrimp (page 176), and the salty sauce is added to Pork Wraps (page 238). Many Koreans include salted fermented shrimp in their kimchi paste when making kimchi. Buy it in Korean grocery stores and store it in the fridge. It will keep for 6 months.

SHORT-GRAIN RICE (Mep-ssal): Short-grain rice, Korea's staple rice, which is also called sushi rice, is stickier and starchier than long-grain rice, but not as sticky as sweet rice (glutinous rice). Buy it in big bags at Korean or Japanese grocery stores, where it will be less expensive than at the supermarket.

SHREDDED DRIED HOT PEPPER (Silgochu): Very thinly sliced dried hot peppers (their name translates literally as "thread pepper") are mostly used as a garnish for vegetable side dishes or Mung Bean Pancakes (page 186). Look for them near the hot pepper flakes at Korean grocery stores.

SHREDDED DRIED POLLOCK (Bug-eo-chae): Pollock (sometimes spelled pollack) is a variety of white fish similar to cod. It is eaten fresh in Korea as it is in North America, but it is also dried for later use; the best is dried by the sea breezes. When it's completely dried, the fish is very hard, like a stick of wood. In the old days, it had to be pounded to soften it before it could be shredded. These days, most dried pollock sold in Korean grocery stores is already shredded. There's no need to wash it, but if the strips are too long, cut them into bite-size pieces. When cooked in soup, the fish softens but stays a little bit chewy. Store dried pollock in an airtight container or zipper-lock bag in the freezer for up to 6 months.

SHREDDED SALTED JELLYFISH (Haepari): Shredded salted jellyfish is flavorless, with a springy, crispy texture. You'll need it for Cold Jellyfish Salad (page 242). Look for it at Korean grocery stores or Chinese markets.

SLICED RICE CAKES (Tteokguk-yong-tteok): Sliced rice cakes are sold in plastic bags in the refrigerated section or in vacuum-sealed packages in the frozen section of Korean grocery stores. Chewier than cooked rice, the rice cakes are used in soup. Store in the freezer for up to 3 months.

SOFT TOFU (Sundubu): Usually sold in tubes, soft, white creamy tofu is an essential ingredient in Spicy Soft Tofu Stew (page 90). It's sold in Korean and Chinese grocery stores; check the expiration date, since it is very perishable, and store in the refrigerator if not using immediately. You can substitute silken tofu.

SOY SAUCE (Jin-ganjang): The familiar Japanese-style soy sauce is relatively new to Korea—unlike Korean soup soy sauce, which has been used for thousands of years. Regular soy sauce, like soup soy sauce, is made from soybeans, but the process is totally different. It is better suited for everyday use as a dipping sauce or as a light flavoring agent rather than for flavoring a whole pot of soup. There are several different Korean brands of soy sauce; I have been using Sempio for decades. But you can use any Japanese brand you like in the recipes in this book.

SOYBEAN SPROUTS (Kongnamul): Sprouted yellow soybeans may be the most popular vegetable in Korea. Don't confuse them with the mung bean sprouts you find in the supermarket. Soybean sprouts are sold in packages alongside the other fresh vegetables at Korean grocery stores. The sprouts are always cooked because they smell fishy when raw but become sweet and nutty tasting when cooked. They can be added to rice and soups or simply served as a side dish. Store them in the fridge and use them quickly; they won't keep for more than a week.

TOASTED SESAME OIL (Cham-gi-reum): Sometimes called Asian sesame oil, toasted sesame oil is different from the sesame oil sold in large bottles alongside the vegetable oil at the supermarket. It adds a nutty flavor and richness to many dishes. Any brand is good.

TOASTED WHITE, BROWN, AND BLACK SESAME SEEDS (Bokkeun-kkae): Toasted white or brown sesame seeds add a nutty flavor to many dishes. You can keep a jar of pretoasted seeds on hand, but you can also buy raw seeds and toast them as you need them. If you buy toasted sesame seeds, there is no need to wash them. Otherwise, washing removes any dust and plumps up the seeds. Toasted black sesame seeds are usually found next to the white sesame seeds on the shelves in Korean grocery stores. They taste slightly nuttier and a little more bitter than ordinary sesame seeds.

To toast sesame seeds: Wash the sesame seeds in a fine strainer under running water. Drain thoroughly. Heat a pan or wok over medium heat and add the washed seeds. Stir with a wooden spoon until they are evenly golden, crisp, and nutty smelling; the timing will depend on how many seeds you are toasting. They'll pop as they cook.

STARTER CULTURE (Nuruk): You'll need this starter culture to make Korean Rice Liquor (page 262). It's available in Korean grocery stores, usually next to malt powder or mung bean starch in the grain section.

TOFU (Dubu): Koreans use medium-firm or firm tofu for panfrying. Store well-wrapped tofu in the refrigerator until its expiration date. If you use only half the package, submerge the remaining half in cold water, cover, and store in the refrigerator. It should be eaten within a few days.

WATER DROPWORT (Minari): Also called Chinese celery or Japanese parsley, water dropwort has crisp stems and leafy tops and an herbal flavor; it's sold in the vegetable section of Korean grocery stores. Fresh minari is not always available, so when I see it, I buy it. It wilts quickly, so use it within a few days. Wrap the minari in a sheet of newspaper or paper towels, put it in a plastic bag, and keep it in the refrigerator until ready to use.

WOOD CHARCOAL (Soot): You'll need hardwood charcoal to make Fermented Soybean Paste (page 253) and Korean Soup Soy Sauce (page 264). Look for it in Korean grocery stores.

YELLOW PICKLED RADISH (Danmuji): Yellow pickled radish is easily recognizable because of its bright yellow color. Sweet, salty, crisp, and tangy, it is an essential ingredient for Seaweed Rice Rolls (page 44). Look for it in the refrigerated section of Korean and Japanese grocery stores. It's sold in airtight plastic packages, either cut into strips or whole, with enough pickling liquid to keep it moist. It keeps in the refrigerator for a few months.

Dried red chili pepper store in Korea

EQUIPMENT FOR KOREAN COOKING

If you have a reasonably well-equipped kitchen, you already have almost everything you need to make the recipes in this book. But here are some items you may not yet have that are useful in Korean cooking. Buy them online (see page 301) or at a Korean grocery store.

BAMBOO MAT: You will need one of these for making Seaweed Rice Rolls (page 44). You can find them in the kitchenware section of Asian grocery stores or near the sushi-making ingredients in the supermarket.

BARBECUE GRILL PAN: This ridged grill pan slopes, so the fat rendered from cooking meat can drain—either through a hole in the center or off the edges—into a pan that fits underneath. You can use a skillet and just drain away the fat as you cook, but a grill pan is inexpensive and convenient, particularly if you're going to make Grilled Pork Belly (page 232) often. Buy grill pans at a Korean market.

KOREAN EARTHENWARE: Traditional Korean earthenware vessels are used for all sorts of tasks in the Korean kitchen. Earthenware pots (*ttukbaegi*), which are fired at high temperatures, can be placed directly on a burner for cooking and then transferred to the table, where they will keep your food hot all through dinner. A medium (1½-quart) pot is big enough for most of the recipes in this book; a larger one is nice for parties. Earthenware pots are available in Korean grocery stores.

Earthenware jars and crocks are beautiful and useful for making Fermented Soybean Paste (page 253), Hot Pepper Paste (page 258), and Korean Rice Liquor (page 262).

ELECTRIC BLANKET: This may seem like an odd item to include in a section on cooking equipment, but I use mine as a stand-in for traditional ondol floor heating (see page 8), creating a warm surface for making Fermented Soybean Paste (page 253) and for Extra-Strong Fermented Soybean Paste (page 256).

FOOD DEHYDRATOR: I discovered electric dehydrators on my first trip to the United States, and I have used one ever since to make traditionally air-dried foods such as Beef Jerky (page 215) quickly and conveniently. I also use it to dry Crunchy Rice-Flour-Coated Kelp Snack (page 202).

FOOD PROCESSOR: I have used my 16-cup food processor to the point where the words on the buttons have literally worn off! I use it to make the noodle dough for Hand-Torn Noodle Soup (page 66), to blend marinades, and for many other tasks.

KOREAN METAL CHOPSTICKS: Koreans use chopsticks to eat the side dishes served with rice and soup. Korean chopsticks are thin, flat, and made of metal, so they are heavier than bamboo chopsticks; the ends are flat and squared off. You can certainly use other types of chopsticks to eat Korean food, but if you want an authentic table setting, seek out these chopsticks at Korean grocery stores.

LARGE SOUP STRAINER: I like to use this when I make Anchovy-Kelp Stock (page 86). You can buy one at Korean grocery stores or any Asian or specialty market.

MORTAR AND PESTLE: I have a couple of mortars and pestles, which I use to pound cooked beans for Fermented Soybean Paste (page 253) and Extra-Strong Fermented Soybean Paste (page 256) and to make rice cakes. They are sold in kitchenware shops and Korean grocery stores.

NINE-SECTION PLATE: This special platter is used for the Platter of Nine Delicacies (page 245). I sometimes fill the sections with different nuts and dried fruits, dried squid, and ginseng candy and serve with beer at a party. Look for platters at Korean grocery stores.

PORTABLE GAS BURNER: These little stoves that run on small canisters of butane are perfect for barbecuing or heating stews at the table. Sure, you could do the same thing on your stove or grill, but this way you're surrounded by family and friends, all talking and enjoying each other's company as the food cooks. The stoves and canisters are inexpensive and can be found at most Asian grocery stores.

RICE COOKER: All of the rice recipes in this book were tested in a pot on my stovetop. That doesn't mean I don't love my Korean rice cooker, which I use all the time when I'm not developing recipes. Rice cookers range in price from $12 to $600, depending on the size and the brand. The most popular one in Korea is Cuckoo brand, and that's what I have. It is also a pressure cooker, so I can use it to make Multigrain Rice (page 38) without having to soak the grains first.

RICE SCOOP: You can use a big spoon to turn over your rice in the pot and to scrape it into serving bowls, but for a few dollars, you can buy a more efficient plastic rice scoop at a Korean grocery store that will scrape every grain from the pot. I sometimes use mine when I am mixing seasonings or making the dough for Sweet Pancakes with Brown Sugar Syrup (page 206) in my stainless bowl, because it does the job quietly.

SHALLOW BAMBOO BASKETS: I have several sizes of bamboo baskets, which I use when making Extra-Strong Fermented Soybean Paste (page 256). Sometimes I use them for serving pancakes or drying vegetables.

SPICE GRINDER: I use my spice grinder to grind sesame seeds to a fine powder for Rice Cake Balls Coated with Black Sesame Seed Powder (page 290) or to grind toasted sesame seeds for Soy Bean Sprout Soup (page 93).

STAINLESS STEEL STEAMER BASKET: A steamer comes in handy for reheating leftover rice over simmering water.

STONE POT (DOLSOT): I use a stone pot to make special rice dishes like Soybean Sprout Rice (page 40) or Multigrain Rice (page 38) for guests. It's fun to place the bowl right on the table and scoop the rice out in front of your guests.

containers for fermentation

Traditionally Koreans used special clay crocks called onggi for fermenting and storing fermented foods such as kimchi, but today they usually use glass jars or plastic containers. Making a lot of kimchi? You'll need a big container.

PLASTIC AND GLASS CONTAINERS

Some people worry that plastic containers are made with chemicals that will leach into foods being fermented and contaminate them. This is true of some but not all such containers. The safest ones to use are made with high-density polyethylene, low-density polyethylene, or polypropylene.

How can you know if your container is made with one of these? An international standard called the Resin Identification Code is stamped on all plastic containers: It's the symbol that is a triangle made of arrows with a number inside it. The number tells you what kind of plastic the container is made of: High-density polyethylene is 2, low-density polyethylene is 4, and polypropylene is 5. Most water and soda bottles are 1. Bacteria can build up in them, so they are not so safe for reuse.

Be warned that if you make kimchi in a plastic container, it will probably stain the container red. Polypropylene is more stain-resistant than polyethylene, but it can stain too!

Many people prefer to use glass containers. They're more fragile and heavier than plastic, but they look nice and never stain. Mason jars are perfect. As far as fermentation is concerned, there's very little difference between using glass and plastic, although plastic can be a bit more permeable.

TRADITIONAL KOREAN EARTHENWARE CROCKS

In Korea, simple earthenware crocks were widely used for fermenting and storage until fairly recently. In the days before refrigeration, the crocks were kept outside, sometimes buried in the ground so the kimchi inside wouldn't freeze in the winter and the temperature would be regulated. Now that everyone has a refrigerator, most Koreans prefer light and stackable plastic and glass containers.

But the traditional crock still has value. I once made kimchi in an onggi crock in the traditional way and shared it with some of my readers at a picnic in New York City's Bryant Park. They loved it, which made me curious. So I did a controlled experiment: I made kimchi and put some of it in a glass container and the rest in an onggi crock. I kept them both in the fridge for two weeks, and then I conducted a blind taste test with friends, some of whom had been eating kimchi their entire lives and some of whom had never had it before. Everyone, including me, chose the kimchi fermented in the crock. The difference was subtle but noticeable. Kimchi fermented in an onggi crock is more vibrant, ripe, flavorful, and complex than kimchi stored in a plastic or glass container. The texture is springier and the color a richer red.

How can a container actually improve the look and taste of food? The secret lies in how the container is made. Onggi potters use unrefined clay, and when the crocks are fired at 2192°F to 2282°F, the impurities in the clay burn away, leaving microscopic holes. These micropores allow some gases to pass in and out, and the porosity of the vessel enables the fermentation process to regulate itself. Take kimchi, for example: At the beginning of the process, aerobic bacteria build up inside the jar and then, ideally, level off as lactic acid is produced, leaving the vegetables fermented but not overripe. Onggi earthenware facilitates this process: Its micropores allow aerobic bacteria to escape constantly, for a perfectly balanced flavor. When kimchi ferments in a plastic or glass container, the gas escapes from the top only when you open it, and the level of aerobic bacteria remains high even after fermentation, which can make the kimchi a little bitter. An onggi crock is also friendly toward lactic acid bacteria, which make the kimchi sharper and fizzier.

Korean earthenware crocks

rice

The first thing I do when I'm expecting guests is make rice. Knowing that my rice, or *bap*, as Koreans call any kind of cooked rice, is ready and sitting warm in the pot (or rice cooker) makes me feel comfortable, and I can turn my attention to the soup or stew and meat, seafood, or vegetable side dishes—the banchan—that will complete the meal. Then my guests can pick and choose the tastes and textures they want to enjoy, taking bites of rice in between morsels of banchan.

Less often, I make one-bowl meals of rice mixed with other ingredients. These can be as simple as Soybean Sprout Rice, rice combined with beef and soybean sprouts, or as elaborate as Bibimbap (the name translates as "mixed rice"), with more than half a dozen vegetables, some meat, and seasoning sauce. Of course, these can also be served with side dishes, depending on your taste and time.

In Korea, we eat short-grain rice. If you are shopping in the supermarket, look for boxes and bags of short-grain or sushi rice in the aisle with other Asian ingredients. If you make rice frequently, buy a larger bag at a Korean or Japanese grocery store, where it will be cheaper.

Properly cooked short-grain rice is slightly sticky, with distinct shiny, fluffy grains that are soft but not mushy. Korean rice is almost always cooked without salt because it will be served with well-seasoned kimchi and side dishes. Making a good pot of rice isn't difficult, but there's an important first step if you are cooking it in a pot on top of the stove: Soak it before cooking. White rice requires a 30-minute soak to soften adequately; brown and multigrain rice blends need 2 hours of soaking.

Soaked rice will cook more quickly than unsoaked rice, so there is no danger that the rice at the bottom of the pot will burn before the rest of it is cooked through. But if you forget to soak your rice or you just don't have time, cook it anyway, knowing that it will take 5 or 10 minutes longer.

It's best to serve rice as soon as it's made, though cooked rice will stay fresh for a few hours in a covered pot off the heat. To make it further in advance (up to 3 days), see page 36. It won't be as fluffy as fresh rice, but it'll be pretty good.

If you are using a rice cooker, there is no need to soak. Just follow the manufacturer's instructions for the type of rice you are cooking.

Fluffy White Rice (page 36)

Fluffy White Rice (Ssalbap)

Makes about 5 cups, 4 servings

Today most Koreans use electric rice cookers, which make perfect rice every time. But if you don't make rice every day, you may not want to invest in this piece of equipment. Not to worry—it is easy to cook rice in a plain old saucepan.

2 cups short-grain white rice
2 cups water

1. Put the rice in a medium heavy saucepan, cover it with cold water, and stir it with your hand, then drain by tilting the pan as far as you can over the sink without pouring out any rice. Stir the rice with your hand to release excess starch. Continue to rinse and drain the rice until the water runs clear. Add the 2 cups water to the pan, cover, and let stand for 30 minutes.

2. Set the covered pan of rice over medium-high heat for 7 to 8 minutes. You will know it is time to turn the rice over when the surface is covered with abundant bubbles that are spluttering noisily and look like they are about to overflow the pan.

3. Take off the lid, turn the rice over with a spoon, and re-cover the pan. Turn the heat to very low and continue to cook until the rice is tender, about 10 minutes longer. Fluff the rice with a wooden spoon or rice scoop to release excess steam and serve immediately. Or let the fluffed rice stand, covered, at room temperature for 2 to 3 hours before serving.

Note: If you want to keep cooked rice longer, you can refrigerate it, covered, for up to 3 days. To serve, reheat it in a steamer basket in a pot of simmering water. Or reheat it in the microwave.

Left, soaking rinsed rice; right, Fluffy White Rice

Toasted Rice (Nurungji)

One advantage to making rice in a pot is that you can make nurungji, which Koreans eat as a snack. It is so popular that snack food companies have started to make it in different flavors, like potato chips. To make nurungji, simply simmer the rice for 12 to 15 minutes instead of just 10. Then scoop the cooked rice out of the pot (to eat now or later), leaving the nurungji rice on the bottom. Cover and cook over low heat for 2 minutes. Uncover and sprinkle some drops of water over the rice with your fingertips, then cover again and cook for another minute. Scrape the nurungji from the pot with a spoon. It comes out more easily if you cook it this way.

But don't wash the pot out yet: Make some toasted rice tea (sung-nyung). After removing as much nurungji from the pot as you can, pour in 2 cups water and bring to a boil over medium-low heat. Pour into mugs or bowls and serve.

Maangchi and Friends

Yeonah: *My mom will have my head if I damage her pot. Is it easier to clean the pot if you make the tea? Or is there anything else I can do to make cleaning it easier?*

Maangchi: *No problem! Use a wire scrubber to remove the tough stuff.*

Karaisoke: *Maangchi, are you telling me that the way I make rice all the time is a thing? Now I'll be telling my parents that the burnt stuff on the bottom of the pot is nurungji!*

Toasted Rice (Nurungji)

Multigrain Rice *(Japgokbap)*
Makes about 5 cups, 4 servings

When I was growing up, white rice was an expensive luxury, so my grandmother made a blend of 70 percent barley (which was relatively cheap) and 30 percent white rice to serve with every meal. These days, everyone is eating multigrain rice for health reasons, and it's more expensive to make than white! I like to blend white rice with barley, brown sweet rice (which is sticky but not sweet), and a couple of tablespoons of black rice, which gives the dish a pretty pale purple color, but you can omit the black rice if you prefer.

The most important thing when making this blend is to soak it for 2 hours before cooking. Soaked grains will cook in about 30 minutes, but unsoaked grains will never fully soften, no matter how long you cook them. Also important: Fluff the rice with a wooden spoon once when it is cooked and then serve immediately.

1 cup short-grain rice
½ cup brown sweet rice (hyeonmi-chapssel)
½ cup barley
2 tablespoons black sweet rice (optional)
2½ cups water

1. Combine the short-grain rice, brown sweet rice, barley, and black sweet rice, if using, in a medium heavy saucepan, cover with cold water, and stir with your hand, then drain by tilting the pan as far as you can over the sink without pouring out any rice. Continue to rinse, stir, and drain the rice until the water runs clear. Add the 2½ cups water to the pan, cover, and let stand for 2 hours.

2. Set the pan over medium-high heat, cover, and cook for about 10 minutes.

3. You will know it is time to turn the rice over when the surface is covered with abundant bubbles that are spluttering noisily and look like they are about to overflow the pan. Turn, scraping the bottom of the pan, then turn the heat to low, cover, and cook until the grains are tender, 10 to 12 minutes longer. Fluff with a wooden spoon to release excess steam and serve immediately. Or let the fluffed rice stand, covered, at room temperature for 2 to 3 hours before serving.

Note: You can refrigerate the cooked rice for up to 3 days. To serve, reheat it in a steamer basket in a pot of simmering water. Or reheat it in the microwave.

Clockwise from top left: black sweet rice; brown sweet rice; short-grain white rice

Soybean Sprout Rice *(Kongnamulbap)*

Serves 2

Koreans make kongnamulbap for lunch or dinner when they want something special but easy to prepare. It combines a variety of tastes and textures, among them crisp fresh soybean sprouts (kongnamul), nutty sesame oil, spicy hot pepper flakes, juicy beef, and savory soy sauce. It is an inexpensive one-bowl meal that you can quickly put together no matter how many people you need to feed.

One of the keys to the dish is not to skimp on the soybean sprouts, because they shrink drastically when they are cooked. The delicious seasoning sauce is also critical because of its many distinct flavors. I mince my own lean beef to make sure there's no extra fat—kongnamulbap should taste clean and light—but you can use ground beef if you're in a hurry.

I serve the rice with kimchi, and I top each portion with a sunny-side-up egg. Anyone who sees a sunny-side-up egg on their food can't help but be happy.

1 cup short-grain white rice

1 (12-ounce) package soybean sprouts (kongnamul)

3 ounces flank steak or brisket, minced (a little more than ½ cup)

Pinch of kosher salt

Pinch of freshly ground black pepper

1 teaspoon toasted sesame oil

1½ cups water

1 tablespoon vegetable oil

2 large eggs

Spicy Soy Seasoning Sauce (page 272)

1. Put the rice in a medium heavy stone pot (dolsot) or a saucepan, cover it with cold water, and stir it with your hand, then drain by tilting the pan as far as you can over the sink without pouring out any rice. Stir the wet rice with your hand to release excess starch. Continue to rinse and drain the rice until the water runs clear.

2. Wash and drain the soybean sprouts and pick out any dead beans or brownish roots. Add to the pan.

3. Combine the beef, salt, pepper, and toasted sesame oil in a small bowl and mix well. Add to the pan, along with the 1½ cups water, cover, and cook over medium-high heat for 20 minutes in a stone pot, 10 to 12 minutes in a pan. The rice should be half cooked.

4. Uncover the pot and turn the rice well with a wooden spoon. Turn the heat down to low, cover, and simmer for 10 to 12 minutes. Taste to check if the rice is fully cooked; if it is still a little uncooked, simmer, covered, for another 5 minutes. Remove from the heat.

Facing page: top row: left, rinsed short-grain white rice in a stone pot; right, soybean sprouts and beef mixture in the pot; center row: left, Spicy Soy Seasoning Sauce (page 272); right, stirring the rice; bottom, Soybean Sprout Rice

5. Meanwhile, heat the vegetable oil in a large skillet. Crack the eggs into the pan and fry sunny-side up.

6. Fluff up and mix the kongnamulbap well with a wooden spoon. Transfer to two serving bowls and place an egg on top of each portion. Serve with seasoning sauce.

Korean-Style Curry Rice *(Ka-re rice)*
Serves 2 or 3

The British introduced curry rice—white rice with a sauce or porridge spiced with curry powder poured over it—to Japan in the late nineteenth century. Koreans learned the recipe from the Japanese, and over the years they adapted it, using local ingredients. Maybe this is why we call it ka-re rice instead of ka-re bap. But it wasn't until 1969, when the Korean company Ottogi began to package its own curry spices, that the dish became popular. Now we are so accustomed to the taste of this version that most of us prefer it over authentic Indian curry. The curry powder you'll need can be found in Korean grocery stores. It comes mild or spicy—buy whichever you prefer.

Clockwise from top left: prepared vegetables and beef; curry powder mixture; Korean-Style Curry Rice; simmering curry

2 tablespoons unsalted butter

½ pound pork loin or flank steak, cut into ¼-inch cubes

2 small russet or Yukon Gold potatoes (about 10 ounces), peeled and cut into ¾-inch cubes

1 large onion (about 8 ounces), cut into ¾-inch cubes

1 medium carrot (about 3 ounces), peeled and cut into ¼-inch cubes

3 cups water

1 (3.52-ounce) package Korean curry powder (ka-re-ga-ru)

Fluffy White Rice (page 36)

1. Heat the butter in a large skillet over medium-high heat. Add the meat and stir-fry until the meat is no longer pink, about 3 minutes. Add the potatoes and stir-fry until slightly translucent, about 3 minutes. Add the onion and carrot and stir-fry until they begin to soften, about 3 minutes.

2. Add 2½ cups of the water, cover, turn the heat down to medium, and cook until the potatoes are tender, 10 to 12 minutes.

3. Meanwhile, mix the curry powder with the remaining ½ cup water in a small bowl.

4. Uncover the skillet, add the curry mixture, and simmer, stirring with a wooden spoon, for a few minutes, until the sauce is thick and creamy. Remove from the heat.

5. Divide the rice among individual serving bowls, ladle the curry sauce on top, and serve.

This recipe makes me think of my grandmother, but not because it comes from her. I went to high school in Seoul, and I lived with my siblings there while my parents remained in the south. Occasionally my grandmother would come to stay, and I was always excited to find out what snacks, like steamed sweet potatoes and corn, she would have waiting for us after school. I always said, "My grandmother is the best cook in the world!" She was so happy to hear my compliments. One day I came home from school and said, "Grandmother! I will make curry rice for dinner." "What is it?" she asked. She had never had it before. While she was eating my dish, she kept saying: "Delicious, delicious. My granddaughter is such a good cook!" My grandmother was the best cook I knew, so this meant a lot to me. This recipe is the one I made for her all those years ago.

Seaweed Rice Rolls *(Gimbap)*

Serves 4

Gimbap is made by rolling up rice and other ingredients in sheets of gim (aka nori, or seaweed paper) and cutting the rolls into bite-size pieces. Gimbap and sushi are similar, but the biggest difference between the two is that the rice in gimbap is seasoned with sesame oil, and the rice in sushi is seasoned with vinegar. Gimbap is a favorite picnic food and a popular choice for lunch boxes—as popular as sandwiches are in the United States. I almost always pack a gimbap lunch with me when I go on a journey. It's simple to make; it's a healthy, affordable alternative to fast food; and it's easy to eat. When I take out my gimbap lunch in the airport, I'm the envy of all the other travelers!

There are no hard-and-fast rules about the fillings, and you can skip whatever you don't like or can't find. Carrots, yellow radish pickle, egg, spinach, and beef or ham are all popular. The one that I just can't leave out is the radish pickle. You can buy yellow radish pickles (which are sold in airtight packages, precut or whole) and a bamboo mat to help you roll up the gimbap at Korean grocery stores.

Keep leftover gimbap in the fridge. When you're ready to eat it, freshen it by dipping each piece in some beaten egg and then panfrying in some vegetable oil until golden brown and crunchy on all sides.

Fluffy White Rice (page 36), freshly cooked

Kosher salt

1 tablespoon toasted sesame oil

3 large eggs

Vegetable oil

8 ounces lean ground beef

1 tablespoon soy sauce

5 garlic cloves, minced

2 tablespoons light brown sugar or granulated sugar

¼ teaspoon freshly ground black pepper

1 pound spinach, blanched in boiling water for 1 minute, rinsed under cold water, squeezed dry, and coarsely chopped

5 (8-inch) crab sticks

5 (7-x-8-inch) sheets dried seaweed paper (gim, aka nori)

5 yellow pickled radish (danmuji), patted dry and cut into strips

1. Transfer the hot cooked rice to a large wide bowl. Gently stir in ½ teaspoon salt and 1 teaspoon of the toasted sesame oil, taking care not to break the grains of rice.

2. Beat the eggs with ¼ teaspoon salt in a small bowl. Heat a 10- to 12-inch non-stick skillet over medium-high heat. Add a few drops of vegetable oil. When the oil is hot, spread it over the bottom of the skillet with a paper towel and then turn the heat to very low. Pour the beaten eggs into the skillet, tilt it so that the eggs cover the bottom evenly, and cook until set but not browned, 30 seconds to 1 minute. Flip the egg sheet over, remove from the heat, and let sit in the skillet for a minute or two to finish cooking. Transfer to a cutting board to cool slightly.

continued

Top row: left, cooked short-grain white rice; right, the beef mixture; second row: left, vegetables for filling; right, spreading rice over gim; third row, left and right, rolling up rolls; bottom, Seaweed Rice Rolls

3. When the eggs are cool enough to handle, cut into ½-inch-wide strips.

4. Combine the beef, soy sauce, three fifths of the minced garlic, the brown sugar, pepper, and 1 teaspoon of the sesame oil in a bowl. Heat a large skillet over high heat. Add the beef and cook, stirring, for 3 to 4 minutes, until most of its moisture has evaporated and the meat is shiny and brown. Remove from the heat and let cool.

5. Mix the spinach with ½ teaspoon salt, the remaining minced garlic, and the remaining 1 teaspoon toasted sesame oil in a bowl.

6. Heat a few drops of vegetable oil in a large skillet over medium-high heat. Add the crab sticks and cook for about 30 seconds, then flip them over and cook for another 30 seconds. Remove from the heat and set aside.

7. Assemble the gimbap: Divide the rice into 5 portions. Hold one edge of a sheet of gim between your thumb and forefinger and move it over a low flame (keep it moving so it doesn't burn) for a few seconds to lightly toast it on one side. You don't want it to become too crispy, or it will crack and crumble when you try to roll it. Place the sheet on a bamboo mat, shiny side down.

8. Spread 1 portion of rice evenly over the gim, leaving a 2-inch border at the top. (This will help you make nice round slices.) Spread ¼ cup of the ground beef mixture in a thin strip across the middle of the rice. Press it down with a spoon so it stays in place. Put one fifth of the spinach, a crab stick, a few egg strips, and a radish strip on top of the beef. Pick up the bottom edge of the mat and use it to roll the gim up and over the fillings, then continue rolling up the gim, using the mat, until you have a neat, clean roll. Remove the roll from the mat and cut into ⅓-inch to ½-inch slices. (For easier slicing, wipe your knife often with a wet kitchen towel or paper towel.) Repeat with the remaining ingredients to make 4 more rolls. Arrange on a plate and then serve.

Variation: Vegetarian Gimbap

Replace the ground beef with several pieces of packaged fried tofu, cut into ½-inch-wide strips, and the crab sticks with carrot strips; skip the egg.

To prepare the tofu, slice several pieces into ½-inch-wide strips. Heat a large skillet lightly filmed with vegetable oil over medium-high heat. Add 2 teaspoons soy sauce, 2 teaspoons light brown sugar, 1 teaspoon toasted sesame oil, and the tofu and cook, stirring, until golden and shiny. Set aside.

To prepare the carrots, cut a medium carrot into matchsticks. Toss with ¼ teaspoon kosher salt in a small bowl and let stand for 5 minutes, then pat dry with a paper towel. Heat a few drops of vegetable oil in a large skillet over medium-high heat, add the carrots, and stir-fry just until barely beginning to soften, about 30 seconds. Proceed as directed.

Steamed Oysters with Rice *(Gulbap)*
Serves 2

When oysters are cooked with rice, they infuse it with a sweet flavor reminiscent of the sea, and radish adds crispness and an earthy sweetness. Koreans call oysters the "milk of the sea," since they consider milk and oysters to be the most nutritious foods of the land and the sea. Fresh oysters are always best, but you can use frozen, available at Korean markets and many supermarkets, if fresh are not available.

   You don't need to soak the rice for this dish.

1 cup short-grain white rice

1 teaspoon toasted sesame oil

8 ounces Korean radish (mu) or daikon, peeled and cut into matchsticks (about 2 cups)

1 cup water

½ teaspoon kosher salt

2 dozen fresh oysters, shucked, rinsed, and patted dry with paper towels, or ½ pound frozen oysters, thawed and drained

Spicy Soy Seasoning Sauce (page 272)

1. Put the rice in a bowl, cover it with cold water, and stir it with your hand, then drain by tilting the bowl as far as you can over the sink without pouring out any rice. Stir the rice with your hand to release excess starch. Continue to rinse and drain the rice until the water runs clear.

2. Heat a large skillet over medium-high heat for 1 minute. Turn the heat down to medium, add the sesame oil and rice, and cook, stirring with a wooden spoon, for 2 minutes until lightly toasted and fragrant. Add the radish matchsticks and cook, stirring to warm through, 1 minute.

3. Add the 1 cup water and salt to the skillet and mix well with the wooden spoon, scraping the bottom of the skillet to prevent the rice from sticking. Cover and cook for 7 minutes. Add the oysters, mixing them in gently, cover, turn the heat down to low, and simmer until the rice is cooked, 7 to 10 minutes.

4. Remove the rice from the heat, fluff with the wooden spoon, and transfer to a serving bowl. Serve with the seasoning sauce.

Maangchi and Friends

Macdawwg: *I'm celebrating St. Patrick's Day by making Steamed Oysters with Rice. The most important ingredient is love, right? How about smoked oysters instead of fresh?*

Maangchi: *Yes, the most important ingredient is love! But smoked oysters don't sound OK. Use fresh or frozen oysters.*

Bibimbap

Serves 4

Bibim translates as "mixed," and *bap* is "cooked rice," So *bibimbap* literally means "mixed rice"—and it's rice mixed with any number of ingredients. Bibimbap that is heated in earthenware pots for serving is called dolsot-bibimbap, but you can just make the bibimbap and serve it in a large shallow bowl.

This bibimbap is special and very colorful. If you are new to Korean cooking, the recipe may seem a little intimidating. There are a lot of components, and preparing them does take a little time. But if you do make such an elaborate bibimbap, you won't need any side dishes. It is a balanced one-dish meal that will make you feel great. For a simpler version, see below. If you want soup to go with your bibimbap, try Egg Soup (page 87), which you can make in 10 minutes.

Most of the vegetables in this dish—spinach, zucchini, cucumber—are familiar, but dried fernbrake and bellflower root are less well known to American cooks. If you can find them, this is the place to try them. Dried bellflower root is chewy and pleasantly bitter, and fernbrake adds a vegetal meatiness. Taken together, these common and exotic vegetables sing in remarkable harmony. Note that the dried bellflower root and fernbrake must be soaked overnight before you make the dish.

If you are not a big fan of spicy foods, you can season your bibimbap with Spicy Soy Seasoning Sauce (page 272) instead of some or all of the hot pepper paste.

For a simpler variation: Pick and choose just a few ingredients to mix into the rice. I suggest soybean sprouts, spinach, and red bell pepper, which will make your bibimbap both pretty and delicious. Place these on top of the cooked rice, along with the hot pepper paste, raw egg yolk, and sesame oil, and you are done.

Maangchi and Friends

Becky: *Is there a quick way to make bibimbap? I was thinking that we could take our ban-chan leftovers from the fridge and mix them with rice and lots of gochujang.*

Maangchi: *That's right! Heat a pot on the stove, add all your leftover vegetables, and stir until warm, then add the rice and hot pepper paste. Keep stirring with the spoon until the rice is hot. Turn the heat off and stir in sesame oil to taste.*

I sometimes make bibimbap with kimchi: For each bowl of rice, chop ¼ cup Napa Cabbage Kimchi (page 114). Put the kimchi in a hot pan on the stove, add some kimchi brine and hot pepper paste if you'd like, and add the rice. Stir until the bibimbap is sizzling, then drizzle with sesame oil. It's like spicy Korean stir-fried rice.

Facing page: top row: left, prepared beef; right, soaking fernbrake root; middle row: left, bellflower root; right, platter of assembled bibimbap ingredients; bottom, bowl of Bibimbap

for the beef
8 ounces flank steak or filet mignon,
    cut into matchsticks
1 tablespoon soy sauce
1 tablespoon honey or sugar
1 tablespoon minced garlic
2 teaspoons toasted sesame oil
1 teaspoon toasted sesame seeds

for the soybean sprouts
2 cups soybean sprouts (kongnamul)
Pinch of kosher salt
¼ teaspoon toasted sesame oil

for the spinach
8 ounces spinach
Pinch of kosher salt
¼ teaspoon toasted sesame oil

for the peppers or carrots
1 teaspoon vegetable oil
2 small or 1 large red bell pepper, cored,
    seeded, and cut into thin strips (about
    1 cup), or 2 carrots, peeled and cut
    into matchsticks

for the zucchini
1 medium zucchini (about 8 ounces),
    cut into thin disks (about 1½ cups)
Pinch of kosher salt
½ teaspoon vegetable oil
¼ teaspoon toasted sesame oil

for the cucumber
1 small English cucumber (about
    6 ounces), cut into thin disks
Pinch of kosher salt
½ teaspoon vegetable oil

for the bellflower root
1 ounce dried bellflower root (doraji),
    soaked in water for 18 to 24 hours
Kosher salt
1 teaspoon vegetable oil

for the fernbrake
½ ounce dried fernbrake (gosari),
    soaked and boiled as described on
    page 146
½ teaspoon vegetable oil
2 teaspoons soy sauce
2 teaspoons sugar
½ teaspoon minced garlic
1 teaspoon toasted sesame oil

Toasted sesame oil
Fluffy White Rice (page 36), freshly
    cooked
4 large egg yolks
¼ cup Korean hot pepper paste
    (gochujang), plus more for serving
1 teaspoon toasted sesame seeds
Spicy Soy Seasoning Sauce (page 272;
    optional)

1. Prepare the beef: Combine the beef, soy sauce, honey, garlic, sesame oil, and sesame seeds in a small bowl. Cover and refrigerate until ready to use.

2. Prepare the soybean sprouts: Rinse the soybean sprouts under cold water; drain. Pick out any dead beans or brownish roots. Put the sprouts in a medium saucepan, add ¼ cup water, cover, and cook over high heat for 5 minutes. Drain and mix with the salt and sesame oil. Place in a pile on a large platter.

3. Prepare the spinach: Blanch the spinach in boiling water for 30 seconds, drain in a colander, and rinse under cold water. Drain well and squeeze out the excess water. Coarsely chop the spinach and mix with the salt and sesame oil. Transfer to the platter.

4. Prepare the red bell peppers: Heat the vegetable oil in a medium skillet over high heat. Add the peppers and cook until warmed through, 30 seconds, or the carrots for 1 minute, then transfer to the platter.

5. Prepare the zucchini: Combine the zucchini and salt in a small bowl and let stand for a few minutes, then pat dry with a kitchen or paper towel. Heat the vegetable oil in a small skillet over high heat. Add the zucchini and sauté until slightly softened, 1 minute. Stir in the sesame oil and transfer to the platter.

6. Prepare the cucumber: Combine the cucumber and salt in a small bowl and let stand for a few minutes, then pat dry with a kitchen or paper towel. Heat the vegetable oil in a small skillet over high heat. Add the cucumber and sauté for 30 seconds until warmed through. Transfer to the platter.

7. Prepare the bellflower root: Drain the bellflower root. Toss with 1 tablespoon salt, then rub the bellflower for a minute to wilt it slightly and release some of its bitterness. Transfer to a sieve and rinse well to remove the salt, then drain thoroughly. Heat the vegetable oil in a small skillet over high heat. Turn down the heat to medium, add the bellflower root, stirring, and cook until wilted and softened, about 3 minutes. Transfer to the platter.

8. Prepare the fernbrake: Cut the fernbrake into 2-inch lengths. Heat the vegetable oil in a small skillet over medium-high heat. Add the fernbrake and cook, stirring, until softened, 3 to 5 minutes. Add the soy sauce, sugar, garlic, and sesame oil and cook, stirring, for 1 minute. Transfer to the platter.

9. If using earthenware pots (dolsots): Put a few drops of sesame oil in the bottom of each of four 4- to 6-cup pots. Divide the rice among the pots. Arrange the vegetables and beef on the rice. Top each serving with an egg yolk and 1 tablespoon hot pepper paste. Set each pot on a burner. Heat over medium-high heat until you hear a ticking sound coming from the rice.

10. If using a large shallow bowl: Put the rice in the bowl and arrange the vegetables and beef on the rice. Top with the egg yolks and pepper paste.

11. To serve: Sprinkle the bibimbap with the sesame seeds, drizzle with sesame oil to taste, and serve hot with more hot pepper paste and/or soy seasoning sauce on the side. Give each diner a spoon for mixing and eating the bibimbap.

Maangchi and Friends

Kat: *I want to make bibimbap for dinner one of these days, but we don't have an Asian store here in Idaho Falls, so there is no way I can get hold of fernbrake. What do I do?*

Maangchi: *Without fernbrake, it will still be fantastic! You can also substitute blanched spinach seasoned with salt and sesame oil or seasoned cooked soybean sprouts.*

Mixed Rice with Raw Fish *(Hoe-deop-bap)*
Serves 4

Hoe-deop-bap (*hoe* means "raw fish," and *deop* means "added") is a deliciously simple dish of rice, raw vegetables, and raw fish served in a big bowl with spicy sauce and toasted sesame oil. It's light, crisp, and incredibly refreshing. You eat it like you eat bibimbap—with a spoon, after mixing it up in the bowl. A spoonful of mild but earthy soup with tofu calms the palate after a bite of fish and vegetables, and then you are ready to enjoy the spicy fish again.

I learned this recipe from a raw fish expert who has prepared it thousands of times for demanding, hungry Koreans. I met Mrs. Park when I was a family counselor in Toronto. She worked at a Korean restaurant, where one of her main duties was the preparation of hoe-deop-bap, and I convinced her to teach some of our group members how to make her specialty. Of course, this was also the perfect opportunity for me to learn from a real expert.

In a Korean restaurant, hoe-deop-bap can be expensive, but if you make it at home, you can use a generous amount of fish without spending too much.

for the sauce
½ cup Korean hot pepper paste (gochujang)
¼ cup distilled white vinegar
2 tablespoons soy sauce
2 tablespoons honey or sugar
6 garlic cloves, minced
2 scallions, chopped
2 teaspoons minced peeled ginger

for the soup
7 cups water
8 large dried anchovies (mareun-myeolchi), heads and guts removed
⅓ cup fermented soybean paste (doenjang)
2 garlic cloves, minced
½ (of a 15-ounce) package medium-firm tofu, cut into ½-inch cubes
2 scallions, chopped

for the mixed rice
4 cups mixed salad greens or chopped lettuce

2 green Korean chili peppers (cheong-gochu), chopped
2 tablespoons chopped red Korean chili pepper (hong-gochu)
10 perilla leaves (kkaennip), cut into thin strips, or ¼ cup thinly sliced mint leaves
¼ cup thinly sliced onion
2 cups peeled, seeded English cucumber matchsticks
1 cup radish sprouts (optional)
1 avocado, halved, pitted, peeled, and cut into ½-inch cubes (optional)
Fluffy White Rice (page 36)
1½ pounds boneless sushi-grade fish, such as salmon, tuna, or flounder, cut into ½-inch cubes and chilled
½ cup flying fish roe (optional)
Toasted sesame seeds
2 sheets dried seaweed paper (gim, aka nori), lightly toasted (see page 53) and sliced into thin strips
Toasted sesame oil

Facing page: left, Mixed Rice with Raw Fish; right, Vegetarian Hoe-deop-bap

1. Make the sauce: Combine all the ingredients in a small bowl.

2. Make the soup: Combine the water, dried anchovies, soybean paste, and garlic in a medium saucepan and cook over medium-high heat until the water is infused with good anchovy flavor, 30 to 35 minutes.

3. Strain the broth and return it to the pan. Add the tofu and cook over medium heat for 5 minutes until heated through. Add the chopped scallions. Cover to keep warm.

4. Assemble the mixed rice: Arrange the greens, both chili peppers, perilla leaves, onion, cucumber, and sprouts and avocado (if using) in the bottom of a large shallow bowl. Spoon the rice on top. Arrange the fish and roe, if using, on top of the rice. Sprinkle with sesame seeds and the seaweed. Serve with the sauce, soup, and sesame oil on the side.

Variation: Vegetarian Hoe-deop-bap

You can use fried tofu in place of the raw fish. Cut one 14-ounce package medium-firm tofu into bite-size cubes and pat dry with paper towels. Panfry in 2 tablespoons oil, turning occasionally, until light golden brown on all sides and crispy.

Don't have tofu? Oh, well! Just mix the rice and vegetables with the hot spicy sauce and the dish will still be delicious. But no matter what, don't skip the sesame oil—it's the special ingredient that brings it all together.

Toasting Dried Seaweed Paper (Gim)

Toasting dried seaweed paper brings out its flavor and fragrance and makes it crisp, so it is easy to crush.

Hold one edge of a sheet of gim between your thumb and forefinger and wave it over a low flame (keep it moving so it doesn't burn) on a gas burner or an electric burner. As it toasts, it will become crisp and turn from almost black to green. Turn the gim periodically to toast it evenly. (The process takes only seconds.) When the gim is very crisp, place it in a plastic bag and crush it into small pieces.

noodles, rice cake soup, and porridge

In Korea, there are just a few acceptable substitutes for a bowl of rice at a meal: noodles, rice cake soup, or porridge. These also replace the usual soup or stew, but they are always served with side dishes and kimchi.

Koreans eat noodles of all types—homemade and store-bought; fresh and dried; noodles made from wheat, buckwheat, or sweet potato starch. The recipes in this chapter give you an idea of this diversity. Some of these dishes are spicy, some are mild. Some are served piping hot, others ice cold. Some are meaty, some taste of the sea. Some appear in soups, others are covered in sauce. One dish takes several days to prepare, another can be made in minutes. Some use noodles roughly torn by hand, others use noodles that are hand-cut with finesse.

With dried noodles in your pantry or rice cakes in your freezer, you can easily make a pot of soup with not much more than some garlic, scallions, hot pepper flakes, and sesame oil. Or mix up a quick dough of flour and water, roll it out, and tear it into rough, tasty noodles. Prepare a simple broth with a few seasonings and a chopped potato, and you have dinner.

Koreans' love of porridges goes a long way back, when mixing rice with some water was an economical way to stretch food in hard times. These porridges are soft and smooth, hearty, healthy, quick to prepare, and easy to digest. There is one for every taste and time of day. Sesame Seed Porridge, lightly sweetened, makes a good breakfast or snack. Winter Squash Porridge with Rice Cake Balls is a sweet-and-savory vegetarian meal in a bowl. And Shrimp Porridge, seasoned with salt or fish sauce, has the briny flavor that all seafood fans crave.

Wheat flour noodles (somyeon)

Cold Noodle Soup *(Mul-naengmyeon)*
Serves 2

This ice-cold noodle soup is so refreshing that I could eat it every day in the summertime. Try it, and you will feel your body temperature cool right down. It is a little tangy from the fermented radish broth, a little sweet from the pear, and rich and meaty from the brisket. I like it best when the broth is almost frozen but still slushy. You've probably never had anything like it, and once you taste it, you will be hooked.

Most Koreans buy the noodles (available in Korean grocery stores) for this soup rather than preparing them from scratch. Made with wheat flour and a little bit of buckwheat, they are quite chewy—a bit like thin red licorice laces in texture.

The broth, a combination of beef brisket broth and the brine from Radish-Water Kimchi, will make your tongue tingle. Note that you need to prepare the broth 7 or 8 hours ahead so you have time to freeze it.

Shortcut: If you're too busy to make the brisket and kimchi broth, use the packet of powdered or liquid concentrated broth included in the package of naengmyeon noodles. Follow the instructions on the package to make the broth. Freeze until slushy before using.

8 ounces beef brisket

7 cups water

4 cups brine from Radish-Water Kimchi (page 126)

2 teaspoons kosher salt

¼ cup plus 1 teaspoon sugar

1 medium Asian pear, or 2 Bosc pears

10 ounces naengmyeon noodles

10 slices Radish-Water Kimchi (page 126), plus more for serving

¼ English cucumber, cut into matchsticks

1 large hard-boiled egg, shelled and cut in half

1 tablespoon toasted sesame seeds

2 teaspoons Korean mustard seed powder (gyeoja-garu; optional)

1. Rinse the brisket under cold running water, then soak in a bowl of cold water for 10 minutes to remove any blood (this will give you a nice, clear broth).

2. Bring the 7 cups water to a boil in a small pot over high heat. Drain the brisket and add to the pot. Turn the heat down to medium and cook, covered, for 1 hour. Turn the heat down to low and cook for another 50 minutes.

3. Remove the brisket from the pot and set the broth aside to cool. Let the beef cool, then thinly slice it. Cover and refrigerate.

4. Combine the beef broth and kimchi brine in a metal bowl. Add the salt and ¼ cup of the sugar and stir to dissolve. Cover and freeze until the mixture is slushy but not completely frozen, 5 to 6 hours.

5. Mix 2 cups water with the remaining 1 teaspoon sugar in a bowl. Shortly before serving, peel, core, and thinly slice the pear. Add the pear to the sugar water and let sit for a minute (this will keep it from turning brown). Drain.

6. When you are ready to serve, bring a large pot of water to a boil. Add the noodles, stirring with a wooden spoon so they won't stick together, and boil until tender but still chewy, 3 to 5 minutes. Drain the noodles in a colander and rinse under cold running water until cooled and no longer slippery.

7. Divide the noodles between two shallow individual serving bowls. Divide the partly frozen broth between the bowls. Arrange the beef, radish kimchi, cucumber, pear, and egg halves on top. Sprinkle with the toasted sesame seeds. If you'd like to make the soup spicy, mix the mustard seed powder with 1 teaspoon water and spoon a little bit into each bowl. Serve immediately, with more radishes on the side.

Clockwise from top left: frozen broth; garnishes for the soup; Cold Noodle Soup

Cold Spicy, Chewy Noodles
(Bibim-naengmyeon)

Serves 2

There are two types of Korean cold noodles. These chewy noodles in a red sauce are sweet, sour, spicy, and intense, while Cold Noodle Soup (page 58) is mild, tangy, and brothy. I can never decide which one I like better!

Mixing the noodles and sauce with the partially frozen brine just before serving helps coat the noodles with the spices. If you don't have Radish-Water Kimchi brine on hand, you can still make the dish using a bit of the ready-to-mix broth that comes with the noodles; see the shortcut on page 58.

In a restaurant, after the dish is presented to you, your server will come with a pair of scissors and ask if you want your long noodles cut in half. If you do, he will snip them right in the bowl. You can do the same at home if you prefer shorter noodles.

for the spicy seasoning sauce

½ Asian pear, or 1 Bosc pear, peeled, cored, and chopped

2 tablespoons minced onion

2 garlic cloves, minced

1 teaspoon minced peeled ginger

¼ cup Korean hot pepper flakes (gochu-garu)

2 tablespoons Korean hot pepper paste (gochujang)

2 scallions, chopped

2 teaspoons toasted sesame oil

1 tablespoon soy sauce

1 teaspoon kosher salt

¼ cup brown rice syrup (ssal-yeot) or honey

2 teaspoons sugar

2 tablespoons distilled white or apple cider vinegar

2 tablespoons beef stock or water

for the noodles

10 ounces naengmyeon noodles

½ Asian pear, or 1 small Bosc pear, peeled and cored

1 cup brine from Radish-Water Kimchi (page 126), frozen until slushy

8 to 12 slices Radish-Water Kimchi (page 126), or ⅓ cup chopped Napa Cabbage Kimchi (page 114)

½ English cucumber, cut into ½-inch-thick matchsticks (about ½ cup)

1 large hard-boiled egg, shelled and halved

1 teaspoon toasted sesame seeds

Distilled white or apple cider vinegar, for serving (optional)

1. Make the spicy seasoning sauce: Put the pear in a food processor and process until smooth.

2. Measure out ½ cup of the pear puree and transfer to a bowl. (Discard the rest of the puree.) Add the onion, garlic, ginger, hot pepper flakes, hot pepper paste, scallions, toasted sesame oil, soy sauce, salt, rice syrup, sugar, vinegar, and beef broth. Combine all the ingredients in the food processor and process until creamy. Cover and refrigerate for up to 1 week.

3. Make the noodles: Bring a large pot of water to a boil. Add the noodles, stirring with a wooden spoon so they won't stick together, and boil until tender but still chewy, 3 to 5 minutes. Drain the noodles in a colander and rinse under cold running water until cooled and no longer slippery. Divide the noodles between two shallow serving bowls.

4. Peel, core, and thinly slice the pear.

5. Spoon seasoning sauce to taste over each portion of noodles. Add ½ cup icy-cold brine to each bowl. Arrange the kimchi, cucumber, pear, and egg halves on top. Sprinkle the toasted sesame seeds over the eggs. Serve immediately, with the remaining seasoning sauce and, if desired, extra vinegar on the side.

Cold Spicy, Chewy Noodles

Noodles with Black Bean Paste *(Jjajangmyeon)*

Serves 2 to 4

Almost every Korean loves these noodles, which are served at Korean restaurants, Chinese restaurants in Korea, and Korean snack bars. My family always considered them special. I will never forget how my father celebrated the day I passed my middle school examination (a big deal in a Korean family) by buying these noodles for everyone. The restaurant delivered them in a special tin box in less than thirty minutes. I was proud to be the reason for this treat.

The thick, pale yellow, chewy noodles are tossed with a dark brown sauce made from fried black bean paste, pork, and fried onions. Pork and potatoes make the dish hearty but not heavy. It's mild, and most children love it.

I can't count how many people have found my website while searching for this recipe. In Korea, the noodles are just a phone call away, but in most places in the world, if you want the dish, you'll have to make it yourself. That is not a bad thing. Having made my own for many years, I know that the homemade version is always superior in taste and quality.

The secret to the dish is to cook the pork belly until very crisp, so that it keeps its crunchiness even after it is coated with the sauce.

3 tablespoons vegetable oil

8 ounces pork belly, cut into ½-inch cubes

1 cup cubed (½-inch) peeled Korean radish (mu) or daikon

1 cup cubed (½-inch) zucchini

1 large russet or Yukon Gold potato, peeled and cut into ½-inch cubes

1 large onion, cut into ½-inch chunks (about 1½ cups)

⅓ cup black bean paste (chunjang)

2¼ cups water

2 tablespoons potato starch or cornstarch

1 teaspoon sugar

1 teaspoon toasted sesame oil

1 pound fresh or frozen jjajangmyeon noodles, thawed if frozen, uncoiled

½ English cucumber, cut into matchsticks (about 1 cup)

1. Heat a large wok or skillet over high heat. Add 1 tablespoon of the vegetable oil and the pork belly and stir-fry until the pork is golden brown and crisp, 3 to 5 minutes. Pour off the fat in the pan.

2. Add the radish to the wok and stir-fry for 1 minute. Add the zucchini, potato, and onion and stir-fry until the potato looks a little translucent, about 3 minutes.

3. Clear a space in the center of the wok, add the remaining 2 tablespoons vegetable oil to the center, and add the black bean paste. Stir the paste for about 1 minute, then mix the pork and vegetables together with the paste so everything is coated and well combined. Add 2 cups of the water to the wok, stir, cover, and cook for 10 minutes.

4. While the pork and vegetables are cooking, whisk together the potato starch, the remaining ¼ cup water, and the sugar in a small bowl.

5. Uncover the wok and taste a piece of radish and one of potato. If they are still hard, cover and cook for a few minutes longer. When they are softened, lower the heat and stir in the potato starch slurry little by little, then keep stirring until the sauce thickens, about 1 minute. Stir in the sesame oil and remove from the heat.

6. Bring a large pot of water to a boil. Add the noodles, stir, and cook until tender but still chewy, 5 to 7 minutes. Drain the noodles in a colander, rinse them under cold running water, and drain again.

7. Reheat the sauce if necessary. Divide the noodles among individual serving bowls. Spoon the sauce over the noodles and garnish with the cucumber strips. Serve immediately.

Variation: Jjajangbap

Serve the jjajang sauce over Fluffy White Rice (page 36) instead of noodles. Top with the cucumber strips and serve with Napa Cabbage Kimchi (page 114) or yellow pickled radish (danmuji).

Top row: left, cubed pork and vegetables; right, stir-frying ingredients;
bottom row: pork and vegetables simmering in black bean paste; right, Noodles with Black Bean paste

Basic Noodle Soup in Anchovy Broth *(Guksu)*
Serves 2

This noodle soup has a clear broth that is slightly fishy and full of umami flavor. Most Korean housewives keep anchovy stock on hand so they can make a satisfying bowl of noodles at a moment's notice; you can substitute a meat-based stock, though the taste will be very different. The recipe scales up (or down) easily. It is also easy to play with: For example, try adding chopped kimchi or cooked finely chopped beef to each bowl before serving for a more complex version.

While noodle soup is great for when friends drop in and you need food in a hurry, it is also a special-occasion dish. Koreans traditionally associate long thin noodles with longevity, so this soup is often served at birthday parties, to wish for a long life, and at weddings, to wish for a long marriage.

1 teaspoon vegetable oil

1 garlic clove, minced

4 pieces packaged fried tofu, sliced into thin strips

Kosher salt

1 teaspoon sugar

2 teaspoons toasted sesame oil, plus more for sprinkling

8 ounces thin wheat flour noodles (somyeon)

3 to 3½ cups Anchovy-Kelp Stock (page 86)

2 scallions, chopped

2 teaspoons Korean hot pepper flakes (gochu-garu; optional)

2 sheets dried seaweed paper (gim, aka nori), toasted and crushed (see page 53)

1. Heat a large skillet over medium-high heat. Add the vegetable oil, garlic, fried tofu strips, and a pinch of salt and cook, stirring, until the garlic is crisp and golden brown, about 1 minute. Add the sugar and toasted sesame oil and stir for another minute to dissolve the sugar. Remove from the heat.

2. Bring a large pot of water to a boil. Add the noodles, stirring with a wooden spoon so that they won't stick to each other, and cook until tender but still chewy, 3 to 4 minutes. Drain the noodles and transfer them to a large bowl of cold water to cool and remove excess starch. Drain. Rinse and drain the noodles under cold running water a couple of times until they are cold and not slippery.

3. Divide the noodles between two soup bowls or put them in earthenware serving pots.

4. Heat the anchovy stock until hot, then pour it over the noodles so the stock covers the noodles by 1 inch. Add half the tofu strips, the scallions, hot pepper flakes (if using), crushed seaweed paper, and a few drops of toasted sesame oil to each bowl. Sprinkle with salt, if desired. Serve immediately.

Top, fried tofu sliced into strips; bottom, Basic Noodle Soup in Anchovy Broth

Hand-Torn Noodle Soup *(Sujebi)*
Serves 2 to 4

Sujebi is a traditional noodle soup that Koreans like to eat on rainy days to keep them warm and cozy. The rustic noodles are made from just flour, water, salt, and oil. To make a meal of it, serve it with kimchi and a few side dishes.

You can knead the dough by hand or make it in a food processor. If you hand-knead it, put some energy into it—the longer you knead, the chewier and better the noodles will be. Resting the dough in the refrigerator makes it easier to work with.

Tearing the noodles from the mass of dough is a fun job for your children, but "hand torn" doesn't mean sloppy or haphazard. The noodles should be stretched into thin, uniform lengths. You can make yours as narrow or wide as you like, but be sure to stretch them very thin, about ⅛ inch. (You could also use a pasta machine.) Koreans judge the skill of a cook by his or her noodles. Practice makes perfect.

for the dough
2 cups all-purpose flour
¾ cup water
½ teaspoon kosher salt
1 tablespoon vegetable oil

for the soup
10 cups water
12 large dried anchovies (mareun-myeolchi), heads and guts removed
1 (4-x-5-inch) piece dried kelp (dasima), cut into strips

2 medium russet or Yukon Gold potatoes, peeled and cut into chunks
½ cup thinly sliced onion
3 garlic cloves, minced
1 tablespoon fish sauce or Korean soup soy sauce, preferably homemade (page 264)
1 scallion, chopped
1 teaspoon toasted sesame oil

1. **Make the dough:** Combine the flour, water, salt, and vegetable oil in a large bowl and knead in the bowl until the dough is smooth (like pizza dough), 10 to 15 minutes. Alternatively, combine the flour, water, salt, and oil in a food processor fitted with the dough blade and process until the dough comes together in a ball, 1 to 2 minutes. Wrap the dough in plastic and refrigerate for 20 to 30 minutes.

2. **Make the soup:** Pour the water into a large pot, add the dried anchovies and dried kelp, cover, and cook over medium-high heat for 20 minutes. Lower the heat and simmer, covered, for another 20 minutes. Turn off the heat and remove the kelp and anchovies with a slotted spoon; discard the anchovies and reserve a few strips of kelp for garnish.

3. Add the potato, onion, and garlic to the pot and cook over medium-high heat until the potatoes are soft but not falling apart, 15 to 20 minutes.

4. Add the fish sauce and reserved kelp strips, cover, and keep at a low boil.

5. Now it's time to make noodles: Fill a small bowl with cold water. Pick up the dough with your left hand (or right hand, if you are left-handed). Dip the fingers of your other hand into the water and pull and stretch a 3-inch portion of the dough with your wet fingers (the water will prevent your fingers from sticking to the dough): Get it as thin and wide as you can as you stretch it. I stretch mine so each noodle is 2 inches wide and ⅛ inch thick. (The length isn't important as long as the noodles are thin.) Tear the noodle from the dough ball and drop it into the boiling soup. Repeat with the remaining dough, working quickly. Cover the pot and cook until the noodles are tender and float to the surface, 2 to 3 minutes.

6. Remove the pot from the heat and stir in the scallion and sesame oil. Ladle the soup into individual bowls and serve immediately.

Top row: left, noodle dough; right, vegetables for soup; bottom row: left, tearing dough into noodles; right, Hand-Torn Noodle Soup

Spicy Seafood Noodle Soup *(Jjampong)*
Serves 2 to 4

The soup, a staple at Chinese restaurants and snack bars in Korea, has a spicy, smoky broth full of seafood, meat, and vegetables. Koreans often have long discussions about its merits relative to noodles with black bean sauce (see page 62) when ordering takeout. Often we'll order both to avoid an argument.

When I lived in Columbia, Missouri, I stopped by a local Korean grocery store one day where the shopkeeper's wife was my good friend, and she urged me to go to the back of the store because her husband was making jjampong. I had never heard of anyone making this soup at home: Everyone orders it from Chinese restaurants. But his was better than any restaurant's. The key is to start with a high-quality broth, which gives the dish real sea flavor. The shopkeeper made his MSG-free broth with dried anchovies and kelp. I have used his method ever since.

10 cups water
10 large dried anchovies (mareun-myeolchi), heads and guts removed
3 dried shiitake mushrooms
1 (4-x-4-inch) piece dried kelp (dasima)
½ cup thinly sliced onion
4 ounces lean pork loin, cut into matchsticks
Kosher salt and freshly ground black pepper
3 tablespoons Korean hot pepper flakes (gochu-garu)
¼ cup vegetable oil
1 tablespoon minced garlic
2 teaspoons minced peeled ginger
1 pound green cabbage or Napa cabbage, cored and cut into bite-size pieces

½ small carrot, peeled and cut into thin 2-inch strips
4 scallions, cut into 2-inch lengths
1 leek (about 5 ounces), white and light green parts, washed and cut into ½-x-2-inch strips
4 white button mushrooms, sliced
4 ounces fresh or frozen cleaned squid bodies, thawed if frozen, cut into ½-x-2-inch strips
8 large shrimp, shelled and deveined
10 mussels, scrubbed and debearded
1 teaspoon fish sauce
1 pound fresh or frozen jjajangmyeon noodles, thawed if frozen, uncoiled
1 teaspoon toasted sesame oil

1. Combine the water, anchovies, shiitake mushrooms, kelp, and onion in a large saucepan, cover, and cook over medium-high heat for 20 minutes. Turn the heat down to low and cook for 20 minutes longer. Strain the stock; discard the solids. You will have 7 to 8 cups stock.

2. Toss the pork with a pinch each of salt and pepper in a small bowl. Combine the hot pepper flakes and 2 tablespoons of the vegetable oil in another small bowl.

3. Heat the remaining 2 tablespoons vegetable oil in a large wok or a large heavy pot over medium-high heat. Add the garlic and ginger and stir-fry until golden, about 1 minute. Add the pork and stir-fry for 2 minutes. Add the cabbage, carrot, scallions, leek, and white mushrooms and cook, stirring, until soft, about 5 minutes. Add the hot pepper flake mixture and mix well. Add the squid, shrimp, and mussels and cook, stirring, over high heat until the shrimp are pink and the mussels have opened, about 5 minutes.

4. Add 7 cups of the stock, cover, and bring to a boil. Uncover and continue to boil until the flavors meld, 7 to 10 minutes. Stir in the fish sauce, 2 teaspoons salt, and a bit of pepper.

5. Add the noodles to the soup and boil until tender but still chewy, 5 to 7 minutes.

6. Stir in the sesame oil. Transfer to individual serving bowls and serve immediately.

Clockwise from top left: jjajangmyeon noodles; stir-frying garlic, ginger, and pork; Spicy Seafood Noodle Soup

Knife-Cut Noodles with Clams *(Jogae-kalguksu)*

Serves 2 to 4

It's a rainy Sunday afternoon and your family is home, watching TV, doing homework, or just relaxing. You are in the kitchen, kneading and rolling out this dough. Everyone is in a good mood because they know that steamy noodle soup is in their future.

The dough is rolled out by hand and cut into noodles with a sharp chef's knife—in fact, *kalguksu* means "knife-noodles." It's crucial that you measure the flour and water carefully. If the dough is too wet, it will be too sticky to roll out; if it's too dry, it will crack and crumble.

The recipe calls for anchovy stock, but in a pinch you can use homemade chicken stock or canned low-sodium chicken broth. The soup has just a touch of sweetness from the zucchini, the noodles are soft but springy, and the clams add a layer of brininess to the full-flavored stock.

Kosher salt

1¼ pounds littleneck clams, scrubbed

for the dough

2 cups all-purpose flour, plus more for dusting

½ cup plus 2 tablespoons water

1 tablespoon vegetable oil

½ teaspoon kosher salt

for the soup

1 teaspoon vegetable oil

1½ cups thinly sliced zucchini (about 4 ounces)

2 teaspoons toasted sesame oil

8 cups Anchovy-Kelp Stock (page 86)

4 garlic cloves, minced

2 scallions, chopped

Shredded dried hot pepper (silgochu; optional)

1. Combine 4 cups water and 1 tablespoon salt in a bowl and stir to dissolve the salt. Add the clams and refrigerate for a few hours to allow the clams to spit any grit.

2. Make the dough: Combine the flour, water, vegetable oil, and salt in a medium bowl and stir with a wooden spoon until a rough dough forms. Knead it in the bowl or on the countertop for about 5 minutes, until the dough is smooth. Alternatively, combine the flour, water, vegetable oil, and salt in a food processor and process until the dough comes together in a ball. Remove the dough and place on a lightly floured countertop and knead by hand for another few minutes, until smooth. Transfer the dough to a plastic bag and set aside for 30 minutes.

3. Remove the dough from the bag and knead until it is soft and smooth, 5 to 7 minutes. Return the dough to the plastic bag so it won't dry out.

4. Make the soup: Heat the vegetable oil in a large skillet over medium-high heat. Add the zucchini and cook, stirring occasionally, until softened, about 3 minutes. Remove from the heat and stir in 1 teaspoon of the toasted sesame oil. Set aside.

5. Combine the anchovy stock and garlic in a large heavy pot and bring to a boil over medium-high heat. Remove from the heat, covering to keep warm.

6. Lightly flour a large cutting board or work surface. Use a rolling pin to roll the dough into a 12-x-15-inch rectangle. (You can also roll it out with a pasta machine.) Sprinkle the dough with flour and fold it over itself two or three times. Use a sharp chef's knife to cut the folded dough into ⅛-inch-wide noodles. Sprinkle the noodles with a handful of flour to prevent sticking, then toss and shake the noodles with both hands to separate them.

7. Bring the stock back to a boil over medium-high heat. Drain the clams and add the noodles, clams, and 1 teaspoon salt to the boiling stock. Cover and cook until the clams open and the noodles float, 4 to 5 minutes. If any clams don't open, cook a little longer until they do; discard any that don't open. Stir in the remaining 1 teaspoon sesame oil. Remove the soup from the heat.

8. Ladle the soup and clams into two large individual serving bowls or four smaller bowls. Add the sautéed zucchini and scallions to the bowls and garnish with shredded red pepper, if desired. Serve immediately.

Top row: left, rolling out noodle dough; right, cutting dough into noodles;
bottom row: left, shaking noodles to separate them; right, Knife-Cut Noodles with Clams

Rice Cake Soup (Tteokguk)
Serves 2 or 3

This soup is served on our New Year's Day for good luck. Traditionally Koreans follow the lunar calendar, so New Year's Day (*seollal*) is the day of the second new moon after the winter solstice and a different date every year, falling sometime in late January or early February. Many Koreans now also enjoy rice cake soup on January 1 too, which makes us twice as lucky!

The cylindrical rice cakes symbolize a long life, and their whiteness represents purity, renewal, and a clean start to the New Year. The cylinders are now cut diagonally, but traditionally the slices were more coin-shaped, symbolizing financial success. Eating rice cake soup with your friends and family is a wonderful way to wish everyone a happy, healthy, and successful New Year.

But of course you can eat it at any other time of year, and you should, because it is easy and delicious—rich and savory from the brisket and egg.

7 cups water
8 ounces beef brisket, chopped into
    small pieces
3 garlic cloves, minced
1 pound sliced rice cakes (tteokguk-
    yong-tteok)
1 tablespoon fish sauce
1 teaspoon kosher salt

1 large egg, lightly beaten
2 scallions, chopped
1 teaspoon toasted sesame oil
½ teaspoon freshly ground black pepper
1 sheet dried seaweed paper (gim,
    aka nori), toasted and crushed (see
    page 53)

1. Bring the water to a boil in a medium heavy pot over high heat. Add the beef and garlic and cook for 5 minutes. Turn the heat down to medium, cover, and cook until the beef is tender and has infused the water with flavor, 20 to 25 minutes.

2. Add the rice cake slices, fish sauce, and salt, cover, and cook until the rice cake slices have floated to the surface and are softened throughout, about 7 minutes.

3. Pour the egg little by little into the soup; do not stir for 30 seconds. Then add the scallions and stir the soup with a ladle. Remove from the heat and add the toasted sesame oil and pepper.

4. Ladle the soup into bowls and sprinkle the crushed gim on top. Serve immediately.

Maangchi and Friends

Rain: *Hi, Maangchi! I made this soup a little while back—it came out wonderfully, and my mom and dad both loved it. The only trouble was that I made it ahead of time and the rice cake slices got very mushy after a few hours. Would it be OK to just throw the rice cakes in right before eating the soup if I wanted to get most of the work done a day or two in advance?*

Maangchi: *Yes! Make the delicious beef broth ahead and keep it in the fridge. When you want to make the soup, reheat the broth. When the broth boils, add the rice cake slices and cook just until they are as soft and chewy as you want. Wait until the last minute to add the egg and sesame oil too.*

A New Year's Ritual

Today most cooks buy rice cakes in the grocery store, but years ago when I lived in Korea, making rice cakes was a real event. A few days before New Year's Day, I would wash a large bowl of rice, drain it, and take it to the local mill. Back then, every neighborhood had a mill where you could have your rice ground and steamed for a reasonable price. In front of the mill were bowls of rice. I'd put mine at the end of the row and then join my friends nearby, where we could chat while the owner of the mill processed our bowls one by one. No one needed to wait in line; our bowls did it for us. Nor did the mill owner need to call our names when the rice cakes were ready: We all watched our own bowl and knew who was next.

First he ground the rice two or three times. Then he put it into the hopper of his big, powerful steamer. He mixed it with water and a little bit of salt, and the machine steamed the mixture into a large, fluffy rice cake. From there, he transferred it to another machine that shaped the hot rice cake into long cylinders, extruding them into a bath of cold water. The first few wouldn't be smooth enough, so he'd put them back into the shaping machine. Eventually they emerged as silky cylinders, which he cut into sections 10 to 12 inches long. I could never resist tasting the fresh rice cakes made from my rice, and I'd tear off a little piece to try.

Then I'd say good-bye to my friends and go home to dry the rice cakes for 10 to 12 hours, so they would be firm enough to cut into thin disks. It was a lot of work, but worth it for New Year's Day. I froze the leftover rice cakes to enjoy for many more meals.

Rice Cake Soup

Sesame Seed Porridge *(Kkaejuk)*

Serves 2

Juk means "porridge," and if you hang around Koreans, you're going to hear that word a lot. Thick and fortifying, with a satisfying nutty flavor, this version can be a quick breakfast for someone on the go or a snack for a student taking a study break.

   When I was young, my mom would wake me up every morning and ask if I wanted to go with her to the open-air market where she did her shopping. I wasn't interested in shopping so much as I wanted a snack of kkaejuk. In the corner of the market was a woman stirring a big, steaming cauldron of it, with an adjacent bench for customers to sit on. She would ladle some of the golden porridge into a bowl and sprinkle some brown sugar on top. If you asked, she would place an egg yolk on top, which cost extra but was worth it. When I make kkaejuk now, I always remember the scene exactly: the woman, the bench, the market, my mom, and even the patterns in the porridge.

⅓ cup toasted sesame seeds

3 cups water

⅓ cup glutinous rice flour (chapssal-garu)

1 teaspoon kosher salt

1 tablespoon light brown sugar (optional)

2 large egg yolks (optional)

1. Combine the sesame seeds and 1 cup of the water in a blender and blend for 1 minute. Add the remaining 2 cups water and the glutinous rice flour and blend for 30 seconds.

2. Transfer the mixture to a small heavy pot, add the salt, and cook over medium heat, stirring occasionally with a wooden spoon, until the porridge thickens and bubbles start popping, 5 to 7 minutes. Then continue to cook, stirring, until the porridge is smooth and has thinned a little bit, another 5 minutes.

3. Transfer to serving bowls, sprinkle with the brown sugar, if using, and place an egg yolk on top of each bowl, if desired. Serve immediately.

Facing page: top, Sesame Seed Porridge; bottom, Shrimp Porridge (page 76)

Shrimp Porridge *(Saeu-juk)*

Serves 2 or 3

If you like shrimp and grits, you will love this. It has a similar texture, but it is a little soupier, and the shrimp give the porridge a sweet brininess. You can replace the shrimp with mussels or clams, or even ground beef. If you are using soup soy sauce instead of fish sauce, it will be less salty, so use more to taste. *The photo is on page 74.*

½ cup short-grain white rice

2 teaspoons toasted sesame oil

1 garlic clove, minced

4 ounces shrimp, shelled, deveined, and chopped

¼ cup chopped peeled carrot

⅓ cup chopped Asian chives or scallions

4 cups water

1 teaspoon fish sauce or Korean soup soy sauce, preferably homemade (page 264), to taste

½ teaspoon kosher salt

1 large egg, lightly beaten

1 sheet dried seaweed paper (gim, aka nori), toasted and crushed (see page 53)

1. Put the rice in a bowl and cover with cold water. Drain the water and scrub the wet rice with one hand. Rinse, drain, and repeat until the water runs clear. Cover with water and let stand for 30 minutes. Drain.

2. Heat a large saucepan over medium heat. Add the rice, sesame oil, and garlic and stir with a wooden spoon until the rice turns translucent, 2 to 3 minutes. Add the shrimp, carrot, and Asian chives and cook, stirring, for 1 minute.

3. Add the water, turn the heat up to medium-high, cover, and cook for 10 minutes. Turn the heat down to low, stir the porridge, cover, and cook for another 5 minutes.

4. Add the fish sauce and salt. Slowly drizzle in the beaten egg. Cover and cook for a minute until the egg is set. Remove from the heat.

5. Ladle the porridge into individual serving bowls, sprinkle with the crushed gim, and serve immediately.

Red Bean Porridge with Rice Cake Balls

(Dongji-patjuk)

Serves 2 or 3

Pat is the name for red azuki beans, which have been used in Korean cuisine for thousands of years. Of all the porridges, patjuk is an all-time favorite, and dongji-patjuk, which contains chewy rice cake balls, is especially beloved.

The flavor of the porridge is nutty and sweet, especially when you add a little sugar, as many Koreans do, and the texture of the mashed beans is similar to Mexican refried beans, but looser. The starch released from the rice cake balls makes the porridge very smooth.

Dongji-patjuk is even tastier the day after it is made. As the porridge cools, it thickens and the rice cake balls become chewier.

for the porridge

1 cup dried azuki beans, picked over, washed, and drained
10 cups water
2 teaspoons kosher salt
Sugar for serving (optional)

for the rice cake balls

2¼ cups glutinous rice flour (chapssal-garu)
½ teaspoon kosher salt
1 tablespoon sugar
1 cup boiling water

1. Make the porridge: Combine the beans and water in a large heavy pot and cook over high heat for 30 minutes. Turn the heat down to low and simmer until the beans are very soft and mash easily, about 1½ hours longer.

2. Set a coarse strainer over a large bowl. Pour the beans and water into the strainer and mash the beans with a spoon, pushing them against the strainer so their soft interiors fall into the bowl. Discard the bean skins left in the strainer and transfer the bean porridge to a medium pot.

3. Make the rice cake balls: Combine 2 cups of the rice flour, the salt, and sugar in a bowl. Add the boiling water and mix well with a wooden spoon. Then knead by hand in the bowl until a smooth dough forms, about 5 minutes. Wrap the dough in plastic and let it rest on the counter for 20 minutes.

4. Put the remaining ¼ cup rice flour in a large shallow bowl or spread it on a cutting board. Dust your fingers with some of the rice flour, pull off small pieces of the dough, roll into ½-inch balls, and place in the bowl or on the cutting board; recoat your hands with flour as necessary. Roll the balls in the rice flour so they won't stick to each other. Transfer the balls to a large floured baking sheet. Use immediately or cover with a paper towel and refrigerate for up to 3 hours.

continued

5. Bring the porridge to a boil over medium-high heat. Add the rice cake balls and the 2 teaspoons salt and cook, stirring, until the rice cake balls float to the surface, 5 to 6 minutes; skim the foam from the surface with a spoon. Then cook for a few more minutes, until the rice cake balls are fully cooked, stirring occasionally so that the porridge on the bottom of the pot doesn't scorch.

6. Ladle the porridge into soup bowls and serve with additional sugar on the side, if desired.

Celebrating Dongjitnal with Patjuk

In Korea, red bean porridge is served year-round. It's a popular snack in shopping center food courts—like French fries in the United States. But it's traditional to make and eat it during Dongjitnal, the winter solstice festival, which takes place on or around December 22. The red bean porridge served then, called dongji-patjuk, is special because it includes rice cake balls. Looking like little birds' eggs, they symbolize new life and prosperity and celebrate the longer days to come. Koreans also believe the red color of the porridge wards off evil spirits. Before eating the porridge on Dongjitnal, people used to smear some of the patjuk on the front door, and my grandmother would leave a bowl at the gate to her house.

When I lived in Korea, I made dongji-patjuk to share with my family, neighbors, and close friends. They also brought their own patjuk to my house, so we had all kinds of porridge made by different people, everyone sharing with each other to protect ourselves from bad luck and to wish each other success in the coming year. It's a beautiful tradition that strengthens family and community bonds.

Winter Squash Porridge with Rice Cake Balls (Hobakjuk)

Serves 2 or 3

Winter squash (*hobak*) porridge is often served as a simple lunch in Korea. When I was young, I used to eat it when I visited my grandmother during winter vacation. She lived on an island and had a patch out back where she grew her hobak. As the squash grew, they became wider and flatter, and their flesh turned orange and sweet. She stockpiled them in a cool place in her house, and they lasted all winter and into early spring.

My grandmother's version of hobakjuk is delicious, and the thick, slightly sweet porridge is a beautiful warm orange color. The tiny, chewy rice cake balls, which I added, contrast with the creamy soup.

for the porridge
2 pounds butternut squash
6 cups water
1 teaspoon kosher salt
3 tablespoons sugar, plus (optional) more for serving
Napa Cabbage Kimchi (page 114)

for the rice cake balls
2 cups glutinous rice flour (chap-ssal-garu), plus more for dusting
¼ teaspoon kosher salt
¾ cup boiling water

1. Cook the squash: Cut the squash lengthwise in half. Scoop out the strings and seeds with a spoon and discard. Cut each half crosswise in half and rinse them.

2. Put the squash in a heavy pot, add 3 cups water, cover, and cook over medium-high heat for 30 minutes. Lower the heat and simmer until the squash is very tender and the flesh can be scooped out easily, another 10 minutes. Drain the squash and let cool slightly. Wipe out the pot with a paper towel.

3. Scoop the cooked squash flesh back into the pot; discard the skins. Mash the squash with a potato masher or the back of a spoon until the large pieces are broken up but the squash still has some texture. (The cooked squash can be placed in an airtight container and frozen for up to 1 month. Defrost in the refrigerator before proceeding.)

continued

Maangchi and Friends

Amanda: *I would like to make hobakjuk ahead of time. Can I prepare it early in the day and serve it for dinner? Will the rice cake balls get too soft? Or should I do everything else but not put the rice cake balls in until right before it's time to serve?*

Maangchi: *You can do it either way. You can make the hobakjuk, with the rice cake balls, and put it in the refrigerator, then reheat it before serving. If the porridge looks too thick, add some water. As you heat it, be sure to stir it so that it doesn't burn. Or refrigerate the squash porridge and the rice cake balls separately (put the balls on a plate, cover with plastic, and refrigerate for up to several hours) and finish the cooking before serving.*

Above: top row: left, cooked squash; right, mashed squash; center row: left, rice cake dough; right, rice cake balls; bottom, Winter Squash Porridge with Rice Cake Balls (page 79)

4. Make the rice cake balls: Combine the rice flour, salt, and boiling water in a medium bowl and mix well. Stir with a wooden spoon until the dough cools down, 2 to 3 minutes. Knead by hand in the bowl until a smooth dough forms, about 5 minutes. Wrap in plastic and let it rest on the counter for about 20 minutes.

5. Take a bit of dough and roll it between your palms into a ½-inch ball. Repeat with the remaining dough, keeping the larger dough ball covered with plastic as you work so it doesn't dry out. Transfer the balls to a large floured baking sheet and dust with rice flour. Use immediately or cover with a paper towel and refrigerate for up to 3 hours.

6. Add the 6 cups water to the mashed squash, cover, and bring to a boil over medium-high heat. Add the rice cake balls, salt, and sugar and cook, stirring occasionally, until the rice cake balls float to the surface, 5 to 6 minutes.

7. Ladle the porridge into serving bowls and serve with the kimchi and additional sugar on the side for those who like their hobakjuk extra sweet.

When I first came to the United States, I assumed I wouldn't be able to make hobakjuk, since that type of winter squash is unavailable here. Then I went to a farmers' market in a small Missouri town and noticed butternut squash. I asked the farmer, "How do you cook this?" She answered, "We usually cut it in half, remove the seeds, put some butter, brown sugar, and ground cinnamon into the hollows, and then microwave it." I followed her directions when I came home and realized that it was very similar to hobak—and very tasty.

soups
and stews

The dishes in this chapter are cornerstones of Korean cuisine, along with rice and kimchi. Almost every Korean meal includes a soup or a stew (sometimes both). Part of their purpose is to add a bit of moisture to the spread, since rice in particular tends to dry the mouth.

Soups are always served in individual portions so everyone will have soup next to his or her rice bowl. Stews, on the other hand, are usually put in the middle of the table in a sizzling-hot pot. They're thicker than the soups, and a little bit saltier.

Both are seasoned with fermented soybean paste, soy sauce, fish sauce, and/or hot pepper paste, or sometimes just salt. While tradition allows for both soup and stew to be served at the same table (especially a lighter soup with a heavier stew), for me, one or the other is usually enough.

There is a Korean soup or stew for every taste and occasion. Soybean Sprout Soup is a particular favorite of mine: I love the nutty beans in the light, fresh broth. Meat eaters watching their saturated fat intake will appreciate Beef Radish Soup; its rich, beefy flavor comes from just a few ounces of brisket. For thrifty cooks, Kimchi Stew with Tuna makes a flavorful meal for pennies a serving. Kitchen novices should begin with Egg Soup, which requires just three ingredients—eggs, chicken broth, and scallions—easily found at any supermarket.

Korean soups and stews are relatively quick to make. While Western soups often call for long-simmered stocks made with quantities of poultry or meat, many of the soups in this chapter are flavored with a quick broth made by boiling a few dried anchovies in water for a few minutes, or simply with fish sauce or fermented soybean paste.

All the recipes here should be served with rice and kimchi at the very least. A small bowl of rice (about 1½ cups) with a bigger bowl of soup (about 3 cups) is right for a nice lunch. For a larger meal, add as many side dishes as you like. If you want to eat like a Korean, use chopsticks for the side dishes and a spoon for the rice and soup. Just remember: Koreans never drink soup straight from the bowl!

Spicy Soft Tofu Stew (page 90)

Anchovy-Kelp Stock *(Myeolchi dasima yuksu)*

Makes 10 cups

This simple stock is as versatile as it is umami-rich. I use it in many recipes: Knife-Cut Noodles with Clams (page 70), Seafood Stew (page 102), and Basic Noodle Soup (page 64), to name a few. Whenever my friends taste these dishes, they can't help but ask, "What's in this?" I experimented with many savory ingredients, including dried shrimp and shiitake mushrooms, before I determined that the best-tasting combination was one of the simplest: Dried anchovies, kelp, radish, and onion give plenty of flavor but the stock won't overpower the other ingredients in your dish.

You can make a larger amount of stock if you like and keep it in the fridge for a week, or in the freezer for up to 1 month, handy for whenever you want to make a delicious soup or stew quickly. In a real pinch, if you have no stock in your fridge or freezer and no time, add a few dried anchovies to your soup or stew, then remove them just before you serve.

3½ quarts water
8 ounces Korean radish (mu) or daikon, cut into ¼-inch disks
1 large onion, sliced (about 2 cups)

20 large dried anchovies (mareun-myeolchi), heads and guts removed
1 (7-x-10-inch) piece dried kelp (dasima)
2½ teaspoons kosher salt

1. Combine the water, radish, and onion in a large saucepan, cover, and cook over medium-high heat for 45 minutes.

2. Add the anchovies and kelp and cook for 15 minutes more.

3. Remove the pan from the heat, strain the stock into another saucepan or a bowl, and stir in the salt until dissolved. Serve hot, or let cool, cover, and refrigerate for up to 1 week. Or transfer to airtight containers and freeze for up to 1 month.

Left to right: dried kelp, an onion, dried anchovies, slices of Korean radish

Egg Soup *(Gyeran-guk)*
Serves 4

This quick soup is often served at Korean snack bars, on the house, when you order spicy rice cakes or kimchi fried rice. It is good with a variety of main dishes that might be dry on their own, such as Fried Dumplings (page 210), Spicy Rice Cakes (page 212), Seaweed Rice Rolls (page 44), or Bibimbap (page 48).

1 (15-ounce) can low-sodium chicken broth, or 2 cups homemade chicken stock

3 cups water

2 large eggs, lightly beaten

Kosher salt

2 scallions, finely chopped

1. Combine the broth and water in a medium saucepan and bring to a boil. Slowly pour the eggs into the pan. Let cook for about 10 seconds without stirring and then stir gently. The soup will be clear and the eggs fluffy.

2. Season the soup with salt and ladle into bowls. Sprinkle with the scallions and serve.

Street snack vendor in Korea

Potato–Soybean Paste Soup

(Gamja-doenjangguk)

Serves 4

You may think you know all about potato soup until you try this and see what you've been missing all your life. Anchovies and fermented soybean paste make it irresistibly savory, and chili peppers give it an undercurrent of heat. Perilla seed powder adds just a hint of nuttiness.

I tie the anchovies up in a piece of cheesecloth so they are easy to remove from the soup before serving. But you can add them directly to the soup and then search around for them and fish them out, or just leave them in and eat them.

8 large dried anchovies (mareun-myeolchi), heads and guts removed

6 cups water

1½ pounds russet or Yukon Gold potatoes, peeled and cut into bite-size pieces

1 medium onion, thinly sliced

4 garlic cloves, minced

¼ cup fermented soybean paste (doenjang)

4 scallions, cut into 1½-inch-long pieces

1 or 2 green Korean chili peppers (cheong-gochu), chopped

¼ cup perilla seed powder (deulkkae-garu)

1. Wrap the anchovies in cheesecloth, if desired. Combine the water, potatoes, onion, garlic, anchovies, and soybean paste in a medium heavy saucepan, cover, and cook over medium-high heat for 40 minutes.

2. Add the scallions, chili peppers, and perilla seed powder, cover, and cook for another 10 minutes. Remove and discard the anchovies, if desired. Remove from the heat, ladle into bowls, and serve.

Seaweed Soup *(Miyeokguk)*

Serves 2 or 3

Korean cuisine has many different styles of seaweed soup. In my hometown, they make it with fresh fish, but this version uses beef brisket. The broth for this soup is light and savory, and the dried seaweed, which is soft yet chewy, adds a touch of ocean flavor.

Because miyeok is rich in iodine and calcium, the soup is ideal for nursing mothers after childbirth. Many new moms eat it for a full month after delivery, for the health of their child as well as their own. That is why we Koreans also call it "birthday soup" and traditionally eat it with rice on our own birthdays.

¾ ounce (about 1 cup) dried seaweed (miyeok)

7 cups water

8 ounces beef brisket or skirt steak, chopped into small pieces

4 garlic cloves, minced

3 tablespoons fish sauce or Korean soup soy sauce, preferably home-made (page 264)

1 teaspoon toasted sesame oil

1. Soak the dried seaweed in a bowl of cold water for 30 minutes. Rinse, drain, and coarsely chop.

2. Combine the seaweed and the 7 cups water in a large saucepan, cover, and cook over medium-high heat for 20 minutes.

3. Add the beef and garlic and boil for another 20 minutes.

4. Add the fish sauce and boil for a few minutes more. Remove the soup from the heat, stir in the sesame oil, and serve immediately.

My mom ate this soup after giving birth to me, and she made it for me after I had each of my children. And when she calls me to wish me a happy birthday, the first thing she asks is if I've made miyeokguk! The day I became a Canadian citizen happened to be my birthday. When I returned to work after getting my citizenship card, my Korean coworker had put a bowl of miyeokguk and rice on my desk with a birthday card, congratulating me on my first day as a Canadian. I couldn't help it—I cried with happiness!

Spicy Soft Tofu Stew *(Sundubu-jjigae)*
Serves 2

The key to this dish is a rich broth, so cook the pork in chicken stock. You can replace the pork with beef brisket. Or, if you're a seafood lover, you can use about 12 clams, mussels, or oysters, and/or 6 shrimp instead of or with the pork, along with the stock of your choice.

This version is quite spicy, but you can adjust the seasonings to taste. For a much milder stew, use 1 tablespoon instead of ¼ cup hot pepper flakes.

Koreans traditionally cook and serve this dish in a heavy earthenware pot (ttukbae-gi) or stone pot (dolsot) but a regular pot will do.

¼ cup Korean hot pepper flakes
   (gochu-garu)
1 tablespoon vegetable oil
1 teaspoon toasted sesame oil
4 ounces pork belly or boneless pork
   shoulder, chopped into small pieces
6 garlic cloves, minced
½ cup chopped Napa Cabbage Kimchi
   (page 114)

1 medium onion, finely chopped
2 cups homemade chicken stock or
   canned low-sodium chicken broth
1 teaspoon kosher salt
2 (11-ounce) tubes soft tofu (sundubu)
2 large eggs
2 scallions, chopped

1. Mix the hot pepper flakes and vegetable oil in a small bowl.

2. Heat a medium heavy pot over medium-high heat. If you are using an earthenware pot (1½-quart pot), this will take a few minutes. Add the sesame oil, pork, and garlic and cook, stirring with a wooden spoon, until the pork is no longer pink and the garlic is fragrant, 2 to 3 minutes.

3. Add the kimchi and onion and cook, stirring, until the onion turns translucent, about 7 minutes. Add 2 tablespoons of the hot pepper flake mixture and mix well. Add the stock and salt, turn the heat down to medium, and cook until bubbling, 10 to 15 minutes.

4. Cut the tubes of tofu in half and squeeze the tofu into the boiling stew. Use a wooden spoon to break the tofu into smaller pieces, then heat until the stew bubbles, a few more minutes.

5. Drizzle the remaining hot pepper flake mixture over the stew, then crack the eggs into the stew, leaving space between them. Add the scallions and cook until the egg whites are set but the yolks are still runny, a few more minutes. Serve immediately.

Facing page: top row: left, cooking pork belly and garlic; right, adding kimchi and onion; second row: left, Korean hot pepper mixture; right, simmering stew; third row: left, adding soft tofu; right, adding eggs; bottom, Spicy Soft Tofu Stew

Top, cooking the soup; bottom, a bowl of Soybean Sprout Soup

Soybean Sprout Soup (Kongnamulguk)

Serves 4

Kongnamulguk is one of the most common soups eaten in Korean homes. The broth is light and the bean sprouts succulent, fresh, and a little nutty tasting. The ground toasted sesame seeds sprinkled on top intensify the nutty flavor. Many families eat this soup at least once a week for breakfast, lunch, or dinner. It's also said to be a great hangover cure.

If you're not a fan of spicy foods, skip the hot pepper flakes. This is one of my favorite soups, and I like it either way.

1 pound soybean sprouts (kongnamul), washed and drained

8 large dried anchovies (mareun-myeolchi), heads and guts removed

6 garlic cloves, minced

½ medium onion, thinly sliced

1 tablespoon soy sauce

1 tablespoon kosher salt

1 tablespoon Korean hot pepper flakes (gochu-garu)

8 cups water

3 scallions, chopped

1 tablespoon toasted sesame oil

¼ cup toasted sesame seeds, finely ground in a spice grinder

1. Combine the soybean sprouts, anchovies, garlic, onion, soy sauce, salt, hot pepper flakes, and water in a large saucepan. Cook, covered, over medium-high heat for 30 minutes.

2. Add the scallions to the pot, stir, and remove from the heat. Remove and discard the anchovies if you'd rather not eat them. Stir in the sesame oil.

3. Ladle the soup into bowls, sprinkle a tablespoon of sesame seed powder over each portion, and serve.

Maangchi and Friends

Jenny: *It's hard to find dried anchovies on Long Island. Can I use anchovy paste? If so, how much would you recommend?*

Maangchi: *I wouldn't replace dried anchovies with anchovy paste. But you could use a 4-x-7-inch piece of dried kelp instead of the anchovies. Or check out the Korean grocery stores in Flushing, Queens, or buy some online.*

Dried Pollock Soup *(Bugeo-guk)*

Serves 2

Because of the high price of dried pollock, dried pollock soup is considered something special to make for someone you love. (It's also a hangover cure.) When the slightly salty, chewy, and flaky fish meets the sweet radish, the result is magical. This soup comes together quickly, and when served with rice, it's light but filling.

1 teaspoon toasted sesame oil
1 ounce shredded dried pollock (bug-eo-chae)
2 garlic cloves, minced
5 cups water
2 cups 1-x-1½-x-⅛-inch pieces peeled Korean radish (mu) or daikon

1 tablespoon fish sauce or Korean soup soy sauce, preferably homemade (page 264)
½ teaspoon kosher salt
1 large egg, beaten
2 scallions, chopped

1. Heat a large saucepan over medium-high heat. Add the sesame oil, pollock, and garlic and stir with a wooden spoon for 30 seconds to combine. Add the water and radish, cover, and cook until fragrant and a little smoky and the radish is soft, about 20 minutes.

2. Add the fish sauce and salt, turn the heat down to medium-low, and cook, covered, until the radishes are translucent, 10 to 15 minutes longer.

3. Pour the beaten egg into the boiling soup and cook, without stirring, until the egg is cooked and floating on the surface, about 10 seconds. Remove the pan from the heat, add the scallions, and serve.

Dried pollock

Beef Radish Soup *(Soegogi-muguk)*

Serves 2 or 3

This soup has a satisfying sweet flavor that Koreans recognize instantly and newcomers to the dish immediately appreciate. I always use well-marbled point-cut brisket, since there should be a little fat in the beef to give the soup richness. The beef is added once the radishes are already boiling in the water, and that helps keep the broth clear.

Beef used to be very expensive in Korea, so much so that it was given as a gift on special occasions. Wrapped in newspaper from the butcher, it didn't look fancy, but everyone was happy to get such a present.

Seasoning the soup with homemade Korean soup soy sauce is the best and most authentic way to finish it. When I taste soegogi-muguk made that way, it brings me right back to the Korean countryside, where soup soy sauce is aged in huge earthenware crocks. But you can use fish sauce and still enjoy the results.

8 ounces Korean radish (mu) or daikon, peeled

7 cups water

8 ounces beef brisket, cut into 1-x-½-x-¼-inch pieces

4 garlic cloves, minced

1 tablespoon fish sauce or Korean soup soy sauce, preferably homemade (page 264)

1 teaspoon kosher salt

¼ teaspoon freshly ground black pepper

2 scallions, thinly sliced on the diagonal

1. Trim the root end of the radish so it lies flat and put it on a cutting board flat end down. Moving around the perimeter of the radish, slice off 1½-inch-square pieces. The pieces should be of uneven thickness, ranging from ⅛ to ¼ inch thick.

2. Combine the radish and water in a large saucepan, cover, and cook over medium-high heat for 15 minutes.

3. Add the beef and garlic to the pan, turn the heat down to medium, and cook, covered, for 25 minutes. Stir in the remaining ingredients and cook for another 5 minutes.

4. Ladle the soup into bowls and serve.

Left, slicing radish; right, Beef Radish Soup

Spicy Beef and Vegetable Soup *(Yukgaejang)*

Serves 3 or 4

This soup is smoky, spicy, and rich, with healthy hunks of sliced beef and plenty of vegetables that are soft, but not mushy—they're full of wild mountain flavor. Served with rice, it is a satisfying, warming meal. (Leftovers will keep in the refrigerator for 1 week, so you can reheat some any time you need a quick bite.)

Traditionally the soup is made with a variety of mountain vegetables, each one cooked separately, which makes it very time-consuming. When I still lived in Korea, a friend who is a very good cook invited me over and served her own version, which was different from what I was used to but tasty. "How did you make it?" I asked. "The easy way," she replied. She had cut back on the number of vegetables and cooked everything together. In fact, she told me, she sometimes made the soup with just brisket and scallions, and it was *still* delicious. Ever since, I've made it her way.

3 quarts water

1 pound beef brisket

1 medium onion, peeled and cut in half

4 dried shiitake mushrooms

6 ounces fernbrake (gosari), soaked and boiled as described on page 146, cut into 2½-inch pieces

2 to 3 cups mung bean sprouts, washed and drained

2 bunches scallions (12 to 14), cut into 2½-inch-long pieces

7 or 8 garlic cloves, minced

¼ cup Korean hot pepper flakes (gochu-garu)

1 tablespoon toasted sesame oil

1 tablespoon vegetable or olive oil

1 tablespoon soy sauce

1 tablespoon kosher salt

1 teaspoon freshly ground black pepper

1. Bring the water to a boil in a large pot over medium-high heat. Meanwhile, soak the brisket in a large bowl of cold water for about 10 minutes; drain.

2. When the water comes to a boil, add the brisket, onion, and shiitake mushrooms, cover, and cook for 1 hour.

3. While the brisket is cooking, combine the fernbrake, mung bean sprouts, scallions, and garlic in a large bowl. Combine the hot pepper flakes, sesame oil, vegetable oil, soy sauce, salt, and black pepper in a small bowl and mix well with a spoon. Stir into the fernbrake mixture.

4. Remove the beef, onion, and mushrooms from the pot. Strain the stock and return it to the pot. Add the seasoned vegetables, cover, and cook over medium-high heat for 20 minutes.

5. Meanwhile, tear or thinly slice the brisket along the grain. Discard the onion. Slice the mushrooms.

6. Add the beef and mushrooms to the pot and cook for 10 more minutes. Serve hot.

Above: top row: left, sliced cooked brisket and shiitake mushrooms; right, mung bean sprouts;
center row: left, hot pepper flakes mixture; right, cooking vegetables; bottom, Spicy Beef and Vegetable Soup

Soybean Paste Soup with Chard

(Geundae-doenjangguk)

Serves 4

Fermented soybean paste, along with dried anchovies, gives doenjangguk a surprisingly complex and layered flavor, at once savory, earthy, and nutty. And it cooks for only 30 minutes. Most Koreans eat it at least once or twice a week, for breakfast or dinner.

Doenjangguk can be made with almost any vegetable you like. This version uses chard, which is easy to find in any supermarket and gives the dish just a bit of sweetness.

1 pound Swiss chard, stems trimmed
⅓ cup fermented soybean paste (doenjang)
4 garlic cloves, minced
1 green Korean chili pepper (cheong-gochu), stemmed and chopped

1 red Korean chili pepper (hong-gochu), stemmed and chopped
2 tablespoons all-purpose flour
10 large dried anchovies (mareun-myeolchi), heads and guts removed
7 cups water

1. Bring a large pot of water to a boil over medium-high heat. Add the chard and cook, stirring with a wooden spoon, until wilted, about 3 minutes. Drain the chard in a colander and rinse under cold running water until cooled. Drain again and squeeze out excess water with your hands.

2. Chop the chard into small pieces and return it to the pot. Add the soybean paste, garlic, chili peppers, and flour and mix well.

3. Tie the dried anchovies up in a piece of cheesecloth and add to the pot. Add the water, cover, and cook over medium-high heat for 20 minutes. Turn the heat down to medium and boil for another 10 minutes.

4. Remove the anchovies from the pot and discard. Ladle the soup into serving bowls. Or let cool and refrigerate for up to 1 week in an airtight container. Reheat before serving.

Left, chard, soybean paste, garlic, chili peppers, and flour; right, Soybean Paste Soup with Chard Facing page, dried anchovies, kelp, and seaweed sheets store in Korea

Extra-Strong Fermented Soybean Paste Stew *(Cheonggukjang-jjigae)*

Serves 2

With extra-strong fermented soybean paste, kimchi, and dried anchovies, this stew has plenty of the pungent flavors Korean cuisine is known for. The kimchi gives it a bit of spicy sourness and the soybeans in the paste are soft yet firm, and a bit slippery in the mouth.

A bubbling pot of cheonggukjang-jjigae is best enjoyed in the cold wintertime, when the pot will provide warmth as well as nourishment. *The photo is on page 100.*

4 large dried anchovies (mareun-
  myeolchi), heads and guts removed
½ cup chopped Napa Cabbage Kimchi
  (page 114)
¼ cup chopped onion
1½ cups water
1 garlic clove, minced

1 ball (3½ ounces) extra-strong
  fermented soybean paste
  (cheongguk-jang)
5 ounces medium-soft tofu, cut into
  bite-size pieces (about ½ cup)
1 scallion, chopped
Kosher salt

1. Wrap the dried anchovies in cheesecloth, if desired. Combine the kimchi, onion, water, anchovies, and garlic in a small heavy saucepan. (I use a 3-cup earthenware pot, but you can use any small heavy pan.) Cover and cook over medium heat for 20 minutes.

2. Stir in the soybean paste, mixing well, turn down the heat to low, and simmer for 10 minutes.

3. Add the tofu and scallion and cook, covered, for 5 minutes. Season with salt to taste. Remove the anchovies with chopsticks if you'd like and discard. Serve.

*Facing page: top, Extra-Strong Fermented Soybean Paste Stew (page 99);
bottom, Kimchi Stew with Tuna (page 104)*

Above: Seafood Stew (page 102)

Seafood Stew *(Haemul-jeongol)*

Serves 2 or 3

This may seem like a lot of seafood for two or three people, but that is the point of this special, generous dish. This is also a very flexible recipe: Feel free to use more of one type of seafood and less of another, depending on your taste and local availability. Two tablespoons of hot pepper flakes will make it nice and spicy; if you prefer a milder version, use a smaller amount. If you are cooking for a group, just double the recipe and use a bigger pan.

The chrysanthemum greens give the broth a great herbal flavor. They taste like celery leaves but sweeter. I used to see them only at Asian markets, but recently I've bought them at the Union Square Greenmarket in New York City, so a wider group of cooks must be catching on to chrysanthemum's appeal. If necessary, use a few sprigs of mint or basil (which have a more concentrated flavor) in place of the chrysanthemum. The anchovy stock gives the stew a deeper flavor, but if there's no time to make stock, you can use 3 cups water and salt to taste instead. *The photo is on page 101.*

Kosher salt

2 littleneck clams, scrubbed

6 mussels, scrubbed and debearded

1 live blue crab

1 (4-ounce) fresh or frozen cleaned squid body, thawed if frozen

1 small zucchini (about 6 ounces)

1 small onion (about 3 ounces), thinly sliced

1 (4-ounce) cod or flounder fillet, rinsed and patted dry with a paper towel, cut into 2-inch pieces

2 large shrimp, preferably with heads on (long antennae removed)

2 ounces (about 1 cup) chrysanthemum greens (ssuk-gat), washed and left whole or cut into 3-inch lengths, or a few sprigs of fresh mint or basil, plus more for garnish

1 red Korean chili pepper (hong-gochu), stemmed and sliced diagonally, or 1 small red bell pepper, sliced into strips

1 green Korean chili pepper (cheong-gochu), stemmed and sliced diagonally, or 1 small green bell pepper, sliced into strips

3 scallions, cut into 1-inch pieces

2 ounces enoki mushrooms, trimmed, washed under cold running water, and shaken dry

1 teaspoon soy sauce

3 garlic cloves, minced

2 tablespoons Korean hot pepper flakes (gochu-garu)

3 cups Anchovy-Kelp Stock (page 86)

1. Combine 2 cups water and 1 teaspoon salt in a small bowl and stir to dissolve the salt. Add the clams and mussels and let soak for a few hours in the refrigerator. Put the crab in the freezer for 2 hours.

2. Slit the squid body open and lay it out flat on a cutting board. Use a sharp chef's knife to score the squid diagonally. Turn it around and score it again to create a diamond pattern. Cut the squid into 1-x-3-inch strips.

3. Pull the apron away from the crab and twist it off. Pull off and reserve the top shell. Remove and discard the gills. Use scissors to cut away the mouth parts. With a sharp chef's knife, cut the body in half. Twist off the large claws and reserve. Rinse the crab well.

4. Drain and rinse the clams and mussels.

5. Cut the zucchini into 2-inch crosswise pieces, then cut each piece in half lengthwise. Slice each half lengthwise into ¼-inch-thick pieces. Scatter the onion and zucchini pieces over the bottom of a 10-inch skillet. Arrange the cod, shrimp, clams, mussels, squid, and crab pieces—including the reserved crab shell—on top of the onion and zucchini. Scatter the chrysanthemum greens, chili peppers, and scallions on top of the crab. Place the mushrooms in the center of the pan in a bunch (like a bouquet of flowers).

6. Combine the soy sauce, garlic, and hot pepper flakes in a small bowl and mix well to make a paste. Form the paste into a ball and place next to the mushrooms.

7. Carefully pour the anchovy stock into the pan. Cook, covered, over medium-high heat for 15 minutes. Uncover and stir to distribute the hot pepper mixture, then continue to cook, uncovered, stirring occasionally, until the crab is cooked through, about 10 minutes.

8. Stir in 1 teaspoon salt until dissolved, garnish with more chrysanthemum leaves, and serve from the pan.

Left, seafood prepared for the stew; right, cooking Seafood Stew

Kimchi Stew with Tuna *(Chamchi-kimchi-jjigae)*

Serves 3 or 4

Everyone who tastes it loves this dish of sweet, sour, slightly crispy cabbage in a savory broth perfumed with sesame oil. A can of tuna adds flavor and protein, but you can substitute 8 ounces pork belly, chopped into bite-size pieces, for a meaty version. Add it along with the kimchi and other ingredients to give it time to cook through.

This recipe calls for a pound of well-fermented kimchi, which may seem like a lot, but it's a reflection of the quantities of kimchi we Koreans consume—and why we make it huge batches. Not only do we eat it as a side dish, but we also use it as a prime ingredient in many traditional dishes, including this one. *The photo is on page 100.*

1 pound Napa Cabbage Kimchi (page 114), cut into 2-inch pieces, plus ¼ cup of the brine

1 medium onion, sliced (about ¾ cup)

2 tablespoons Korean hot pepper flakes (gochu-garu)

2 teaspoons sugar

1 teaspoon kosher salt

2 teaspoons toasted sesame oil

3 scallions, 2 sliced into 1-inch pieces, 1 chopped

2½ cups water

1 (5-ounce) can chunk light tuna packed in oil, drained

8 ounces medium-firm tofu, cut into ½-inch slices and then into bite-size pieces

1. Combine the kimchi, kimchi brine, onion, hot pepper flakes, sugar, salt, sesame oil, and sliced scallions in a large skillet. Add the water, cover, and cook over medium-high heat for 25 minutes.

2. Stir the stew well with a spoon. Add the tuna and tofu, stirring gently so as not to break up the tofu. Cover and cook until the kimchi is softened but still a little crisp and the tofu is soft, fluffy, and hot, 5 to 7 minutes.

3. Sprinkle the chopped scallion on top of the stew and serve.

Spicy Pollock Roe Stew *(Altang)*

Serves 2 to 4

The fish roe in this stew adds a pleasantly soft, pebbly texture, and chrysanthemum greens impart an herbal edge. This is a simpler dish, as there's no stock to prepare, and there are no fish bones in it, so it's easy to eat too. With a bowl of rice, it makes a good quick meal.

I use frozen pollock roe because it's easy to find in a Korean grocery store, but you can use any kind of fresh fish roe sold in a fish market, including salmon roe, if you prefer.

5 ounces Korean radish (mu) or daikon, peeled and cut into ⅛-inch slices and then into bite-size pieces (about 1 cup)

1 medium onion, sliced

2 tablespoons fermented soybean paste (doenjang)

3 cups water

1 (12-ounce) package frozen pollock roe (naengdong-myeong-ran), thawed in the refrigerator

4 or 5 garlic cloves, minced

3 tablespoons Korean hot pepper flakes (gochu-garu)

1 teaspoon kosher salt

3 scallions, cut diagonally into ½-inch pieces

1 green Korean chili pepper (cheong-gochu), stemmed and sliced

1 red Korean chili pepper (hong-gochu), stemmed and sliced

1 ounce (about ½ cup) chrysanthemum greens (ssuk-gat), washed and left whole or cut into 3-inch lengths, or a small handful of basil

1. Combine the radish, onion, soybean paste, and water in a shallow 10-inch pot or sauté pan. Cover and cook over medium-high heat until the onion is almost translucent, about 12 minutes.

2. Add the fish roe, garlic, hot pepper flakes, and salt, turn the heat down to medium, cover, and cook for 10 minutes.

3. Scatter the scallions, chili peppers, and chrysanthemum greens over the top of the boiling stew, cover, and cook for another 3 minutes. Serve.

Left, pollock roe; right, Spicy Pollock Roe Stew

Soybean Paste Soup with Spinach and Clams *(Sigeumchi-jogae-doenjangguk)*

Serves 4

I usually make the broth for doenjangguk with dried anchovies, as in the recipe on page 108, but when I find good-quality clams and spinach at the market, I make this version of the soup, which is a Korean classic. With the combination of soybean paste and the shellfish, the dish tastes like the sea and the earth all at once.

1 tablespoon kosher salt

12 littleneck clams, scrubbed

1 teaspoon toasted sesame oil

4 ounces beef brisket, chopped

4 garlic cloves, minced

7 cups water

¼ cup fermented soybean paste (doenjang)

1 tablespoon Korean hot pepper paste (gochujang)

1 (10-ounce) bunch spinach, washed and drained

1 green Korean chili pepper (cheong-gochu), stemmed and chopped

1 red Korean chili pepper (hong-gochu), stemmed and chopped

1. Put the salt in a bowl of cold water (about 4 cups). Stir to dissolve. Add the clams and stir well. Let sit for a few hours in the refrigerator so that the clams spit out any grit. Drain and rinse the clams.

2. Combine the sesame oil, beef, and garlic in a large heavy pot over medium-high heat. Cook, stirring, for a few minutes, until the beef loses its pink color and the garlic is fragrant.

3. Add the water to the pot, cover, and cook over medium-high heat for 25 minutes.

4. Stir the soybean paste and hot pepper paste into the boiling beef stock, then add the spinach and clams, cover, and cook for 10 minutes. Add the chili peppers and cook for another 5 minutes.

5. Ladle the soup into bowls and serve.

Above: top row: left, littleneck clams; right, cooking beef and garlic; center row: left, simmering stock; right, adding spinach and clams to stock; bottom, Soybean Paste Soup with Spinach and Clams

Soybean Paste Stew with Dried Anchovies

(Myeolchi doenjang-jjigae)

Serves 2 to 4

There is no other stew as beloved in Korean cuisine as doenjang-jjigae. It's been part of our culture for centuries, in good times and bad, always convenient, savory, and satisfying. If you can make good rice, kimchi, and doenjang-jjigae, you can lay claim to being a good Korean cook, and no one will ever dispute you.

The significance of doenjang—fermented soybean paste—in Korean cuisine dictates that the stew be named after it, no matter how many other ingredients are added. Salty, earthy, and fermented, it's uniquely Korean and it pretty much guarantees a delicious stew or soup. Dried anchovies deepen the stew's flavor.

I always make it in an earthenware pot, which looks beautiful on the table and keeps the stew piping hot until it's all gone, but if you don't have one, don't worry—any heavy pot will work. For an even spicier dish, you can add some Korean hot pepper paste or hot pepper flakes along with the soybean paste.

With rice alone, the stew will serve two people. It will serve four or more as part of a more elaborate meal with lots of side dishes.

1 medium russet potato, peeled and cut into ½-inch cubes (about 1 cup)

1 medium onion, cut into ½-inch pieces (about 1 cup)

1 small zucchini, cut into ½-inch pieces (about 1 cup)

1 green Korean chili pepper (cheong-gochu), stemmed and chopped

4 garlic cloves, minced

4 large shrimp, shelled, deveined, and coarsely chopped (about ⅓ cup; optional)

2½ cups water

7 dried anchovies (mareun-myeolchi), heads and guts removed

5 tablespoons fermented soybean paste (doenjang)

6 ounces medium-firm tofu, cut into ½-inch cubes (about 1 cup)

2 scallions, chopped

1. Combine the potato, onion, zucchini, chili pepper, garlic, shrimp (if using), and water in a 1½-quart flameproof earthenware or other heavy pot. Wrap the dried anchovies in cheesecloth, if desired, and place them on top of the other ingredients. Cover and cook over medium-high heat for 15 minutes.

2. Stir in the soybean paste, mixing well. Cover and cook for 20 minutes longer. Add the tofu and cook for another 3 minutes. Remove the anchovies with chopsticks if you'd like and discard.

3. Serve directly from the pot, or transfer to a serving bowl. Sprinkle with the scallions and serve.

Facing page: top, vegetables, shrimp, and anchovies in an earthenware pot before cooking; bottom, Soybean Paste Stew with Dried Anchovies

kimchi
and pickles

Koreans mastered the art of preserving wild vegetables in ancient times, for year-round eating. The techniques of pickling, drying, and fermenting also infused vegetables with flavor, firming and crisping them as they absorbed the salt.

Kimchi, the best-known example of these foods, has long been at the heart of Korean culture. Spicy, sour, a little sweet, and crisp, it lends remarkable complexity to a plain bowl of rice. Like wine, cheese, and sourdough bread, kimchi is a fermented food highly valued for its character. Among other such health-enhancing fermented foods as yogurt and kombucha, it stands out for its fiber as well as its beneficial bacteria. In addition to the vitamins, minerals, and fiber in the vegetables themselves, the healthy bacteria produced during fermentation have been linked to digestive health, and current research is demonstrating that those microorganisms living in our gut are key to our very survival.

You can purchase good-quality kimchi at any Korean grocery store, but there is nothing like the flavor and the satisfaction you will get from homemade kimchi. It's not difficult: All you have to do is to salt your vegetables, mix them with a paste made of chili flakes, garlic, ginger, and fish sauce, and let them stand at room temperature in a sealed container until they become slightly sour.

Today kimchi making has changed a bit, to reflect current cooking practices and tastes. My grandmother used much more salt than I do—she had to, because she didn't have a refrigerator, and the salt kept her kimchi from fermenting too fast. She spent a lot of effort trying to slow the fermentation process. She buried her kimchi crock in the ground to keep it at a constant temperature all winter. Even so, by the end of winter, her kimchi was super sour. In the summer, she made smaller batches, storing them in a basin half-filled with cold water from her well and changing the water a few times a day to keep the kimchi as cool as possible.

Kimchi will reach its peak in flavor after two weeks in the fridge or within a day or two outside of the fridge, depending on how warm your house is. When I make a new batch, I like to leave some of it at room temperature for a day or two so it ferments quickly and put the rest in the refrigerator so it ferments slowly. That way I have a range of flavors, from fresh to sour, to choose from.

Napa Cabbage Kimchi (page 114)

A Quick Kimchi Primer

Microscopic living bacteria are everywhere around us: floating in the air, on our skin, and even on our food. Some bacteria (think E. coli and salmonella) can be deadly. But most are harmless, and some are downright healthy. When cabbage or other vegetables are salted and left to stand, these healthy bacteria proliferate, not only producing tasty acids that give kimchi its trademark pickled flavor, but also keeping it from going bad.

That is why kimchi can be kept for a long time, even years! After you put your fresh kimchi into a container or jar, be sure to press down on the kimchi—by hand or with the back of a wooden spoon—to remove any air pockets that might encourage the growth of harmful bacteria. First-time kimchi makers, especially those who have experience with wine making or canning, are surprised to learn that sterilizing jars and utensils is unnecessary, because of the abundant amount of salt.

After a day or two at room temperature, the kimchi will have a sour smell and it might begin to bubble. These are signs of the acids produced by the good bacteria and are exactly what you want. As the kimchi ferments, and even as it sits in a cold refrigerator, its taste and texture will continue to change because of these living bacteria.

Many of my Western readers think that kimchi is only "ready" after it is well fermented and ask me how they can ferment their kimchi faster. I urge them not to wait. I love kimchi right after I make it. I tear some leaves from Napa Cabbage Kimchi, dip them in a bowl of toasted sesame seeds, and devour them with warm rice. At this stage, the flavors are very distinct and fresh, and the combination of crisp cabbage, nutty toasted seeds, and spices is irresistible—like a spicy salad. My children also like it this way.

Then I seal the container and let the kimchi ferment for a day or so at room temperature, until it is a little sweet and sour and a bit tingly on the tongue. Refrigerating it now will slow the fermentation so you can enjoy your kimchi until it's gone and it's time to make another batch.

Napa Cabbage Kimchi (Baechu-kimchi)
Makes about 8 pounds

There are hundreds of different kinds of kimchi, but the baechu-kimchi is king of them all. Sometimes my readers and friends ask me, "How many servings does it make?" My answer: "Please don't torture me with that question!"

Koreans don't think of kimchi in terms of servings: We make a lot of it and use it for all kinds of things. If you keep this kimchi in your refrigerator, you can easily make soup, stew, dumplings, pancakes, or fried rice. Then, when it runs out, make more. It's an easy habit to get into if you make Korean food often. Many of my non-Korean readers have told me that they make 8 pounds at a time on a regular basis. To make the job easier, you can use your food processor to grind the garlic, ginger, and onions.

The glutinous rice flour acts like a glue, helping the seasonings to cling to the cabbage. Without it, the hot pepper flakes would fall off the cabbage. If you've never used Korean hot pepper flakes and don't know if they will irritate your skin, you might want to mix your first batch wearing rubber gloves. *The photo is on page 117.*

6 pounds Napa cabbage (about 2 large or 3 or 4 small)

¾ cup kosher salt

3 tablespoons glutinous rice flour (chapssal-garu)

2½ cups water

2 tablespoons granulated or turbinado sugar

20 garlic cloves, minced (½ cup)

2 teaspoons minced peeled ginger

1 small onion, minced (½ cup)

½ cup fish sauce

1½ cups Korean hot pepper flakes (gochu-garu)

12 ounces Korean radish (mu) or daikon, peeled and cut into matchsticks (1½ cups)

1 medium carrot, peeled and cut into matchsticks (1 cup)

10 scallions, chopped

3 ounces Asian chives or additional scallions, chopped (1 cup)

1. Cut each cabbage in half through the core, then cut a slit through the core 2 inches above the stem so that the leaves are loosened but still attached. Dunk the halves in a large bowl of water to moisten all the leaves. Place on a work surface. Sprinkle the salt between the leaves and put the cabbage in a large bowl. Let stand for 1½ hours, turning the cabbage over every 30 minutes.

2. Meanwhile, combine the rice flour and water in a saucepan and cook over medium heat, stirring, until it bubbles, about 10 minutes. Add the sugar and cook, stirring, until the porridge is a little translucent and thinner, a few more minutes. Remove from the heat and let cool to room temperature.

3. Rinse the cabbage halves under cold running water, ruffling the leaves to remove any dirt and the excess salt. Split each half lengthwise into 2 pieces. Drain well.

4. Put the cooled porridge, garlic, ginger, onion, fish sauce, hot pepper flakes, radish, carrot, scallions, and chives in a large bowl. Mix well. (This is the kimchi paste.)

5. Leaving the cabbage quarters intact, spread some kimchi paste over each leaf. Pack the cabbage quarters into glass jars or other airtight containers and cover. Let stand at cool room temperature until the surface bubbles and the kimchi smells and tastes sour, 1 to 2 days, depending on how warm your kitchen is. Once the kimchi is fermented, store in the refrigerator to use as needed.

Maangchi and Friends

Rain: *I started making kimchi and realized that I was out of red pepper flakes. I'm not going to be able to get to the store that carries them until tomorrow, and I've already salted and washed my cabbage. Can I store the cabbage until tomorrow, when I can complete the process?*

Maangchi: *Wash the salted cabbage and drain it well, then put it in the fridge until your kimchi paste is ready. It will keep for a day or two.*

*Facing page: top row: left, cutting Napa cabbage in half; right, pulling apart cabbage halves;
second row: left, cabbage with core slit; right, salting the cabbage leaves
third row: left, prepared vegetables; right, rice porridge;
bottom row: left, rinsed salted cabbage leaves; right, mixing vegetables, seasonings, and
Korean hot pepper flakes; above: left, kimchi paste; right; spreading kimchi paste on
cabbage leaves; bottom, Napa Cabbage Kimchi (page 114)*

Perilla Leaf Kimchi *(Kkaennip-kimchi)*

Makes about 1 pound

When I first posted this recipe, it got a lot of attention: Many North Americans had been trying to eradicate perilla leaves from their yards and gardens for years. I was surprised to hear this, since in Korea perilla is much loved and the basis for many recipes, this spicy lightweight kimchi among them.

Perilla leaves have a minty flavor and a slightly fibrous texture. To enjoy this special kimchi, take a spoonful of rice, lay the perilla leaf with the spicy paste on top, and eat in one bite. The combination of mint and spices, along with the chewy texture of the leaf, transforms the rice into something exceptional.

If you don't grow your own, you can buy perilla leaves in Korean grocery stores. May and June is the best time for perilla leaves, and every year I go to the same stretch of Union Street in Flushing, Queens, where local Korean women sell their personal harvests on the street. The women change from year to year, but I can always expect to get the leaves.

As with stuffed cucumber kimchi, I make this in small batches and I always eat some immediately. Then I put the rest of it in the refrigerator, where it will get a little sour, for up to 2 weeks.

7 ounces perilla leaves (kkaennip)
½ cup Korean hot pepper flakes
   (gochu-garu)
5 tablespoons fish sauce
1 tablespoon sugar
1 tablespoon toasted sesame seeds

1 large onion, thinly sliced (about
   1½ cups)
6 scallions, chopped
4 garlic cloves, minced
1 large carrot, peeled and cut into
   matchsticks (about 1½ cups)

1. Fill a large bowl with cold water. One by one, dip the perilla leaves into the water to remove any dust. Then stack them neatly, with the stems pointing in the same direction, pick up the stack of leaves with both hands, and hold it under cold running water, letting the water run between leaves to clean them thoroughly. Shake the bunch of leaves to remove excess water.

2. Combine the hot pepper flakes, fish sauce, sugar, and sesame seeds in a small bowl and mix well. Add the onion, scallions, garlic, and carrot and mix well. Use your hand to spread some of the kimchi paste in between every other leaf (wear rubber gloves, if you'd like).

3. Serve immediately, or store in an airtight container in the refrigerator for up to 2 weeks.

Facing page: top row: left, washed perilla leaves; right, prepared vegetables;
center row; left, mixing vegetables with spicy paste; right, spreading kimchi paste on perilla leaves;
bottom; Perilla Leaf Kimchi

Diced Radish Kimchi *(Kkakdugi)*
Makes about 5 pounds

Made from Korean radishes, this kimchi is juicy, spicy, crisp, cold, and just a little sweet. Kkakdugi is great when it's fresh, but it's even better when it ages. As it ferments, it gets sour, the spiciness deepens, and the ginger and garlic flavors get more complex.

Kkakdugi is omnipresent on the Korean table and is an essential side dish for beefy soups like Beef and Radish Soup (page 95) or a spicy counterpart to Soybean Sprout Soup (page 93). When I serve the soybean sprout soup, I put some rice in my bowl, ladle some soup in, and top it off with some radish kimchi and a few spoons of the sour brine.

The radishes should be firm and fresh, and the skin should have a slight sheen, with no bruises and a nice gradation between the white and the green. The bigger the green part, the sweeter the radish. If you can't get Korean radishes, use firm daikon.

4 pounds Korean radishes (mu) or daikon, peeled, and cut into ¾- to 1-inch cubes
2 tablespoons kosher salt
2 tablespoons sugar
5 or 6 garlic cloves, minced
1 teaspoon minced peeled ginger
4 scallions, chopped
⅔ cup Korean hot pepper flakes (gochu-garu)
¼ cup fish sauce

1. Combine the radishes with the salt and sugar in a large bowl, toss to coat, and let stand for 30 minutes to 1 hour.

2. Reserve ⅓ cup of the liquid, then drain the radishes. Transfer them to another bowl and stir in the garlic, ginger, scallions, hot pepper flakes, fish sauce, and the reserved liquid. Mix well with your hands (use rubber gloves, if you'd like).

3. Transfer the radishes to glass jars or other airtight containers, pressing on them with the back of a spoon to pack them tightly to avoid air pockets. Cover and let stand at cool room temperature until the kimchi tastes and smells sour (it might also bubble on the surface), 1 to 2 days, depending on the temperature of the room.

4. Once the kimchi is fermented, store in the refrigerator to use as needed.

Spicy Stuffed Cucumber Kimchi *(Oi-sobagi)*

Makes about 4 pounds

This kimchi is great in the summertime, when cucumbers are in season, but you can make it at any time of the year. It's usually made with Korean cucumbers, which can be hard to find (check your farmers' market), but Kirby and English cucumbers work very well. If you use Korean or English cucumbers, cut them into 4-inch lengths; Kirby cucumbers don't need to be cut at all. Oi-sobagi is very easy to make. Just mix some Korean seasonings together and stuff your cucumbers.

I like this kimchi fresh and crisp, so I always eat some right away, with rice. Others like it to ferment a bit before digging in. It's up to you. Some people cut off the ends of the cucumbers before serving them, releasing them into manageable strips. But I like to give everyone their own cucumber, with the ends intact. Be warned: Eating cucumber kimchi this way is not pretty. But among close friends and family, that's not a problem, right?

3 pounds Kirby cucumbers (about 12), about 4 inches long, washed

3 tablespoons kosher salt

1 medium carrot, peeled and cut into matchsticks (about 1 cup)

1 large onion, thinly sliced (about 1½ cups)

4 ounces Asian chives, or 10 to 12 scallions, chopped

6 garlic cloves, minced

¾ cup Korean hot pepper flakes (gochu-garu)

¼ cup fish sauce

4 teaspoons sugar

⅓ cup water

1. Cut each cucumber lengthwise into quarters, stopping about ½ inch before the end so that the quarters are still connected. Sprinkle the salt all over the insides of the cucumbers and gently rub it in. Put the salted cucumbers in a bowl and sprinkle evenly with any remaining salt. Let stand for 20 minutes.

2. Rinse the cucumbers under cold running water to remove excess salt. Drain.

3. Combine the remaining ingredients in a small bowl.

4. Stuff the kimchi paste into the quartered cucumbers (wear rubber gloves, if you'd like); apply some kimchi paste to the outside of the cucumber as well. Serve immediately, or put the cucumbers in glass jars or other airtight containers, cover, and refrigerate. Or, to ferment the kimchi, leave it on the countertop until slightly sour, 1 to 2 days, before refrigerating. The kimchi will keep in the refrigerator, covered, for up to 1 month.

Facing page: top row: left, cutting cucumbers; right, salting cucumbers; center row; left, prepared vegetables; right, mixing vegetables and hot pepper flakes; bottom; Spicy Stuffed Cucumber Kimchi

Vegetable-and-Fruit-Water Kimchi

(Nabak-kimchi)

Makes 9 to 10 pounds

Essentially sliced vegetables and fruits in a pinkish water, this is a very mild kimchi and incredibly refreshing. I like to make it in the summer and serve it as a cold soup, along with rice. Nabak-kimchi also pairs well with heartier dishes like rice cakes, bulgogi, pancakes, and substantial noodle dishes. The light, tangy broth and crisp fruits and vegetables offset the heaviness of those foods.

You can eat this kimchi as soon as you make it, but I prefer it fermented for a bit.

1 medium Napa cabbage (about 3 pounds)

Kosher salt

1 pound Korean radish (mu) or daikon, peeled

1 small English cucumber, cut into ¼-inch-thick rounds (about 1½ cups)

½ cup thinly sliced onion

2 green Korean chili peppers (cheong-gochu), stemmed and chopped

1 red Korean chili pepper (hong-gochu), stemmed and chopped

3 garlic cloves, thinly sliced

1 tablespoon thinly sliced peeled ginger

5 scallions, cut into 1½-inch lengths

1 Gala, Fuji, Golden Delicious, or other sweet apple, peeled, cored, and cut into 1-x-1-x-¼-inch slices

1 Asian pear, peeled, cored, and cut into 1-x-1-x-¼-inch slices

10 cups water

2 tablespoons Korean hot pepper flakes (gochu-garu)

1. Cut the cabbage lengthwise into quarters and then trim the stem ends. Cut each quarter crosswise into 1½-inch slices. Put the cabbage into a large bowl, add 3 cups water, and sprinkle with 3 tablespoons salt. Mix well by hand to dissolve the salt and make sure each piece of cabbage is salted evenly. Let stand for 30 minutes, then toss the cabbage well with your hands and let stand for another 30 minutes.

2. Meanwhile, cut the radish into 1-x-1-x-¼-inch pieces. Put in a bowl, mix with 1 teaspoon salt, and let stand for 1 hour.

3. Rinse the salted cabbage under cold running water to remove excess salt. Drain and transfer to a large bowl.

4. Add the radish, along with its salty liquid, to the bowl with the cabbage. Add the cucumber, onion, chili peppers, garlic, ginger, scallions, apple, and pear and mix everything together with your hands.

5. Combine the 10 cups water and ¼ cup salt in another large bowl and stir well to dissolve the salt.

Facing page: clockwise from top left: hot pepper flakes in cheesecloth bag infusing salty water; vegetables and fruit; Vegetable-and-Fruit-Water Kimchi

6. Tie the pepper flakes up in a piece of cheesecloth. Immerse the cheesecloth pouch in the water and squeeze the pouch several times, until the water turns pink. Remove and discard the pouch.

7. Pour the brine over the vegetables and fruits. Stir well with a wooden spoon. Transfer to glass jars or other airtight containers.

8. Serve some of the kimchi immediately, or cover it all and let stand at room temperature until fermented and a little bit sour, 1 to 2 days.

9. Once the kimchi is fermented, refrigerate for up to 1 month. (You can keep the kimchi longer than this, but it will become very sour and the fruits and vegetables may become soggy.)

Radish-Water Kimchi for Cold Noodle Soup *(Naengmyeonyong mu mulkimchi)*

Makes about 2 pounds kimchi, with 12 cups brine

Cold noodle soup is a hugely popular dish in Korea, and one of my favorites. There's a spicy version without a lot of broth (bibim-naengmyeon; page 60), and a nonspicy version that does have a lot (mul-naengmyeon; page 58). The best noodle soup broth is made with a mix of brine from radish-water kimchi and chicken or beef stock.

I developed this recipe specifically to get a high yield of brine for the soup. It's made with much more water than is usual. After just a few minutes of work and then a few days of waiting as it ferments, you will have a perfect brine: subtly sour, salty, and tangy. It's wonderfully thirst-quenching when chilled.

To use this kimchi as a side dish for rice, ladle the cold broth into serving bowls, along with several radish disks; cut the disks in half if they are large. You can also use some of the radishes as an ingredient in your cold noodle soup.

2 pounds Korean radishes (mu) or daikon, washed, peeled and cut into very thin (⅛ inch thick or less) disks
Kosher salt
13¼ cups water
2 Gala, Fuji, Golden Delicious, or other sweet apples, cored and thinly sliced
1 medium onion, thinly sliced (about 1 cup)

1 teaspoon all-purpose flour
5 garlic cloves, minced
2 green Korean chili peppers (cheong-gochu), stemmed and chopped
1 red Korean chili pepper (hong-gochu), stemmed and chopped
2 scallions

1. Combine the radishes with 3 tablespoons salt in a bowl and mix well. Put the salted radishes in a 1-gallon glass jar or other airtight container, cover, and let stand at room temperature for 24 hours, stirring once or twice to distribute the salt evenly.

2. Pour 13 cups of the water into a large pot, add the apples and onion, cover, and cook over medium heat until the apples and onion are translucent and the broth tastes sweet, about 1 hour. Refrigerated, the kimchi will last for 1 month.

3. Mix the flour and the remaining ¼ cup cold water in a small bowl until completely smooth. Pour it into the boiling broth, stirring to dissolve. The broth will turn a little milky. Add 2 tablespoons salt and mix well. Remove from the heat and let cool completely.

4. Tie the garlic and chili peppers up tightly in a piece of cheesecloth. Add the seasoning pouch and the scallions to the jar with the radishes. Strain the cooled broth into the jar. Cover and let stand until the brine is a little sour with a good flavor, about 2 days.

5. Remove the seasoning pouch and scallions and discard. Cover and refrigerate until you are ready to make cold noodle soup, or for up to 1 month.

Radish Pickles *(Mu-pickle)*

Makes about 2 pounds

These sweet, sour, crispy pickles are the perfect side dish for Fried Dumplings (page 210) or Korean Fried Chicken (page 220). In fact, most fried chicken restaurants in Korea serve them as a complimentary side dish, and even home delivery businesses include a little plastic bag of mu-pickle.

  However, the pickles can be easily made at home, and then you can enjoy them any time you want. You can eat them right away, but it's best to wait 24 hours so the flavorful brine has time to seep into the radishes. Be sure to dice the radishes small enough so they will pickle quickly. The radish cubes also look a lot prettier when they are small and uniform.

⅔ cup sugar
⅔ cup distilled white vinegar
2 tablespoons kosher salt
1½ cups water

2 pounds Korean radishes (mu) or
   daikon, peeled and cut into ⅓-inch
   cubes

1. Combine the sugar, vinegar, and salt in a small bowl. Add the water and stir to dissolve the sugar and salt.

2. Put the radishes in a glass jar or other airtight container and pour in the pickling solution. Cover and refrigerate for at least 1 day, and up to 1 month before serving.

Left, Radish-Water Kimchi for Cold Noodle Soup (page 126); Radish Pickles (above)

side dishes

At a typical Korean meal, rice is a given, kimchi is a constant, and there is usually a soup or stew. But it is the side dishes (banchan) that round out the meal and give it personality. This category encompasses dozens, if not hundreds, of dishes, which can consist of vegetables, meat, nuts, grains, tofu, and/or seafood. Some are hot, others are cold. Some are spicy, others soothingly mild. Some are fresh, others fermented. Each one contributes particular colors, flavors, and textures. These side dishes, many of which can be kept on hand in the refrigerator, are a quick way to put together an interesting dinner. For special occasions, Korean cooks can show off their skill and taste with an artful array of different ones.

Choosing your side dishes depends on your mood, your taste, the seasons, and what else will be on the table. Say you have a craving for the simple flavors of soy, sesame, and pepper flakes at the end of the summer. Steamed Eggplant is just the thing. Cooked and Seasoned Soybean Sprouts bring healthy protein to the meal. Seasoned Dried Filefish adds a pleasant chewiness. Use common sense, so you present a selection that has a variety of tastes and textures. Don't serve Soybean Paste Soup with Spinach and Clams (page 106) if you are planning on making Blanched Spinach with Scallions and Sesame. Pair something sweet like Braised Black Beans with crisp Green Chili Peppers Seasoned with Soybean Paste.

Coming up with a variety of banchan for a weeknight meal may seem daunting, but with a little organization, anyone can put together a nutritious Korean dinner at the drop of a hat. The key to doing so is relying on mitbanchan, a category of side dishes that Koreans prepare in quantity and keep in the refrigerator to round out any meal. Braised Black Beans, Spicy Raw Crab, Braised Lotus Root, Braised Burdock Root, Braised Beef in Soy Sauce, Seasoned Dried Filefish, Dried Anchovies and Nuts: All of these, and others too, will keep in the refrigerator for more than a week to be served alongside rice, soup or stew, kimchi, and freshly made banchan.

Finally, a note on portion sizes: The number of servings you will get from the following recipes will depend on how many side dishes you are serving at a particular meal. The yields given for the recipes assume that you are likely (at least at first) to make just one or two banchan per meal. If you make more than that, these recipes will go further.

Green Chili Peppers Seasoned with Soybean Paste *(Putgochu-doenjang-muchim)*

Serves 4

Whenever my grandmother made fermented soybean paste, she buried a bunch of green chili peppers in the paste in her earthenware crock. After a few months of fermentation, she dug the peppers out and served them as a side dish. They were pickled and super-salty, delicious in small quantities with rice. It was one of my favorite things to eat, but hardly practical for the modern cook.

That's why I was overjoyed to discover this interpretation on a recent trip to Los Angeles. Someone there must have been inspired by that traditional pickle to create this dish, which takes only minutes to make and is fresher tasting and much less salty than the original, but still spicy, garlicky, nutty, and a little sweet from the honey, just like my grandmother's peppers. That recipe was made with long green chili peppers, which are more widely available here than Korean chili peppers. After a few experiments in my kitchen, I figured out how to make it myself.

3 tablespoons fermented soybean paste (doenjang)
1 garlic clove, minced
1 scallion, chopped
1 tablespoon honey

1 teaspoon toasted sesame seeds
4 or 5 long green chili peppers or Anaheim chili peppers, or 10 green Korean chili peppers (cheong-gochu), stemmed and cut into ½-inch slices

Combine the soybean paste, garlic, scallion, honey, and sesame seeds in a small bowl and mix well. Add the peppers and mix well. Serve immediately, so the peppers are still crispy and refreshing.

Scallion Salad *(Pajeori)*

Serves 2 or 3

Enjoy this crisp, simple salad, which has just a hint of heat, with Bulgogi (page 223), Grilled Pork Belly (page 232), or L.A.–Style Beef Short Ribs (page 226).

7 scallions

2 tablespoons soy sauce

1 teaspoon sugar or honey

1 tablespoon distilled white vinegar

1 tablespoon Korean hot pepper flakes (gochu-garu)

1 tablespoon toasted sesame seeds

1. Cut the scallions into 3- to 4- inch lengths, then cut each piece lengthwise into very thin strips. Soak the shredded scallions in a bowl of cold water for 5 minutes.

2. Drain the scallions in a colander and rinse under cold running water, stirring with your hand, for 30 seconds. This will remove some of the scallions' bite. Drain well. Divide the scallions into small serving bowls.

3. Combine the remaining ingredients in a small bowl and mix well.

4. Just before serving, pour the dressing over the scallions and mix well.

Clockwise from top left: slicing scallions; soaking scallions; mixing the sauce; Scallion Salad

Seaweed Salad *(Miyeok-muchim)*

Serves 4 to 6 as a side dish or appetizer, 2 to 3 as a main course

The dried sea plant miyeok (called wakame in Japan) is papery, dry, and black in the bag, but it turns deep green and soft when soaked in water. This salad, which is sweet-and-sour, juicy, and garlicky, is a good appetizer choice if you want to add a Korean dish to a Western-style meal. If you like your seaweed salad spicy, add 1 tablespoon Korean hot red pepper paste (gochujang) to the dressing.

¾ ounce (a little less than 1 cup) dried seaweed (miyeok), soaked in cold water for 30 minutes

3 tablespoons soy sauce

¼ cup cider vinegar or distilled white vinegar

1 tablespoon honey or sugar

2 garlic cloves, minced

2 teaspoons toasted sesame seeds

1. Bring a large saucepan of water to a boil. Drain the soaked seaweed, add it to the boiling water, and blanch for 30 seconds, stirring so it cooks evenly. Drain in a colander, rinse under very cold running water to stop the cooking, and drain well. Squeeze out excess water and chop the seaweed into bite-size pieces.

2. Combine the soy sauce, vinegar, honey, and garlic in a medium bowl and mix well. Add the seaweed and mix well with a spoon. (The salad can be covered and refrigerated for up to 3 days.)

3. To serve, transfer to a serving dish and sprinkle with the sesame seeds.

Spicy Cucumber Salad *(Oi-muchim)*

Serves 4

Try this instead of your usual salad when you're looking for something cool, crisp, and spicy. The dish should be assembled just before serving; if you have to prepare it ahead of time, keep the cucumber and seasoning sauce separate from each other and mix them together at the last minute. Also, it's best to make only what you need for one meal; leftovers will never be as good as the just-made salad.

1 English cucumber, or 2 or 3 Kirby cucumbers (about 12 ounces)
2 garlic cloves, minced
1 scallion, chopped
¼ cup thinly sliced onion
2 tablespoons soy sauce

2 teaspoons Korean hot pepper flakes (gochu-garu)
1 teaspoon sugar
2 teaspoons toasted sesame oil
2 teaspoons toasted sesame seeds

1. Cut the cucumber lengthwise in half (if using Kirby cucumbers, remove the seeds). Cut diagonally into thin slices.

2. Put the cucumbers in a bowl, add all the remaining ingredients, and mix well with a wooden spoon or your hands. Transfer to a serving bowl and serve immediately.

Cold Cucumber Soup *(Oi-naengguk)*
Serves 4

With just a hint of spice, this cool, sharp, salty soup is great for stimulating the appetite in the summertime, when the heat is oppressive and you don't feel like eating much. My Western friends say it is a Korean version of gazpacho, but it doesn't have a tomato base. (I loved gazpacho so much when I first had it in Spain that I started garnishing my cucumber soup with a little tomato, but that is not traditional.) And, unlike gazpacho, cold cucumber soup is not served on its own, but with rice, to balance its saltiness.

I learned how to make the soup in middle school in Korea. My home ec teacher revealed the secret: Mix the cucumbers and seasonings first, so they are well combined, before you add the cold water and ice cubes. Once the ice cubes are added, the soup is a lot harder to mix.

Seedless cucumbers are best for this dish. You can substitute 2 or 3 Kirby cucumbers, but halve them lengthwise and scrape the seeds out with a spoon before slicing them into matchsticks.

1 English cucumber, peeled and cut into 3-inch-long matchsticks
1 garlic clove, minced
¼ cup thinly sliced onion
1 tablespoon chopped green (cheong-gochu) or red (hong-gochu) Korean chili pepper (optional)
1 scallion, chopped
1 teaspoon soy sauce
1½ teaspoons kosher salt
2 teaspoons sugar
4 teaspoons distilled white or cider vinegar
7 or 8 ice cubes (about 1 cup)
1 cup cold water
1 teaspoon toasted sesame seeds
A few slices of tomato for garnish (optional)

1. Combine the cucumber, garlic, onion, chili pepper, scallion, soy sauce, salt, sugar, and vinegar in a medium bowl and mix well with a spoon. Add the ice cubes and water and stir well.

2. Transfer the soup to a serving bowl. Crush the sesame seeds between your thumb and index finger and sprinkle them over the soup. Garnish with the tomato, if desired, and serve immediately.

Maangchi and Friends
Lucca: *There wasn't any red chili at the market, so I used a sweet red pepper and it worked very well. Oi means cucumber, right? Is it also a person's name?*
Maangchi: *I sometimes use red bell pepper in my oi-naengguk too. My Thai friend's name is Oi. I tease her, "Cucumber, where have you been?"*

Blanched Spinach with Scallions and Sesame *(Sigeumchi-namul)*

Serves 4

This is one of the most common Korean side dishes, along with Cooked and Seasoned Soybean Sprouts (page 140). Most people eat it at least once a week. It's mild, soft, salty, and garlicky but not spicy. Many of my readers had never heard of this dish until I posted the recipe. Now they tell me they can't live without it!

I had a potluck dinner with some of my readers once, and someone brought a dish I didn't recognize. When I asked her what it was, she told me it was this recipe made with kale. What a great idea! If using kale, be sure to chop it fine, because it's tougher than spinach. Since then, I've also tried Chinese broccoli and bok choy in place of the spinach, and both were good. Maybe you can think of something else to try? If so, let me know how it turns out.

1 pound spinach with large leaves, trimmed, leaving the sweet, tender reddish tops of the roots

2 scallions, chopped

3 garlic cloves, minced

1 tablespoon soy sauce

2 teaspoons toasted sesame oil

1 teaspoon toasted sesame seeds

1. Bring 8 cups water to a boil in a large saucepan. Add the spinach and blanch for 1 minute, then drain in a colander and rinse under cold running water to stop the cooking. Drain and squeeze out excess water with your hands, then chop into ½-inch pieces.

2. Combine the remaining ingredients in a medium bowl. Add the spinach and toss to coat. Serve right away, or cover and refrigerate for up to 2 days.

Stir-Fried Kale with Soybean Paste

(Keil-doenjang-bokkeum)

Serves 4

It was only after I came to America that I started to cook with kale. It was so readily available and inexpensive that I thought, "Why not try using it in Korean cuisine?" My first experiments were terrific, and I soon realized that kale is a great substitute for less readily available Korean vegetables.

This recipe is traditionally made with Korean radish tops or Napa cabbage. But either way—authentic or Westernized—it's earthy, mild, and healthy. It tastes like the Korean countryside, no matter where you are.

1 pound kale, tough stems trimmed
2 tablespoons vegetable oil
⅓ cup thinly sliced onion
3 garlic cloves, minced

¼ cup fermented soybean paste
    (doenjang)
1 tablespoon honey
2 scallions, chopped

1. Bring a large pot of water to a boil. Add the kale and blanch until soft and wilted, 2 to 3 minutes. Drain in a colander and rinse under cold running water to stop the cooking. Drain and squeeze out excess water with your hands. Chop into small pieces.

2. Heat a large skillet over high heat and add the vegetable oil. Add the onion and garlic and stir-fry for 1 minute. Add the chopped kale and cook, stirring, for 3 minutes. Add the soybean paste and honey and cook, stirring, until the kale is coated and hot, another 3 minutes. Add the chopped scallions and stir well.

3. Transfer to a serving plate and serve immediately. Leftovers can be refrigerated for up to 3 days.

Top, Stir-Fried Kale with Soybean Paste; bottom, Cooked and Seasoned Soybean Sprouts (page 140)

Cooked and Seasoned Soybean Sprouts

(Kongnamul-muchim)

Serves 4

Because it is so easy and good, this is probably the number-one Korean side dish. It's served every day on Korean tables, as well as on special occasions. If I'm making it for just four, I put it together right before serving. But if I'm making a big bowl for a party, I cook the sprouts ahead of time, refrigerate them, and then toss them with the dressing before the party starts.

Soybean sprouts shouldn't be eaten raw. They have an unpleasant odor and flavor. Cooked, they become mild and nutty. They are healthy, too, full of protein. I season them with salt and soy sauce. *The photo is on page 139.*

1 pound soybean sprouts (kongnamul)
Kosher salt
2 garlic cloves, minced
1 scallion, chopped
1 teaspoon Korean hot pepper flakes
   (gochu-garu; optional)

1 teaspoon soy sauce
2 teaspoons toasted sesame oil
2 teaspoons toasted sesame seeds

1. Put the soybean sprouts in a large bowl, cover with water, and gently stir with your hand to clean them. Pick out any dead beans and loosened skins, then drain. Repeat a few times, again removing any dead beans or loosened skins, until the water remains clear.

2. Transfer the bean sprouts to a large saucepan. Add 1 cup water and 1 teaspoon salt, cover, and cook over medium-high heat for 10 minutes. Taste to see if the beans are cooked; if not, cook for an additional 2 minutes or so. Drain and set aside in a bowl to cool slightly so you can handle them. (At this point, the sprouts can be covered and refrigerated overnight.)

3. Add another 1 teaspoon salt and the rest of the ingredients to the bowl and mix gently with your hands. Transfer to a serving plate and serve. Leftover sprouts will keep in an airtight container in the refrigerator for up to 2 days.

Steamed Eggplant *(Gaji-namul)*

Serves 4

I've been making gaji-namul for so long that I can't remember where I got the recipe. The steamed eggplant is soft, sweet, salty, a little spicy, and meaty. It's a Korean staple. My version is pretty traditional, except for the amount of garlic I use. When I was a kid, I overheard my grandmother telling my aunts that a copious amount of garlic is the important thing, and that tip has stuck with me.

Korean eggplant is thinner than Western eggplant and lavender instead of dark purple. You can use Western eggplant here, but you may have to peel it first, because the skin is tougher than the Asian kind.

1 pound Korean or other small Asian eggplants (2 or 3), washed, cut lengthwise in half and then crosswise into 2½-inch pieces

1 teaspoon fish sauce or Korean soup soy sauce, preferably homemade (page 264)

1 tablespoon soy sauce

3 garlic cloves, minced

2 scallions, chopped

1 teaspoon Korean hot pepper flakes (gochu-garu)

2 teaspoons toasted sesame oil

2 teaspoons toasted sesame seeds

1. Pour 2 cups water into a medium pot and set a steamer basket over it. Bring the water to a boil over medium-high heat. Add the eggplant, cover, and steam until soft, about 5 minutes. Remove the pot from the heat, uncover, and let the eggplant cool.

2. When the eggplant is cool enough to handle, tear each piece lengthwise into strips about ⅓ inch thick. Transfer the eggplant strips to a large bowl. Add the remaining ingredients and toss well to combine. Transfer to a serving plate and serve.

Braised Dried Sweet Potato Stems

(Mallin-goguma-julgi-bokkeum)

Serves 4

In Korea, sweet potatoes are harvested in the fall, so that's when we get the freshest sweet potato stems. The stems are long, narrow, green, and very succulent and sweet, and Koreans use them in soups, stews, side dishes, and even kimchi. Farmers also dry some of the stems until they look like hard threads.

I learned this method for preparing the dried stems from one of my friends in Korea, who had learned it from her mother-in-law in the country. Small pieces of pork belly and a bit of ground perilla seeds give the rehydrated stems a deep, rich flavor.

Be sure to soak the stems thoroughly. This is a long process, so start the day before. You'll be surprised at how juicy and succulent the stick-like stems become.

1 ounce dried sweet potato stems
   (mallin-goguma-julgi)
¼ cup perilla seed powder
   (deulkkae-garu)
1½ cups water
1 tablespoon vegetable oil
4 ounces pork belly, chopped into small
   pieces

2 garlic cloves, minced
1 tablespoon fish sauce or Korean soup
   soy sauce, preferably homemade
   (page 264)
3 scallions, chopped
1 teaspoon toasted sesame oil

1. One day ahead, combine the potato stems with 10 cups water in a large pot and cook over medium-high heat for 30 minutes. Remove from the heat, cover, and let stand for 3 hours.

2. Drain the stems in a colander and rinse well. Transfer to a large bowl, cover with cold water, and let soak at room temperature overnight.

3. The next day, taste the stems: They should be soft, like cooked spinach. If they are still tough, boil them in a fresh pot of water for about 30 minutes and let sit, covered, until soft.

4. Drain the stems and cut into 2-inch pieces.

5. Put the perilla seed powder in a small bowl and stir in the 1½ cups water.

6. Heat a medium heavy pot over medium-high heat. Add the vegetable oil, pork, and garlic and cook, stirring with a wooden spoon, until the pork is no longer pink, about 3 minutes. Add the sweet potato stems and fish sauce. Set a fine strainer over the pot and strain the perilla seed mixture into the pot; discard the coarse skins of the seeds.

7. Give the stems a good stir, cover, turn the heat down, and simmer until the stems are very soft, 25 to 30 minutes. (If they are still tough, add a little more water and continue to cook until they soften.)

8. Stir in the scallions and sesame oil. Transfer the stems, along with the milky broth, to a shallow bowl and serve.

Clockwise from top left: cooking sweet potato stems; cooked potato stems, scallions, garlic, and pork; Braised Dried Sweet Potato Stems

Steamed Shishito Peppers *(Kkwarigochu-jjim)*

Serves 4

Shishito peppers are light green, thin-walled, small, and sweet. In Korea, we use them whole. Coating them with flour before steaming them gives them a nice chewy texture. The little bit of dried anchovy broth used to finish cooking the peppers makes them so tasty. Served with rice and soup, they can be a complete meal. Leftovers are popular in lunch boxes, and my American friends like them as a snack with cocktails or cold beer.

8 ounces shishito peppers (kkwari-gochu), stemmed

2 tablespoons all-purpose flour

1 teaspoon vegetable oil

2 garlic cloves, minced

¼ cup thinly sliced onion

5 large dried anchovies (mareun-myeolchi), heads and guts removed

¼ cup water

2 tablespoons plus 1 teaspoon soy sauce

1 tablespoon Korean hot pepper flakes (gochu-garu)

1 teaspoon toasted sesame oil

1 teaspoon toasted sesame seeds

1. Rinse and drain the peppers. Put them in a bowl and toss with the flour.

2. Bring a cup or so of water to a boil in a saucepan fitted with a steamer basket. Add the peppers, cover, and cook for 5 minutes over medium-high heat. Remove the pan from the heat and uncover.

3. Heat a large skillet over high heat. Add the vegetable oil, garlic, onion, and anchovies and cook, stirring, for 1 minute. Add the water, soy sauce, and hot pepper flakes, turn the heat down to low, and simmer, stirring, until the broth becomes delicious from the anchovies, a few minutes.

4. Add the peppers, mix well, and stir with a wooden spoon until they are shiny and tender, about 2 minutes.

5. Remove from the heat and stir in the sesame oil. Transfer the peppers to a serving plate, sprinkle with the sesame seeds, and serve.

Left, shishito peppers; right, cooking Steamed Shishito Peppers

Braised Lotus Root *(Yeon-geun-jorim)*

Serves 4 to 6

Lacy white lotus root attracts attention on any party table. All Koreans love its texture, which is crisp-tender, like a cross between a radish and a cooked potato. Cooked in soy sauce and rice syrup, the slices become shiny, sticky, salty, and sweet. It is a popular addition to Korean lunch boxes, because it retains its crunch over time. Keep leftovers in the refrigerator, and you can put together a quick meal by serving it with rice and other side dishes.

1 pound lotus root (yeon-geun), peeled, washed, sliced ⅓ inch thick, and soaked in cold water for 10 minutes
1 teaspoon distilled white vinegar
1 tablespoon vegetable oil

¼ cup soy sauce
3 garlic cloves, minced
2¼ cups water
¾ cup brown rice syrup (ssal-yeot)
1 tablespoon toasted sesame oil
1 teaspoon toasted sesame seeds

1. Bring 4 cups water to a boil in a medium saucepan. Add the lotus root and vinegar and cook, uncovered, for 5 minutes. Drain the lotus root in a colander and rinse under cold running water to stop the cooking. Drain.

2. Heat the oil in a medium heavy pot over medium-high heat. Add the lotus root and stir-fry until it looks a little translucent, a few minutes. Add the soy sauce, garlic, and water, cover, and cook over medium heat for 40 minutes.

3. Uncover the pot and stir the lotus root. Stir in the rice syrup, cover, and cook for another 20 minutes, until the lotus root is tender, replenishing the water if necessary. Uncover and cook, stirring occasionally, until the lotus root is shiny and the liquid has almost evaporated, 7 to 10 minutes.

4. Remove from the heat and stir in the sesame oil. Transfer to a serving plate, sprinkle with the sesame seeds, and serve. Store leftovers in an airtight container in the refrigerator for up to 1 week and serve cold.

Left, sliced peeled lotus root; right, Braised Lotus Root

Fernbrake with Garlic and Soy (Gosari-namul)

Serves 4

Similar to fiddleheads in taste and texture, fernbrake is foraged in the mountains of Korea in the spring. My grandmother picked it every year with her friends. She would dry it in the sun and it would keep for a full year, until she went again the next spring.

These days most people buy fernbrake in grocery stores. You may find it dried, presoaked, or fresh. I always buy dried, because it will keep in my pantry for months if it has to. If you buy vacuum-packed presoaked fernbrake, you need to use it within a few days once it's opened.

This is one of my favorite mountain vegetable dishes. It's so substantial that some Koreans call it "mountain beef." It's a little salty, and sweet, and has a meaty texture.

Fernbrake needs a long soak, so it's best to start this recipe the day before you plan to serve it. If you'd like, in the spring, you can substitute fresh fiddleheads. Just blanch them in boiling water for 1 minute instead of soaking, and stir-fry briefly (they'll cook more quickly than fernbrake).

1 tablespoon vegetable oil

½ cup thinly sliced onion

2 garlic cloves, minced

1 ounce (about ¼ cup) dried fernbrake (gosari), soaked, drained, and cut into bite-size pieces (see below)

2 tablespoons soy sauce

2 teaspoons sugar or honey

1 teaspoon toasted sesame oil

1 teaspoon toasted sesame seeds

1. Heat a large skillet over medium-high heat. Add the vegetable oil, onion, and garlic and stir until fragrant, about 30 seconds. Add the fernbrake and cook, stirring, for 5 minutes. Turn the heat down to low, add the soy sauce and sugar, and cook, stirring occasionally, until the fernbrake is soft, about 5 minutes.

2. Remove the pan from the heat and stir in the sesame oil and sesame seeds. Transfer to a serving plate and serve.

Preparing Dried Fernbrake

1 ounce (about ¼ cup) dried fernbrake (gosari)

1. Combine the fernbrake and 10 cups water in a large saucepan, bring to a boil over medium-high heat, and boil for 30 minutes. Cover and let stand until cool, 2 to 3 hours.

2. Drain the fernbrake and put it in a bowl. Cover with fresh cold water and let soak for at least 8 hours, or overnight, in a cool place, changing the water 2 or 3 times during the soaking.

3. Taste the fernbrake: It should be soft. If it is tough, boil it again in a fresh pot of water for about 30 minutes and then let it sit, covered, until soft. Drain the fernbrake and cut into bite-size pieces.

Top, cooking dried fernbrake; bottom, Fernbrake with Garlic and Soy

Vegetable Leaf Wraps with Rice and Apple Dipping Sauce *(Sagwa-ssamjang-ssam)*

Serves 2 or 3

Composed of crisp lettuce and herb leaves, fresh rice, and a savory-sweet apple dipping sauce of my own invention, this dish is eaten traditional ssam style: Spoon some rice and dipping sauce onto a couple of leafy greens, wrap them up into a manageable bite, and eat the whole package in one shot.

Ssamjang, the traditional Korean dipping sauce, is made with fermented soybean paste, Korean hot pepper paste, and sugar. My version was inspired by apple season at the Union Square Greenmarket here in New York City, where I decided to use a Royal Gala apple as a natural sweetener. It also added a crunchiness that's not traditional. It's important to keep the apple chunky and crisp by hand-chopping it.

This dish is best eaten right away, as the ssamjang will separate if left to sit too long.

¼ cup fermented soybean paste (doenjang)

1 tablespoon Korean hot pepper paste (gochujang)

1 small sweet apple, such as Gala, Fuji, or Golden Delicious, peeled, cored, and cut into ⅛-inch dice (about ¾ cup)

2 garlic cloves, minced

2 scallions, chopped

1 tablespoon toasted sesame oil

1 teaspoon toasted sesame seeds

Green lettuce, red lettuce, chicory, or perilla (kkaenip) leaves for serving

Chrysanthemum greens (ssuk-gat) and fresh cilantro sprigs for serving

Fluffy White Rice (page 36)

1. Combine the soybean paste, hot pepper paste, apple, garlic, scallions, and sesame oil in a small bowl and mix well. Transfer to a serving bowl and sprinkle with the sesame seeds.

2. Arrange the greens and herbs in a shallow basket or on a platter.

3. Tell your guests to hold a lettuce leaf on their palm, arrange a few chrysanthemum greens and a cilantro sprig on the lettuce, and scoop some rice on top. Spoon some of the apple ssamjang on top of the rice, wrap the lettuce around the rice and sauce, and enjoy immediately.

Top row: left, chrysanthemum leaves; right, mixing apple dipping sauce; center row: left, apple dipping sauce; right, arranged dish, ready to eat; bottom, a Vegetable Leaf Wrap with Rice and Apple Dipping Sauce

Stir-Fried Bellflower Root

(Doraji-namul-bokkeum)

Serves 4

Bellflower grows wild in the mountains and fields of Korea, although these days it's also cultivated on farms. Its roots are used extensively in Korean cuisine. The fresh roots look a little like ginseng roots and are bitter like ginseng. Sliced and dried, the roots are used medicinally in the form of tea, boiled in water and served with honey.

The large amount of salt in this recipe helps reduce the natural bitterness of the roots, as does the rice syrup. The result is chewy, juicy, and crisp, with a pleasant herbal flavor.

4 ounces dried bellflower roots (doraji)
Kosher salt
2 tablespoons vegetable oil
½ medium onion, sliced (½ cup)
4 garlic cloves, minced
1 tablespoon brown rice syrup
  (ssal-yeot)

2 teaspoons toasted sesame oil
1 teaspoon toasted sesame seeds
A few strips of shredded dried hot
  pepper (silgochu; optional)

1. Soak the bellflower roots in 3 quarts water in a large bowl for 7 to 8 hours (they will expand to about 4 cups).

2. Drain the soaked roots and put in a bowl. Add 2 tablespoons salt and mix vigorously with your hands for about 3 minutes. Transfer to a colander and rinse under cold running water to remove excess salt; drain. (This process will help reduce the bitterness of the roots.)

3. Heat the vegetable oil in a large skillet over medium-high heat. Add the bellflower roots and stir-fry for 5 minutes. Add the onion, garlic, and 2 teaspoons salt, turn the heat down to medium, and cook, stirring, until the bellflower roots are softened and a little translucent, about 7 minutes.

4. Remove from the heat, stir in the rice syrup and toasted sesame oil, and mix well. Transfer to a serving plate. Sprinkle with the sesame seeds and garnish with the shredded hot pepper, if desired. Serve warm or cold. Refrigerate leftovers in an airtight container for up to 1 week.

Maangchi and Friends

Cutemom: *I just scrubbed fresh doraji once with salt, then rinsed it thoroughly before I mixed it with the seasonings. It was very tasty, and my mom thought it was young ginseng. We finished the whole thing in one day.*

Maangchi: *Yes, it tastes like ginseng! Your mom is right!*

Braised Burdock Root *(Ueong-jorim)*

Serves 4

If you enjoy something herbal and a little sweet, you will love braised burdock root. When you first see this root, you'll probably be a little surprised: It looks like a long gray branch, not something you would eat. When it's fully grown, it can be more than two feet long. Look for it in Asian grocery stores, where they sell whole roots as well as packages of smaller pieces.

   You can serve this as a side dish or use it as a filling for Seaweed Rice Rolls (gim-bap; page 44). Koreans make this mitbanchan in quantity so it's ready to add variety to any meal.

1 pound burdock root (ueong-ppuri)

1 teaspoon distilled white or apple cider vinegar

1 tablespoon vegetable oil

2 garlic cloves, minced

3 tablespoons soy sauce

1 tablespoon light brown sugar

1 cup water

⅓ cup brown rice syrup (ssal-yeot)

1 teaspoon toasted sesame oil

1 teaspoon toasted sesame seeds

1. Peel the burdock root with a vegetable peeler or a sharp spoon. Cut the roots into 2½-inch pieces, then cut into matchsticks.

2. Bring 5 cups water to a boil in a medium saucepan over high heat. Add the root and vinegar, cover, and boil for 10 minutes. Drain and rinse the root under cold running water until the water runs clear. Drain and let cool.

3. Heat a medium heavy pot over medium-high heat. Add the vegetable oil, then add the root and stir-fry until slightly softened, 5 minutes. Add the garlic, soy sauce, brown sugar, and the 1 cup water, turn the heat down to low, cover, and simmer for 30 minutes.

4. Uncover the pot and stir well. Turn the heat up to medium, add the rice syrup, and cook, stirring occasionally, until the sauce is thickened and the root is dark brown and shiny, 10 to 12 minutes.

5. Remove from the heat and stir in the sesame oil. Transfer to a serving plate, sprinkle with the sesame seeds, and serve. Store leftovers in an airtight container in the refrigerator for up to 1 week; serve cold.

Thick Soybean Paste Stew (Gang-doenjang)

Serves 4

Gang-doenjang is usually brought to the table sizzling in an earthenware pot. The salty, earthy, beefy stew is thickened with some potatoes and made a little sweet with onions. I like to serve it in the classic Korean style—with some steamed cabbage (see below) that you use to wrap some rice and stew into little packages and pop into your mouth.

1 teaspoon vegetable oil

2 garlic cloves, minced

3 ounces lean ground beef (about ½ cup)

¾ cup chopped onion

1 medium russet potato, peeled and cut into ¼-inch cubes (about ¾ cup)

1 green Korean chili pepper (cheong-gochu), stemmed and chopped

¼ cup fermented soybean paste (doenjang)

½ cup water

Fluffy White Rice (page 36)

Steamed Cabbage (recipe follows)

1. Heat a 3-cup flameproof earthenware pot or a medium saucepan over medium heat. Add the vegetable oil, garlic, and beef and stir-fry until the beef is no longer pink, a few minutes.

2. Add the onion, potato, and chili pepper and cook, stirring, until the vegetables are beginning to soften, about 5 minutes. Add the soybean paste and water and mix well with a wooden spoon. Cover, turn the heat down to low, and cook for about 10 minutes. The vegetables should be fully cooked but not mushy. Uncover and stir.

3. Spoon some rice onto a cabbage leaf, top with some stew, roll up, and enjoy.

Steamed Cabbage (Yangbaechu-jjim)

Serves 2 to 4

This is how to prepare cabbage leaves to be used as a wrapping for rice with Thick Soybean Paste Stew (see above) or Soybean Paste Dipping Sauce (page 272).

1 medium head green cabbage (about 1 pound)

1. Remove the tough outer leaves of the cabbage. Cut the cabbage in half through the core and use a sharp paring knife to cut out the core in each half.

2. Pour about 3 cups water into a large pot and set a steamer basket or rack over it. Rinse the cabbage under cold running water and put it in the steamer, cut side down. Cover and cook over medium-high heat for 20 minutes. Turn the heat to low and cook for another 10 minutes. Remove the cabbage halves from the steamer basket and let cool completely. Use immediately or refrigerate for up to 3 days.

Braised Black Beans *(Geomeunkong-jorim)*

Serves 12

Black beans are nutritious and full of protein, but they're usually not visually appealing. These beans, though, look like shiny black jewels. I eat them by the spoonful because I'm just too impatient to pick them up with chopsticks.

The beans keep well in the refrigerator, so it makes sense to make a large batch. When just made, they're served warm with rice, and then leftovers are usually served cold over the course of a week or two, so they are a good lunch box item. You can substitute dried yellow soybeans for the black beans.

8 ounces (1⅓ cups) dried Korean black beans (geomeun-kong)
¼ cup soy sauce
2 cups water

4 garlic cloves, minced
3 tablespoons light brown sugar
¼ cup brown rice syrup (ssal-yeot)
Toasted sesame seeds for garnish

1. Cover the beans with 5 cups cold water in a large bowl and soak for 8 hours.

2. Drain the beans in a colander, rinse under cold running water, and drain again. Put the beans in a large skillet, add the soy sauce and the 2 cups water, cover, and cook over medium-high heat for 30 minutes. If the water becomes foamy and boils over, adjust the lid so the skillet is only partially covered and stir occasionally.

3. Add the garlic, brown sugar, and rice syrup to the beans and mix well. Turn the heat down to low and simmer, covered, for 30 minutes.

4. Uncover and stir the beans with a wooden spoon. Turn the heat up to medium-high and cook, stirring, until the beans look shiny, sticky, and a little wrinkly, about 3 minutes. Remove from the heat and transfer to a serving bowl. Sprinkle with toasted sesame seeds. Leftover black beans can be kept in an airtight container in the refrigerator for up to 2 weeks.

Left, Thick Soybean Paste Stew; right, Braised Black Beans

Clockwise from top left: drying tofu; frying tofu; Panfried Tofu with Spicy Seasoning Sauce

Panfried Tofu with Spicy Seasoning Sauce
(Dububuchim-yangnyeomjang)

Serves 4

This side dish is very common on Korean dining tables and in lunch boxes. The seasoning sauce, a mixture of soy sauce, sesame oil, scallions, garlic, sugar, and hot pepper flakes, is finished with sesame seeds. It's versatile: I use it in bibimbap, on fish, and in many other ways.

   You need medium-firm tofu for this dish. Firm is too dry, and soft will not keep its shape in the frying pan.

for the sauce
2 tablespoons soy sauce
2 scallions, chopped
1 garlic clove, minced
½ teaspoon sugar
1 teaspoon Korean hot pepper flakes
   (gochu-garu)
1 teaspoon toasted sesame oil

for the tofu
1 (14-ounce) package medium-firm tofu
2 tablespoons vegetable oil
1 teaspoon toasted sesame seeds,
   plus extra seeds for garnish

1. Make the sauce: Combine the soy sauce, scallions, garlic, sugar, hot pepper flakes, sesame oil, and the 1 teaspoon sesame seeds in a small bowl.

2. Make the tofu: Rinse the tofu under cold water and pat dry with paper towels. Cut it in half lengthwise, then cut each half crosswise into 10 pieces, so you have a total of 20 pieces, each ¼ inch thick.

3. Heat a 12-inch skillet over medium-high heat. Add 1 tablespoon of the vegetable oil and tilt the skillet to spread it over the bottom. Add the tofu and fry until the bottoms turn golden brown and crisp, 6 to 7 minutes. Turn the tofu with a spatula, then drizzle the remaining 1 tablespoon vegetable oil around the edges of the skillet and tilt the skillet to spread it evenly. Cook until the other side of the tofu is golden brown and crisp, another 6 to 7 minutes.

4. Transfer the tofu to a serving plate. Spoon the seasoning sauce on top, sprinkle with the extra sesame seeds, and serve.

Maangchi and Friends

Yire: Is there anything that is a tofu stew or other side dish that doesn't have to be fried?

Maangchi: I sometimes blanch medium-firm tofu lightly and cut it into cubes or slices, then wrap it in Napa Cabbage Kimchi (page 114). As you know, tofu itself has no taste, so it should always be served with a sauce or kimchi.

Steamed Eggs in an Earthenware Bowl

(Ttukbaegi-gyeran-jjim)

Serves 2 to 4

If you've ever seen steamed eggs served in a hot, dark earthenware bowl at a Korean restaurant, you know that the dish commands attention. It is usually still sizzling when it comes to the table, and it is a showstopper. Light, fluffy, salty, and sweet from the scallions, the eggs are further enhanced by an irresistible savory broth.

What most people don't realize is how easy the dish is to make at home. If you have the ingredients on hand, it takes only 10 minutes. The broth can be chicken or anchovy stock. If you don't have an earthenware pot, you can use a heavy stainless-steel pan. Serve with rice.

3 large eggs
1 large egg yolk
1 teaspoon fish sauce or kosher salt
1 scallion, chopped

1½ cups canned low-sodium chicken broth or Anchovy-Kelp Stock (page 86)
1 teaspoon toasted sesame oil

1. Beat the eggs and egg yolk with the fish sauce and scallion in a small bowl.

2. Pour the chicken broth into 3-cup flameproof earthenware bowl or a small heavy stainless-steel pot and bring to a boil over medium-high heat. Turn the heat down to very low and slowly pour the beaten eggs into the broth, stirring with a fork. Cover and simmer until the eggs are cooked and fluffy, 5 to 6 minutes.

3. Drizzle the sesame oil over the eggs and serve immediately. (If you use a stainless-steel pot, transfer to a bowl to serve.)

Dried Anchovies and Nuts
(Janmyeolchi-ttangkong-bokkeum)

Serves 8 to 12

Koreans use large dried anchovies to make delicious stocks and use the small ones in all kinds of snacks and side dishes. In this recipe, tiny dried anchovies are toasted in a skillet until crisp and then combined with peanuts, rice syrup, and sesame oil for an addictive snack or side dish. I often make this dish in larger quantities, because it keeps in the refrigerator for up to 1 month and is nice to have on hand as a last-minute addition to a meal.

You can use almost any kind of nut: Peanuts, walnuts, pine nuts, almonds, or pecans are all good. But if you don't like nuts, you can leave them out and you will still have a tasty snack.

4 ounces small dried anchovies (mareun-myeolchi), heads and guts removed

¼ cup roasted peanuts (salted or unsalted)

2 teaspoons vegetable oil

1 garlic clove, minced

1 green Korean chili pepper (cheong-gochu), stemmed and chopped into small pieces (optional)

1 to 2 tablespoons brown rice syrup (ssal-yeot), honey, or light brown sugar

1 teaspoon toasted sesame oil

1 tablespoon toasted sesame seeds

1. Cook the anchovies in a large skillet over medium heat, stirring with a wooden spoon, until crispy and light brown, 3 to 4 minutes. Transfer to a bowl.

2. Add the peanuts to the skillet and cook, stirring, for 1 minute. Add the vegetable oil, garlic, and chili pepper, if using, and stir-fry for another minute.

3. Remove from the heat and stir in the rice syrup, sesame oil, sesame seeds, and anchovies (the residual heat will warm the mixture). Transfer to a serving bowl or plate and serve warm or at room temperature. Refrigerate leftovers in an airtight container for up to 1 month and serve cold.

Braised Beef in Soy Sauce *(Jangjorim)*
Serves 8 to 12

For this traditional dish of beef with soy sauce, hard-boiled eggs, green chili peppers, and lots of garlic, be sure to choose a lean cut so the broth won't be greasy. Flank steak is lean and also tears nicely into strips once cooked. Don't throw away any leftover broth: You can make a quick bibimbap with it by mixing some of it with your warm rice.

Jangjorim is another good example of mitbanchan—side dishes that can be made in large batches, ready for pulling out of the refrigerator at the drop of a hat.

When I was young, beef was expensive, so this dish was a special treat—and it still is. It's always served in very small portions. To save time, I cook the eggs in the shell right in with the beef.

8 ounces flank steak, cut along the grain into 2½-x-1½-x-¼-inch strips

1 cup soy sauce

1 (4-x-6-inch) piece dried kelp (dasima; optional)

2 cups water

½ cup peeled garlic cloves

3 large green Korean chili peppers (cheong-gochu), stemmed and cut crosswise into 1-inch pieces

3 large eggs in the shell, washed, and patted dry with paper towels

1 tablespoon light brown sugar

1 red Korean chili pepper (hong-gochu), stemmed and chopped into small pieces, for garnish (optional)

1. Put the beef in a medium pot and add water to cover. Cover and cook over medium-high heat for 10 minutes. Drain, rinse the beef under cold running water, and drain again. Wash out the pot.

2. Return the beef to the clean pot. Add the soy sauce, dried kelp (if using), and water, cover, and cook over medium-high heat for 20 minutes.

3. Add the garlic, green chili peppers, and eggs and turn the heat down to low. Cover and cook for 5 minutes. Uncover the pot and gently turn the eggs over (this will help keep the yolks in the center of the eggs). Cover and cook until the flavors meld, 30 to 40 minutes, stirring a few times.

4. Remove the eggs, let stand until just cool enough to handle, shell them, and put them back in the pot. Add the brown sugar and mix well. Remove the pot from the heat and cool until the beef is cool enough to handle.

5. Remove the kelp if you used it. The soy sauce–infused kelp can be eaten as a side dish with rice. Remove the beef, tear it into thin strips with your fingers, and put it in a serving bowl. Cut the eggs into a few pieces each and add them to the serving bowl. Add the garlic and green chili pepper, along with some of the braising liquid. Garnish with the red chili pepper, if using, and serve. Refrigerate leftovers in an airtight container for up to 1 week.

Top, cooking eggs in soy sauce; bottom, Braised Beef in Soy Sauce

Top, mixing the ingredients before stir-frying; bottom, Spicy Stir-Fried Pork

Spicy Stir-Fried Pork *(Dwaejigogi-bokkeum)*

Serves 4

Whenever I make this glistening dish of thin slices of pork and caramelized onions, spicy-hot with hot pepper paste, hot pepper flakes, and green chili, people go crazy. If you need a great dish in a hurry, this is the way to go.

1 pound pork belly or boneless pork shoulder, cut into about 1½-x-1-x-¼-inch pieces

¼ cup Korean hot pepper paste (gochujang)

1 tablespoon Korean hot pepper flakes (gochu-garu)

1 tablespoon soy sauce

1 tablespoon plus 1 teaspoon sugar or honey

½ cup sliced onion

3 garlic cloves, minced

½ teaspoon minced peeled ginger

1 scallion, chopped

¼ teaspoon freshly ground black pepper

1 green Korean chili pepper (cheong-gochu), stemmed and chopped

2 teaspoons toasted sesame oil

1 teaspoon toasted sesame seeds

1. Combine the pork, hot pepper paste, hot pepper flakes, soy sauce, sugar, onion, garlic, ginger, scallion, black pepper, chili pepper, and sesame oil in a large skillet and mix together with a wooden spoon. Set the pan over high heat and stir-fry until the pork is cooked through but still juicy and the onion is caramelized, 10 to 12 minutes.

2. Transfer to a serving plate, sprinkle with the sesame seeds, and serve.

Sweet, Sour, and Spicy Squid with Water Dropwort *(Ojingeo-minari-chomuchim)*

Serves 4

Water dropwort has crisp green stems and leafy tops. Its herbal, earthy flavor is a great match for squid with spicy seasoning paste. Outside of Korean markets, water dropwort can be hard to find, but you can use another green or vegetable in its place. Blanched watercress works well. Or try cucumber (a favorite of mine): Thinly slice it, sprinkle with salt, let stand for 10 minutes, and squeeze all the water out. Just don't try to forage for your own water dropwort: To the untrained eye, its relative, the highly toxic hemlock plant, can be mistaken for it. Buy your water dropwort at a Korean grocery store.

This spicy squid goes well alongside alcoholic beverages like Korean Rice Liquor (page 270).

¼ cup Korean hot pepper paste (gochujang)

1 tablespoon Korean hot pepper flakes (gochu-garu)

2 garlic cloves, minced

1 tablespoon honey or sugar

3 tablespoons distilled white or apple cider vinegar

1 teaspoon kosher salt

2 teaspoons toasted sesame oil

8 ounces fresh or frozen cleaned squid bodies, thawed if frozen, cut into about 2½-x-½-inch strips

1 bunch (about 5 ounces) water dropwort (minari), tips of roots trimmed

½ cup thinly sliced onion

1 medium carrot, peeled and cut into 3-x-½-x-⅛-inch strips

1 green Korean chili pepper (cheong-gochu), stemmed and chopped

1 teaspoon toasted sesame seeds

1. Combine the hot pepper paste, hot pepper flakes, garlic, honey, vinegar, salt, and sesame oil in a small bowl and mix well with a spoon to make the seasoning paste.

2. Bring a large pot of water to a boil. Put the squid in a strainer with a handle, lower the strainer into the boiling water, and stir the squid for 30 seconds, then lift the strainer from the pot and transfer the squid to a bowl.

3. Add the water dropwort to the boiling water and blanch for 30 seconds. Drain in a colander and rinse under cold running water to stop the cooking. Drain again and squeeze out excess water. Cut into bite-size pieces.

4. Add the water dropwort, onion, carrot, and chili pepper to the bowl with the squid. Add the seasoning paste and mix well. Transfer to a serving plate, sprinkle with the sesame seeds, and serve.

Top row: left, seasoning paste; right, blanched squid; center row: left, cutting blanched water dropwort; right, mixing ingredients; bottom, Sweet, Sour, and Spicy Squid with Water Dropwort

How to Cut Up Live Crabs

1. Put the crabs in a paper bag or wrap them in newspaper and freeze for 2 hours. This will make them groggy and easy to handle (but longer freezing will kill them and the meat will be soggy).

2. Chop (or break) off the tips of the claws with the back of your chef's knife (so if the crabs wake up, they can't pinch you). Put the crabs in a large bowl, set it under cold running water, and scrub each one with a kitchen brush; change the water a couple of times during cleaning. Drain.

3. Grab a crab and place it on a cutting board, belly up. Remove the apron, which looks like a flap, by lifting it up and then twisting it off.

4. Flip the crab over and pull off the top shell. Remove the feathery gills with your fingers. Use scissors to cut away the antennae, eyes, mouth parts, and the ends of the back legs (which don't have any meat). Use a sharp chef's knife to cut the crab body into 7 or 8 pieces.

5. Crack the claws with the back of the knife so that the seasoning sauce can be absorbed easily and the shell will be easy to remove before eating.

6. Put the crab pieces into a bowl. Use a spoon to scoop out the tomalley and roe from the top shell and add it to the bowl. Repeat with the remaining crabs.

Spicy Raw Crab *(Maeun-gejang)*
Serves 8 to 12

In the southern harbor city of Yeosu, where I lived until I went to high school, every family has its own version of this dish—crabs marinated in a mix of seasonings. This recipe is my mom's. I once made it for some Japanese friends who had never had it, and the husband couldn't stop eating it. Even though the pepper flakes made his face drip with sweat, he kept saying, "Delicious, delicious, delicious," as he plowed through it.

Getting live crabs is crucial: They will guarantee the freshest taste and the best texture. I use Atlantic blue crabs, which are smaller and easier to handle than the giant crabs my mom had to deal with. And I've developed my own humane way of preparing them; see the box above.

Female crabs are best, because their orange roe and yellow tomalley (often called the "mustard" in Maryland) make the dish more colorful, sweet, and rich. How can you tell if a crab is male or female? Flip it over and look at the apron. If it is dome shaped, it's female; if it's narrow and pointed, it's male.

Start this the day before so the crab has time to marinate.

1½ pounds live female blue crabs
   (4 or 5 crabs)
¼ cup soy sauce
¼ cup Korean hot pepper flakes
   (gochu-garu)
2 scallions, chopped

6 garlic cloves, minced
1 teaspoon minced peeled ginger
1 tablespoon sugar
2 teaspoons toasted sesame oil
Pinch of freshly ground black pepper
1 tablespoon toasted sesame seeds

1. Freeze the crabs for 2 hours to anesthetize them, then chop into bite-size pieces (see the box, opposite).

2. Combine the soy sauce, hot pepper flakes, scallions, garlic, ginger, sugar, sesame oil, and black pepper in a large bowl and mix until well combined. Add the crabs and turn to coat. Sprinkle with the sesame seeds. Transfer to an airtight container and refrigerate for at least 12 hours (you can eat the crab immediately, but it will taste better after it has had time to absorb the sauce).

3. The spicy crab will keep for up to 1 week. Serve cold.

Seasoned Dried Filefish (Juipo-muchim)

Serves 8 to 12

When dried and shredded filefish is seasoned with a sweet and spicy sauce, it makes a great side dish. The hard dried fish softens and takes on a nutty sesame-oil flavor.

You'll need to get to a Korean grocery store to find dried filefish. You can substitute shredded dried squid or shredded dried pollock, if you'd like.

8 ounces dried filefish (juipo)
⅓ cup Korean hot pepper paste
  (gochujang)
2 tablespoons vegetable or olive oil
1 tablespoon toasted sesame oil

3 garlic cloves, minced
¼ cup brown rice syrup (ssal-yeot),
  or 2 to 3 tablespoons sugar
2 teaspoons toasted sesame seeds

1. Wipe each piece of filefish on both sides with a wet cloth or paper towel to remove any dusty residue. Use scissors to cut each piece into thin 2-x-⅓-inch strips.

2. Heat a large skillet over medium heat. Add the filefish and cook, stirring, for 2 minutes, until slightly cooked. Remove from the heat.

3. Combine the hot pepper paste, vegetable oil, sesame oil, garlic, and rice syrup in a large bowl and mix well with a wooden spoon until the mixture is creamy and shiny. Add the filefish and mix well with the spoon or your hands. (If you mix this by hand, you might want to wear disposable gloves.) Add the sesame seeds and mix again. Refrigerate for 4 to 6 hours.

4. Transfer the fish to a bowl and serve. Refrigerate leftovers in an airtight container for up to 1 month; serve cold.

Seasoned Oysters *(Gulmuchim)*

Serves 4

In the early mornings in the harbor city of Yeosu, I used to follow my mother to the open-air market. There was always a gaggle of women who came daily from a nearby island to sell oysters that they had harvested among the rocks by the shore. They squatted behind their bowls of very small, very sweet wild oysters, shucking them and selling them to passersby.

My mom would bring the oysters home, mix them with a quick seasoning sauce, and serve them as a breakfast side dish. They were full of the flavor of the fresh sea.

If you live in a place where very fresh oysters are available, use them. You may be able to find containers of shucked oysters at your fish market or grocery store. If not, the frozen oysters you can buy in Korean grocery stores in the United States make a good substitute, since they are flash-frozen as soon as they are gathered and are good raw.

8 ounces shucked fresh oysters, or
  1 (8-ounce) package frozen oysters,
  thawed in the refrigerator
2 tablespoons soy sauce
2 tablespoons Korean hot pepper flakes
  (gochu-garu)

1 teaspoon sugar
2 or 3 scallions, thinly sliced
3 garlic cloves, minced
1 tablespoon toasted sesame oil
1 tablespoon toasted sesame seeds

1. Rinse the oysters under cold running water and drain. If they are large, cut them into bite-size pieces.

2. Put the oysters in a bowl and add the soy sauce, hot pepper flakes, sugar, scallions, garlic, sesame oil, and sesame seeds. Mix well.

3. Transfer to a serving bowl and serve immediately. The oysters are best eaten on the day they are prepared, but you can refrigerate leftovers for up to 3 days.

Braised Beltfish (*Galchi-jorim*)

Serves 4

Flavored with aromatics and cooked with vegetables, this fish side dish comes with a broth that is satisfying and hearty. You can scoop the flesh from the fish with a spoon—it will come away from the bones easily. In Korea, this kind of dish is known as a "rice thief" (*bapdoduk*)—it goes so well with rice that it makes the rice disappear as though it were stolen.

So named because it resembles a long belt, beltfish is also known as hairtail. It is popular in Korea but less well known here. Fresh mackerel is a good substitute that's widely available.

8 to 10 garlic cloves, minced

1 teaspoon minced peeled ginger

¼ cup soy sauce

1 tablespoon Korean hot pepper flakes (gochu-garu)

1 teaspoon sugar

1 (1-pound) fresh beltfish (galchi) or mackerel, or 1 pound frozen beltfish, thawed in the refrigerator

8 ounces Korean radish (mu) or daikon, peeled and sliced into ¼-inch-thick disks

1 medium onion, sliced

1½ cups water

1 scallion, thinly sliced on the diagonal

1 green Korean chili pepper (cheong-gochu), stemmed and thinly sliced on the diagonal

1 red Korean chili pepper (hong-gochu), stemmed and thinly sliced on the diagonal

1. Combine the garlic, ginger, soy sauce, hot pepper flakes, and sugar in a small bowl.

2. If using whole fresh fish, remove the head and guts and snip off the fins, or ask your fishmonger to do this. Cut the fish into 3-inch pieces (frozen fish will have already been cut). Rinse the fish under cold running water and pat dry.

3. Arrange the radish disks in the bottom of a large heavy skillet. Arrange the onion slices over the radish. Place the fish pieces on top and spoon the seasoning mixture over the fish. Add the water, cover, and cook over medium heat for 25 minutes.

4. Uncover the pan and turn the heat up to high. Scatter the scallion and chili peppers over and around the fish. Cook, uncovered to allow some of the broth to evaporate, for 7 to 10 minutes. Occasionally spoon some of the broth over the top of the fish to season it evenly.

5. Remove from the heat and serve.

Top, beltfish ready for cooking; bottom, Braised Beltfish

Stir-Fried Fish Cakes with Soy Sauce

(Ganjang-eomuk-bokkeum)

Serves 4

I often get requests for this recipe from readers who have tried it at Korean restaurants. They ask for it not by name but by description: "It's fishy, a little sweet, somewhat chewy, a little brown, and salty. Do you have a recipe?"

It is remarkably easy to make: It's just fish cakes from a Korean grocery store, stir-fried with soy sauce and rice syrup. It is popular in Korean lunch boxes, because it packs well and doesn't become watery by midday. You can swap hot pepper paste for the soy sauce to make spicy red fish cakes.

When shopping for the fish cakes—which are made from pollock, squid, or, sometimes, shrimp—you'll see that price depends on the percentage of real fish in the cakes. Cheaper fish cakes have a higher starch content. More expensive ones are worth the money.

8 ounces fish cakes (eomuk), rinsed under hot water and patted dry with paper towels

2 teaspoons vegetable oil

¼ cup thinly sliced onion

1 garlic clove, minced

½ small carrot, peeled and cut into matchsticks (about ¼ cup)

1 green Korean chili pepper (cheong-gochu), stemmed and thinly sliced

1 tablespoon soy sauce

1 tablespoon brown rice syrup (ssal-yeot)

1 teaspoon toasted sesame oil

1 teaspoon toasted sesame seeds

1. If the fish cakes are rectangular, cut them into 2-x-¼-inch strips. If they are cylindrical, cut them diagonally into ¼-inch slices.

2. Heat a large skillet over medium heat. Add the vegetable oil. Add the fish cake pieces and stir-fry until golden brown, 2 to 3 minutes. Add the onion, garlic, carrot, and chili pepper and stir-fry until the onion starts to become translucent, about 2 minutes.

3. Remove the pan from the heat and stir in the soy sauce and rice syrup. Return the pan to the heat and stir-fry until the fish cakes are glistening, about 1 minute.

4. Remove from the heat and stir in the sesame oil and sesame seeds. Transfer to a serving plate and serve. Refrigerate leftovers for up to 3 days; serve cold.

Clockwise from top left: fish cakes; stir-frying fish cakes; Stir-Fried Fish Cakes with Soy Sauce

Spicy Stir-Fried Squid (Ojingeo-bokkeum)
Serves 4

This squid stir-fried with lots of scallions is nice and spicy. It's not all heat, however; the onion and squid are both sweet and chewy, in contrast to the fiery sauce. You won't need to prepare any other side dishes—just serve this with rice, and you will have a meal with a full range of textures and flavors.

It's not always easy to find fresh squid, so I sometimes buy frozen. The quality is good because the squid is flash-frozen right on the fishing boats. Make sure not to overcook the squid, or it will be rubbery.

6 garlic cloves, minced

½ teaspoon minced peeled ginger

3 tablespoons soy sauce

2 teaspoons sugar

2 tablespoons Korean hot pepper flakes (gochu-garu)

1 teaspoon potato starch or cornstarch

¼ cup water

1 tablespoon vegetable oil

1 small carrot, cut into 3-x-½-inch-thick strips (about ½ cup)

1 large onion, sliced (about 1½ cups)

12 scallions, cut into 3-inch pieces on the diagonal

1 pound fresh or frozen cleaned squid bodies and tentacles, thawed if frozen, cut into about 3-x-½-inch pieces

1 green Korean chili pepper (cheong-gochu), stemmed and thinly sliced on the diagonal

1. Combine the garlic, ginger, soy sauce, sugar, and hot pepper flakes in a small bowl. Mix the potato starch with the water in another small bowl.

2. Heat a large nonstick skillet over medium-high heat. Add the vegetable oil, carrot, and onion and stir-fry for 1 minute. Add the scallions and stir-fry until wilted and beginning to soften, 5 to 7 minutes.

3. Add the squid and the seasoning mixture and cook, stirring, until the squid is just opaque, 2 to 3 minutes. Add the potato starch slurry and stir until the sauce thickens, about 30 seconds.

4. Transfer to a serving plate and serve immediately.

Facing page: top row: left, whole uncleaned squid; right, pulling tentacles and innards from body; second row: left, body and tentacles, head, beak, innards, and cartilage removed; right, pulling off skin; third row: left, trimming squid; right, slicing squid; bottom, Spicy Stir-Fried Squid

Top, roasted porgy; bottom, spooning Spicy Seasoning Sauce over roasted porgy

Roasted Porgy with Spicy Seasoning Sauce *(Pogi-yangnyeom-gui)*

Serves 4

Roast a whole fish and cover it with a spicy seasoning sauce, and it becomes very special indeed. The lettuce on the serving platter is not merely decorative: The juices from the fish and the sauce soak into it, turning the leaves into a delicious salad to eat once the fish is gone. Serve the dish with rice to temper its spiciness.

When I find large fresh porgies for sale in Chinatown fish markets, I usually buy three or four, sprinkle them with a little salt, and freeze them for later. If you're not crazy about cleaning fish, ask the fishmonger to do it for you.

1 (1½-pound) porgy, guts removed, scaled, washed, and patted dry with paper towels
1 teaspoon kosher salt
1 tablespoon vegetable oil

Lettuce leaves for serving (optional)
Spicy Soy Seasoning Sauce (page 272)
1 scallion, chopped
¼ cup sliced onion
1 teaspoon toasted sesame seeds

1. Score both sides of the fish diagonally three or four times. Sprinkle both sides of the fish evenly with the salt. Put it in a zipper-lock bag and refrigerate for 30 minutes. (You can freeze the fish for up to 3 months; defrost in the refrigerator overnight before proceeding.)

2. Set a rack in the center of the oven and preheat the oven to 375°F. Brush the fish all over with the oil and place it on a baking sheet. Roast for 30 minutes, then turn with a large spatula and roast until the fish is opaque throughout when pierced with a knife, about 30 minutes longer.

3. Turn the oven to broil and broil the fish until crispy and golden brown, about 5 minutes.

4. Line a large platter with lettuce leaves. Transfer the fish to the platter. Pour the sauce over the fish, sprinkle with the scallion, onion slices, and sesame seeds, and serve.

Seasoned Fermented Sardine Side Dish
(Jeong-eo-ri jeotgal-muchim)

Serves 6 to 8

If you love stinky cheese, you'll appreciate this dish, and you can classify yourself as a hard-core Korean food lover.

If you've taken the time to make your own Fermented Sardines (page 266), you already have the main ingredient for this quick and tasty side dish. You can also make it with fermented salted anchovies from a Korean grocery store. Just choose a few good firm ones from the jar.

3 or 4 large Fermented Sardines (page 266), or 5 or 6 fermented anchovies
1 garlic clove, chopped
1 scallion, chopped
1 green Korean chili pepper (cheong-gochu), stemmed and chopped

½ teaspoon sugar
1 teaspoon Korean hot pepper flakes (gochu-garu)
1 tablespoon toasted sesame seeds
2 teaspoons toasted sesame oil

1. Press down on the fermented sardines with your fingers and then pull away the flesh from the bones and heads. Discard the bones and heads, or return them to the jar with the rest of your fermenting fish.

2. With a chef's knife, chop the fish fillets into a paste. Combine the chopped fish, garlic, scallion, chili pepper, sugar, hot pepper flakes, sesame seeds, and sesame oil in a small bowl and mix well.

3. Serve immediately. Refrigerate leftovers for up to 2 weeks.

Sautéed Zucchini and Shrimp
(Hobak-saeu-bokkeum)

Serves 4

This eye-catching dish of soft green squash and pink shrimp goes well with Bulgogi (page 223), Grilled Pork Belly (page 232), or L.A.–Style Beef Short Ribs (page 226) and rice. Traditionally it is seasoned with salted fermented shrimp, which lend a deep, savory flavor. They are available at any Korean or Asian grocery store, but you can use fish sauce in their place.

Facing page: clockwise from top left: prepared ingredients; stir-frying vegetables and shrimp; Sautéed Zucchini and Shrimp

1 pound zucchini or Korean squash (often sold as "avocado squash"), cut into bite-size pieces

1 teaspoon kosher salt

1 tablespoon vegetable oil

½ cup sliced onion

2 garlic cloves, minced

4 ounces large shrimp, shelled, deveined, and cut lengthwise in half

1 tablespoon salted fermented shrimp (saeujeot) or fish sauce

1 red Korean chili pepper (hong-gochu), stemmed and chopped

1 teaspoon toasted sesame oil

1. Combine the zucchini and salt in a bowl and leave it on the counter for 5 to 10 minutes. Drain and pat dry with paper towels.

2. Heat a large skillet over medium-high heat. Add the oil, onion, and garlic and stir-fry for 1 minute. Turn the heat down to medium, add the zucchini, shrimp, and salted fermented shrimp, and cook, stirring occasionally, until the zucchini becomes a little bit translucent and the shrimp turns pink, 5 to 7 minutes. Stir in the chili pepper.

3. Remove from the heat and stir in the sesame oil. Transfer to a serving plate and serve. Refrigerate leftovers for up to 3 days; serve cold.

pancakes

Korean pancakes, called *jeon*, are many things, but they are not like American pancakes, dollops of batter cooked in a skillet and served for breakfast. Our pancakes are savory and crisp. They can be anything dipped in flour or mixed with a batter and then panfried. They can be rounds of sweet potato or zucchini, seasoned meat patties, or stuffed chili peppers. For larger pancakes, batter holds together flavorful ingredients like kimchi, seafood, and scallions.

Korean pancakes are served as side dishes, snacks, or light bites with alcoholic drinks. No party is complete without plenty of Pollock Pancakes. Larger pancakes are shared among friends and family, placed on the table so that everyone can tear off bite-size pieces with their chopsticks. They are also a popular choice on rainy days, served with Korean Rice Liquor (page 262).

My best advice when it comes to pancakes of all kinds is to have patience while you're cooking them. For most recipes, medium heat is best. You want the inside of your pancake to cook through before the exterior burns. Flip pancakes a few times to ensure even cooking.

Pancake vendor in a local market in Korea

Kimchi Pancake *(Kimchijeon)*

Serves 2 to 4

Kimchijeon are hot, a little sweet, sour, spicy, and satisfying. These are one of the many dishes that you can make on the spot if you have Napa Cabbage Kimchi on hand.

Since kimchijeon is a little salty, it's most often served with rice. But it also makes a good snack on its own, and it's a popular item for Korean lunch boxes. Make 2-inch pancakes for a quick appetizer with drinks when guests come over at the last minute. *The photo is on page 184.*

½ pound Napa Cabbage Kimchi (page 114), chopped into small pieces, plus 2 tablespoons of the brine

3 scallions, chopped

1 teaspoon sugar

½ cup all-purpose flour

½ cup water

4 tablespoons vegetable oil

1. Combine the kimchi, kimchi brine, scallions, sugar, flour, and water in a medium bowl and mix well with a spoon.

2. Heat a 12-inch nonstick skillet over medium heat. (If you don't have a 12-inch skillet, use a smaller skillet to make 2 pancakes.) Add 2 tablespoons of the vegetable oil and swirl to coat the bottom of the pan. Pour the batter into the pan and spread it with the back of a spoon or a spatula to make a large circle. Cook until the bottom is golden brown and crisp, 3 to 5 minutes.

3. Carefully turn the pancake over. Drizzle the remaining 2 tablespoons oil around the edges of the skillet, then lift the pancake with a thin spatula to allow the oil to run underneath and tilt the pan to spread it evenly. Cook until the bottom of the pancake is light golden brown and crisp, 3 to 5 minutes. Flip it one more time and cook for another minute.

4. Slide onto a large serving platter and serve immediately.

Maangchi and Friends

Mark: *What exactly is "kimchi brine"? Is it just the liquid that is with the kimchi when you make it? Or is it something else?*

Maangchi: *When you first make kimchi, you won't see much liquid. But 1 or 2 days later, the water from the cabbage or radish is drawn out, and it mixes with the kimchi paste. That's "kimchi brine."*

Potato Pancakes *(Gamjajeon)*

Serves 2

If you didn't make these potato pancakes yourself, you would never know they were made from potatoes. The inside is smooth and silky, but also chewy like a rice cake. And, if done right, the crisp outside tastes like a perfectly fried potato chip.

Gamjajeon is a specialty of Gangwon Province, which is famous for its potatoes. It is very mountainous, so it's difficult to grow rice there, but potatoes do just fine. The traditional recipe calls for grated potatoes, which produce coarse pancakes that are always a little brown. I like mine smooth and white, so I use a food processor instead of a grater, and I work fast so the potatoes never get a chance to oxidize. A little salt in the puree helps keep them white too.

This recipe is perfect for people who say they have no time to cook, or say they can't cook at all. *The photo is on page 185.*

for the pancakes

1 pound russet potatoes, peeled
½ teaspoon kosher salt
¼ cup water
2 scallions, chopped

Vegetable oil for frying

for the dipping sauce

2 tablespoons soy sauce
1 tablespoon distilled white vinegar
Pinch of toasted sesame seeds

1. Make the pancakes: Cut the potatoes into small chunks and put in a food processor. Add the salt and water and process until pureed and creamy.

2. Scrape the potato puree into a fine strainer set over a bowl. Press down on it gently with a spoon. Let stand for 1 minute to allow the starchy liquid to drain into the bowl.

3. Transfer the drained potato puree to another bowl and let the starch in the drained liquid settle to the bottom of the bowl, then pour off the liquid and scrape the starch into the potato puree. Add the scallions and stir to combine.

4. Heat a large nonstick skillet over medium heat. Add a few drops of vegetable oil to the pan, then drop heaping tablespoonfuls of the potato batter into the pan and spread into 2-inch disks with the back of a spoon or a spatula. Cook until the bottoms of the pancakes are lightly browned, about 2 minutes. Turn and cook until the other sides are crisp and light golden, 1 to 2 minutes, adding more vegetable oil as necessary. Transfer to a serving plate and repeat with the remaining batter. You should wind up with about 10 pancakes.

5. Meanwhile, make the dipping sauce: While the pancakes are cooking, combine all the ingredients in a small bowl.

6. Serve the dipping sauce with the hot pancakes.

Facing page: top, Kimchi Pancake (page 184); bottom, Potato Pancakes (page 185)

Above: top row: left, dried peeled split mung beans and glutinous rice; right, soaked mung beans and rice; second row: left, mung bean batter; right, vegetable and beef mixture; bottom; frying Mung Bean Pancakes (page 188)

Mung Bean Pancakes *(Bindaetteok)*
Serves 4 to 6

Packed full of meat and vegetables, this pancake is a meal in itself. The batter—made of dried mung beans and glutinous rice that have been soaked overnight—is a perfect foil for the tastes and textures of the pork, kimchi, fernbrake, sprouts, and other ingredients.

Cook the pancakes so they are a little crisp; you want that satisfying crunch when you bite into one. The inside should still be juicy, the meat and veggies firm and distinct.

I prepare these pancakes in big batches and freeze the extras, wrapping them individually in plastic wrap and then putting them into a zipper-lock bag. Whenever I want them as a quick meal, I thaw them in the fridge and then panfry them in a few drops of vegetable oil until they're hot and crisp again.

The beans, rice, and dried fernbrake need to soak, so start this recipe a day ahead. *The photos are on page 188.*

for the pancakes

1 cup dried peeled split mung beans (geopi-nokdu)
¼ cup glutinous rice (chap-ssal)
¾ cup water
4 ounces ground pork
¾ cup well-fermented, sour Napa Cabbage Kimchi (page 114), chopped
4 ounces fresh or soaked and boiled (see page 146) fernbrake (gosari), cut into 1½-inch pieces (about 1 cup)
6 ounces (about 2½ cups) mung bean sprouts, washed and drained

1 large egg
4 scallions, chopped
2 garlic cloves, minced
2 teaspoons kosher salt
¼ teaspoon freshly ground black pepper
2 teaspoons toasted sesame oil

for the dipping sauce

2 tablespoons soy sauce
1 tablespoon distilled white vinegar

Vegetable oil for frying
Shredded dried hot pepper (silgochu) for garnish (optional)

1. Soak the beans and rice: Combine the mung beans and rice in a large bowl, add cold water to cover, rinse in cold water, and drain. Cover with water by 3 inches and soak overnight. Drain.

2. Make the pancakes: Combine the soaked beans and rice and the ¾ cup water in a food processor and process until smooth and creamy, 1 to 2 minutes. Transfer to a large bowl. Add the pork, kimchi, fernbrake, mung bean sprouts, egg, scallions, garlic, salt, pepper, and sesame oil and mix well.

3. Heat a large skillet over medium-high heat. Add 1 tablespoon vegetable oil, swirl to coat the bottom of the pan, and then add 1 cup of the batter. Spread with the back of a spoon to make a 6-inch round and cook until the bottom turns golden, 2 to 3 minutes. Turn the pancake over, adding more vegetable oil to the pan if needed, and cook until the second side turns golden brown, another 2 minutes. Turn it over once more and cook for another 2 minutes on the first side until golden brown and crispy. Transfer to a large plate. Repeat with the remaining batter, making 6 pancakes in all.

4. Make the dipping sauce: Combine the soy sauce and vinegar in a small bowl.

5. Put a few threads of dried hot pepper on top of each pancake, if desired. Serve immediately, with the dipping sauce on the side.

I learned this recipe from a friend in Korea, who learned it from her mother-in-law from North Korea. My friend was the wife of the first son and, following Korean custom, she had a lot of responsibilities. One of them was to prepare the food offerings to dead ancestors for her family's memorial rites (*jesa*). This is an important tradition for Korean families, carried out every year on the anniversary of the death of the relative to pay respect. When the ancestral rites are over, everyone eats the food that's been prepared for the ceremony.

Her father-in-law always asked that the offerings include bindaetteok, and one day she gave me some leftover bindaetteok. It was by far the best I had ever eaten. I made her promise that the next time she was making it, she would show me how she did it.

Soon afterward, she invited me over. She was waiting for me with all the ingredients ready to mix, and I learned that her secret was to use generous amounts of kimchi and raw mung bean sprouts, which made the pancakes crisp and flavorful.

While we were working, I asked her, "By the way, which dead relative are you making this for?"

She answered, "I don't know. I do so many of these I can never keep track." I thought that was very funny.

Top, cooking pancake; bottom, Seafood-Scallion Pancake

Seafood-Scallion Pancake *(Haemul-pajeon)*
Serves 2 or 3

Unlike the flaky, puffy Chinese scallion pancakes you may have had, this is made with a rich, light batter so it's soft and fluffy inside and crunchy outside. It is filled with scallions, which give it a fresh sweetness. It's popular as a quick meal or snack, or as a side dish with Korean Rice Liquor (page 262). It's almost always shared in the middle of the table, with everyone tearing off bits with their chopsticks and dipping them into a savory vinegar–soy sauce dipping sauce.

The squid and shrimp are mild; for a stronger version, use shucked oysters instead.

for the dipping sauce
2 tablespoons soy sauce
1 tablespoon distilled white vinegar

for the pancake
¾ cup all-purpose flour
1 large egg
1 teaspoon kosher salt
¾ cup water

8 scallions, cut into 2-inch pieces
¼ cup vegetable oil
2 ounces fresh or frozen cleaned squid bodies, thawed if frozen, chopped into small pieces
2 ounces shrimp, shelled, deveined, and chopped into small pieces

1. Make the dipping sauce: Combine the soy sauce and vinegar in a small bowl.

2. Make the pancake: Combine the flour, egg, salt, and water in a bowl and mix well. Add the scallions and mix well.

3. Heat a 12-inch skillet over medium-high heat. (If you don't have a 12-inch skillet, use a smaller skillet to make 2 pancakes.) When the skillet is hot, turn the heat down to medium, add 2 tablespoons of the vegetable oil, and swirl to coat the bottom of the skillet evenly. Pour the batter into the skillet and spread it into a large circle with the back of a spoon or a spatula. Scatter the squid and shrimp over the pancake, pressing the seafood into the batter and shaping the edges with a spatula to form the pancake. Cook until the bottom turns light golden brown and crispy, 5 to 6 minutes, loosening the pancake with a spatula as it cooks.

4. Turn the pancake over with the spatula. Drizzle the remaining 2 tablespoons vegetable oil around the edges of the pancake, lifting the pancake with the spatula to let the oil run underneath. Shake the pan to distribute the oil evenly. Cook until the bottom is light golden brown and crispy, 5 to 6 minutes. Turn the pancake once more and cook for 2 minutes.

5. Slide onto a large platter and serve immediately with the dipping sauce.

Korean-Style Zucchini Pancakes (Hobakjeon)

Serves 4

These battered zucchini disks are light and crispy on the outside, moist inside. They go perfectly with the Creamy Pine Nut Sauce, and you'll turn to them often when you want to get something fresh on the table in a hurry. You can prepare disks of eggplant the same way.

The pancakes can be served as a side dish with rice, or as a quick snack all on their own. Make the pine nut sauce in the blender while the pancakes cook, or, for an even quicker dipping sauce, simply mix 2 tablespoons soy sauce and 1 tablespoon distilled white vinegar in a small bowl. Whichever sauce you choose, take care not to overcook the pancakes, so they keep all their flavor.

1 medium zucchini (about 8 ounces),
  sliced into ⅛-inch disks
Kosher salt
¼ cup all-purpose flour

2 large eggs
About 3 tablespoons vegetable oil
Creamy Pine Nut Sauce (page 275)

1. Arrange the zucchini slices in a single layer on a cutting board and sprinkle evenly with ½ teaspoon salt. Let stand for 5 to 7 minutes. They will sweat out some of their liquid and become little soft.

2. Gently blot the zucchini dry with paper towels. Transfer to a bowl. Add the flour and toss well to coat.

3. Beat the eggs in a small bowl with a pinch of salt.

4. Heat a large skillet over medium-high heat for 2 minutes. Turn the heat down to medium. Add 1 tablespoon of the vegetable oil and swirl to coat the bottom of the pan. Working in batches, one by one, dip each of the flour-coated zucchini slices in the eggs and place in the pan; do not crowd. Cook, turning the slices once or twice, until they are light golden brown and crisp, 3 to 5 minutes; add more oil to the pan as needed. Transfer to a plate. Serve with the pine nut sauce.

Left, Korean-Style Zucchini Pancake; left, Meat and Tofu Patties

Meat and Tofu Patties *(Wanjajeon)*

Serves 3 or 4

Wanjajeon are Korean-style beef patties served as a side dish with rice and soup, or made by moms for their children's lunch boxes. The secret to their succulence is the tofu.

If you'd like, use half beef and half pork instead of all ground beef. The egg coating gives the patties a beautiful golden color. My Western friends are big fans of this recipe. Everyone who's not a vegetarian likes meatballs, right?

for the dipping sauce
2 tablespoons soy sauce
1 tablespoon distilled white vinegar

for the patties
¼ cup medium-soft tofu
8 ounces lean ground beef
Kosher salt

¼ teaspoon freshly ground black pepper
1 garlic clove, minced
2 tablespoons chopped onion
1 teaspoon toasted sesame oil
2 tablespoons all-purpose flour
1 large egg
1 large egg yolk
2 to 3 tablespoons vegetable oil

1. Make the dipping sauce: Combine the soy sauce and vinegar in a small bowl.

2. Make the patties: Wrap the tofu in a paper towel or piece of cheesecloth and squeeze to remove excess water.

3. Combine the tofu, beef, 1 teaspoon salt, the pepper, garlic, onion, and sesame oil in a large bowl and mix well with your hands. Divide the meat mixture into 16 equal portions. Roll each piece between your palms into a ball and flatten into a 2-inch disk, about ¼ inch thick.

4. Put the flour in a shallow bowl. Coat each patty with flour. Transfer to a platter.

5. Whisk together the egg, egg yolk, and a pinch of salt in another shallow bowl.

6. Heat a large nonstick skillet over medium heat. Add about 1 tablespoon of the oil. Working in batches, one by one, dip each patty in the beaten egg and place in the pan, taking care not to overcrowd the pan. Cook until light golden brown on the first side, about 2 minutes. Turn and cook until the other side is light golden brown, about 2 minutes longer. Transfer to a serving platter. Add more oil to the pan as needed to cook the remaining patties.

7. Serve the patties hot or at room temperature, with the dipping sauce on the side.

Pollock Pancakes *(Dongtaejeon)*

Serves 4

These pancakes are made with slices of mild pollock cooked in a light, slightly salty, egg batter. It's important to cook them without browning the batter, so the pancakes are just golden and moist throughout.

Pollock is commonly sold frozen in Korean markets, and it is easiest to cut into neat pieces while it is still partially frozen. If you use a fresh fillet, put it in the freezer for an hour or so to firm it up. You can replace the pollock with other white-fleshed fish like snapper, cod, or flounder.

for the dipping sauce

2 tablespoons soy sauce

1 tablespoon apple cider vinegar
   or distilled white vinegar

1 teaspoon toasted sesame seeds

for the pancakes

8 ounces frozen pollock fillet, partially
   thawed (see above)

1 garlic clove, minced

½ teaspoon kosher salt

½ teaspoon freshly ground black
   or white pepper

⅓ cup all-purpose flour

1 large egg

2 large egg yolks

1 to 2 tablespoons vegetable oil

1. Make the dipping sauce: Combine all the ingredients in a small bowl.

2. Make the pancakes: Cut the fish into 2-x-2¼-inch thick pieces. Transfer to a bowl, add the garlic, salt, and pepper, and gently toss to coat.

3. Put the flour in a shallow bowl and coat each piece of fish in flour.

4. Combine the egg and egg yolks in a shallow bowl and beat together.

5. Heat a large nonstick skillet over medium-high heat. Add the vegetable oil and reduce the heat to medium-low. One by one, dip the fish pieces into the beaten eggs and place in the pan, in batches if necessary. Cook just until light golden brown, turning once, 2 to 3 minutes.

6. Transfer the pancakes to a platter and serve immediately with the dipping sauce.

In Korea, this is one of the recipes used to judge the skill of a cook. When we have big parties, a bunch of neighborhood women will get together to do the cooking. Usually one woman is especially good at pancake making, and she will fry her pancakes just until they turn a nice golden color but never brown. "Wow," people will say. "She is very good!"

This is usually considered special-occasion food, so my Korean coworkers in Toronto were always surprised when I had dongtaejeon in my lunch box. But it is really very simple and I make it often. It reminds me of my grandmother and her friends cooking together for a wedding.

Chili Pepper Pancakes *(Gochujeon)*

Serves 4

A panfried chili pepper filled with a seasoned mixture of beef and tofu is equally at home as a side dish, a snack, or an appetizer with drinks.

Korean chili peppers vary in spiciness. At the market, they are usually labeled, so you know if you are buying hot or mild peppers. Jalapeños are a little smaller than Korean chili peppers, if you'd like a hotter substitute.

If you have leftover filling, you can make small meatballs, flatten them, coat them with some flour and dip in beaten egg, then panfry them.

for the dipping sauce

1 tablespoon soy sauce

1½ teapoons distilled white or apple cider vinegar

Pinch of toasted sesame seeds

for the pancakes

¼ cup medium-soft tofu

4 ounces beef sirloin or tenderloin, minced, or ground beef

1 garlic clove, minced

2 tablespoons chopped onion

1 scallion, chopped

2 teaspoons soy sauce

1 teaspoon toasted sesame oil

Pinch of freshly ground black pepper

½ teaspoon sugar

⅓ cup all-purpose flour

15 to 20 mixed red (hong-gochu) and green (cheong-gochu) Korean chili peppers

1 large egg

Pinch of kosher salt

2 to 3 tablespoons vegetable oil

1. Make the dipping sauce: Combine the soy sauce and vinegar in a small bowl and sprinkle in the sesame seeds.

2. Make the pancakes: Wrap the tofu in a paper towel or piece of cheesecloth and squeeze to remove excess water.

3. Combine the tofu, beef, garlic, onion, scallion, soy sauce, sesame oil, black pepper, and sugar in a medium bowl and mix well with your hands or a wooden spoon.

4. Put the flour in a shallow bowl. Cut each pepper lengthwise in half, leaving the stems intact. Remove the seeds with a small spoon. Dip each pepper half in the flour to coat it inside and out. Fill each pepper half with some of the meat mixture, then roll the pepper in the flour to coat the meat and the outside.

5. Lightly beat the egg with the salt in a shallow bowl.

6. Heat a large nonstick skillet over medium-high heat. Add 1 tablespoon of the vegetable oil to the skillet and swirl to coat the bottom. Dip a pepper in the egg to coat and place it in the skillet, filling side down. Repeat with enough peppers to fill the skillet without overcrowding. Cook until well browned on the first side, 2 to 3 minutes. Turn and cook for another 2 to 3 minutes. If the peppers are browning too quickly, turn the heat down to medium. Transfer to a serving plate. Repeat with the remaining peppers, adding more vegetable oil to the skillet as necessary.

7. Serve the peppers hot with the dipping sauce.

Clockwise from top left: seeding chili peppers; filled peppers; Chili Pepper Pancakes

Perilla Leaf Pancakes *(Kkaennip-jeon)*
Serves 4

Perilla leaves have a distinctive minty, herbal taste that goes well with meat. Here they are folded over a savory filling of beef, tofu, onion, soy sauce, and garlic, then dipped in a light egg batter and fried. Koreans make these pancakes for parties and special occasions, not only because they taste great, but also because the green pouches look pretty on the table. Serve them as a snack, an appetizer with drinks, or as a side dish with rice.

This recipe uses the same savory meat filling as Chili Pepper Pancakes (page 194), so you can easily double the filling and make them both at once. If you have leftover beef mixture, make little meatballs about 1 inch in diameter, coat them with flour and beaten egg, and panfry them in a nonstick skillet in a little bit of vegetable oil.

You can buy perilla leaves at Korean markets, and you can also grow them at home. You might even have some growing near your house if you have Koreans in the neighborhood.

for the dipping sauce
1 tablespoon soy sauce
1½ teaspoons apple cider vinegar or
   distilled white vinegar
Pinch of toasted sesame seeds

for the filling
4 ounces beef sirloin, or tenderloin,
   minced, or ground beef
1 garlic clove, minced
2 tablespoons chopped onion
1 scallion, finely chopped
¼ cup medium-soft tofu, drained and
   patted dry

2 teaspoons soy sauce
1 teaspoon toasted sesame oil
Pinch of freshly ground black pepper
½ teaspoon sugar

3 tablespoons all-purpose flour
1 large egg
Pinch of kosher salt
20 perilla leaves (kkaennip), washed
   and drained
Vegetable oil for frying

1. Make the dipping sauce: Combine the soy sauce and vinegar in a small bowl and sprinkle in the sesame seeds.

2. Make the filling: Wrap the tofu in a paper towel or piece of cheesecloth and squeeze to remove excess water.

3. Combine the beef, garlic, onion, scallion, tofu, soy sauce, sesame oil, pepper, and sugar in a bowl and mix well.

4. Put the flour in a shallow bowl. Lightly beat the egg with the salt in another shallow bowl.

5. Dust both sides of a perilla leaf lightly with flour. Place a heaping tablespoon of the beef filling on one half of the leaf, spreading it to the edges. Fold the other half of the leaf over the meat and press to seal. Coat the packet with flour again. Repeat with the remaining leaves and filling. Transfer to a plate.

6. Heat a large nonstick skillet over medium heat. Add 1 tablespoon vegetable oil and swirl to coat the bottom of the skillet. Working in batches, so you don't over-crowd the pan, dip the packets into the beaten egg and place in the skillet. Cook until lightly crisped and light golden brown on the first side, about 2 minutes. Flip and cook until the other side is lightly crisp and golden, 2 minutes. Transfer to a platter. Serve the pancakes with the dipping sauce on the side.

Clockwise from top left: perilla leaves; filling perilla leaves with beef mixture; frying Perilla Leaf Pancakes

snacks

Korea throngs with vendors selling a delightful variety of street foods, and many Korean TV dramas include scenes of young people snacking on the various delicacies. Because some of these television shows are available online, a steady stream of Westerners come to my website seeking information and recipes for the dishes they've seen. (What are those rice cakes that the guys in the show eat with such gusto?)

You may live far from the streets of Seoul, but you can explore a wide range of Korean snacks and street food in your own kitchen. You may never have tried Hotteok, a sweet pancake with brown sugar syrup. Creamy and crispy Potato Croquettes, served warm, are more substantial. Korean-Style Fried Dumplings can be made ahead of time and frozen, ready to be the perfect bite with cocktails or beer, or even a light meal in a pinch.

Street food vendor in a market in Korea

Crunchy Rice Flour–Coated Kelp Snack
(Dasima-bugak)

Serves 10 to 12

Westerners don't think of sea vegetables when they think of snacks, but this kelp preparation deserves worldwide popularity. It is crisp, a little chewy, and full of the hearty taste of the sea.

This technique is a time-tested way to preserve other ingredients such as dried seaweed paper, perilla leaves, and chili peppers, in addition to kelp. The traditional method is time-consuming and labor-intensive: The kelp is brushed with a thick layer of glutinous rice porridge and then dehydrated in the wind and sun for a few days. In my New York kitchen, I skip the sun and wind and use a food dehydrator, and the kelp is ready to fry in a matter of hours.

When the kelp is fried, the glutinous rice porridge expands, covering the seaweed like snow. When you bite into it, the rice porridge is crispy and chewy and the kelp releases its intoxicating ocean fragrance. The kelp must be fried just long enough: If overcooked, it will be bitter; if undercooked, it will be difficult to chew. After frying a few pieces, you will get the hang of it.

Be sure to prepare more than you think you'll need. These go fast!

2 ounces (about 2 wide strips) dried kelp (dasima)

¼ cup glutinous rice flour (chapssal-garu)

1 cup water

1 tablespoon toasted sesame seeds

2 cups corn oil

Sugar

1. Wipe both sides of the dried kelp with a damp kitchen towel or paper towels to remove any dust. Use scissors to cut the kelp into 4-x-6-inch pieces.

2. Combine the rice flour and water in a small saucepan, mix well with a wooden spoon, and cook, stirring, over medium heat until the mixture turns thick, milky, and sticky, about 3 minutes. Then continue to cook, stirring, until the porridge becomes a little more fluid and a little translucent and bubbles pop up, about 2 minutes. Remove from the heat and let cool slightly.

3. Put the kelp on a cutting board. Brush one side of each piece with some of the porridge. Repeat, so the kelp has two coatings of porridge on one side. Sprinkle with the sesame seeds.

4. Put the coated kelp pieces on the trays of your food dehydrator, taking care that they don't touch and stick to each other. Set on the vegetable setting, about 140°F, and dry until breakable, 5 to 6 hours. (At this point, you can put the dried kelp in a zipper-lock bag and freeze it for up to 3 months.)

5. Fry the kelp: Heat the oil in a large deep skillet over medium-high heat until the temperature reaches 330°F. Turn the heat down to medium. Add 2 or 3 kelp strips to the hot oil, coated side down, and press down with a spatula to flatten the kelp while it cooks. The dried rice porridge will puff like a white flower. Turn the kelp over with tongs after 30 seconds and press down again with the spatula. Continue to cook, turning every 30 seconds, until the kelp is very crisp and light brown, 4 to 5 minutes. Adjust the heat as necessary so the kelp doesn't brown too quickly. If it overcooks, it will become black and bitter. If the fried kelp is not crunchy enough, fry it again briefly. Transfer to a paper-towel-lined baking sheet or platter to drain. Sprinkle with a little sugar, about ¼ teaspoon per strip. Repeat with the remaining kelp strips. Let cool and serve. To save for later use, transfer to an airtight container or zipper-lock bag and freeze for up to 1 month. There's no need to defrost before serving.

Clockwise from top left: rice porridge; sprinkling sesame seeds on rice porridge–coated kelp; Crunchy Rice Flour–Coated Kelp Snack

Potato Croquettes *(Gamja-croquettes)*
Serves 4

Koreans love these croquettes for the same reason Westerners do: They're crunchy outside and creamy inside. Watch the croquettes carefully as they cook: If the oil gets too hot, they may overbrown or burst; if the oil isn't hot enough, they won't get crisp enough. When properly cooked, they will stay crisp for several hours.

for the dipping sauce
2 tablespoons soy sauce
1 tablespoon distilled white vinegar
    or apple cider vinegar
1 tablespoon chopped scallion
¼ teaspoon toasted sesame seeds

for the croquettes
2 cups plus 1 teaspoon vegetable oil
¼ cup minced extra-lean beef, such as
    flank steak

Kosher salt
1 tablespoon minced green bell pepper
2 tablespoons minced peeled carrot
¼ cup minced onion
1 pound russet potatoes, peeled
1 cup water
¼ cup all-purpose flour
1 large egg
1 cup Korean bread crumbs (ppang-
    garu) or panko

1. Make the dipping sauce: Combine all the ingredients in a small bowl.

2. Make the croquettes: Heat 1 teaspoon of the vegetable oil in a small skillet. Add the beef and a pinch of salt and cook, stirring, for 1 minute. Add the bell pepper, carrot, and onion and stir-fry for another 1 minute to soften slightly. Remove from the heat.

3. Cut the potatoes into ½-inch-thick slices and put them in a large heavy skillet. Add the 1 cup water and 1 teaspoon salt, cover, and cook over medium heat until the potatoes are soft and almost all the water has evaporated, about 20 minutes.

4. Drain the potatoes, transfer to a bowl, and mash them. Stir in the vegetables and beef, mixing well. Divide the mixture into 16 equal portions. Roll each one into a ball and flatten into a 2-inch disk.

When I was in middle school, my homeroom teacher, who was also my home ec teacher, asked me to come with her to the market to shop for the day's class. This was the kind of job reserved for the classroom's top student, so I was honored to be asked. She took me by the hand as we walked to the market, where we bought potatoes, onions, and beef. We made these croquettes in class that day, and everyone had a lot of fun. It was the first time I had ever tasted them.

5. Put the flour in a shallow bowl. Beat the egg in another shallow bowl. Put the bread crumbs in a third shallow bowl. Coat each croquette with flour, dip into the egg, and coat with bread crumbs. Transfer to a large platter or baking sheet.

6. Heat the remaining 2 cups vegetable oil in a large deep skillet over medium-high heat until it reaches 330°F. Add the croquettes and cook in batches, turning several times, until they are golden brown and very crisp outside, about 10 minutes. Adjust the heat as necessary as they cook, lowering it if they are browning too quickly or if it looks like they are about to burst.

7. Drain the croquettes briefly on a paper-towel-lined plate and serve hot, with the dipping sauce.

Top row: left, formed croquettes; right, breaded croquettes; bottom row: left, frying potato croquettes; right, Potato Croquettes

Sweet Pancakes with Brown Sugar Syrup
(Hotteok)

Make 8 to 10 hotteok; serves 4 to 8

Many Koreans buy this delicious warm street food snack in the wintertime. The hotteok vendor shapes the dough, presses the pancake down on the griddle, and fries it. It doesn't take long, but the anticipation of eating the piping-hot pancake in the cold can make the delay seem endless. And once the pancake is ready, you have to wait a little longer for the hot sugar to cool down enough so you can eat it without burning your tongue.

At home, you can use less oil and be more generous with filling ingredients like peanuts or walnuts than the street vendors. But you must still eat the pancakes immediately after making them, since they will be heavy and tough if allowed to cool.

When I first posted a version of this recipe online, I was surprised at how quickly it became popular. I was happy to hear how some of my readers got creative with the pancakes, filling them with Nutella or omitting the sugar in the filling and making savory versions with meat or cheese. *The photos are on page 208.*

for the dough
1 cup warm water
2 tablespoons sugar
2 teaspoons active dry yeast
½ teaspoon kosher salt
1 tablespoon vegetable oil
2 cups all-purpose flour

for the filling
¾ cup packed light brown sugar
1 tablespoon ground cinnamon
2 tablespoons chopped walnuts or
   unsalted peanuts
⅓ cup all-purpose flour
Vegetable oil for cooking

1. Make the dough: Combine the water, sugar, yeast, salt, and vegetable oil in a medium bowl and stir well to dissolve the yeast. Stir in the flour and knead the dough in the bowl until smooth, about 2 minutes. Cover the bowl with plastic wrap and let stand at room temperature until the dough doubles in volume, 1 to 1½ hours.

2. Make the filling: Combine all the ingredients in a small bowl.

3. Knead the dough in the bowl for about 5 minutes to deflate the gas bubbles and make it smooth. Re-cover with the plastic wrap and let rest for 30 minutes.

4. Assemble and cook the pancakes: Knead the dough in the bowl again to deflate all the gas bubbles, about 5 minutes. Dust a large cutting board with the ⅓ cup flour. Transfer the dough to the board and shape it into a ball. With floured hands (the dough will be sticky), divide the dough into 8 to 10 equal pieces and shape each one into a ball. Cover the balls with plastic wrap to prevent them from drying out.

5. Heat a 10- to 12-inch nonstick skillet over medium heat. Add about 1 tablespoon vegetable oil and swirl the skillet to coat it evenly. Flour your hands, flatten one ball of dough, and place about 2 tablespoons of the filling in the center. Gather the edges together and pinch to seal.

6. Place the hotteok in the skillet, sealed side down. Repeat with another ball of dough and filling and place in the skillet. When the bottoms turn light golden brown, about 2 minutes, turn the hotteok over and press each one down with a spatula to make a thin 4-inch disk. Cook for 1 minute and turn again. Press down with the spatula. Cover the skillet, turn the heat down to very low, and cook until the hotteok are puffy and the brown sugar inside has melted into syrup, 2 to 3 minutes—you will see the brown syrup through the dough.

7. Transfer the first hotteok to an individual plate and serve. About 30 seconds later, transfer the second hotteok to another individual plate and serve. Repeat with the remaining dough balls, using more vegetable oil as needed.

Maangchi and Friends

ChaMee: *I nearly cried when I found this recipe! I remember walking with my twin sister and our mother through the markets in Seoul when I was very young and eating one of these. Since coming to the United States through adoption, I have never forgotten these snacks that our mother always bought for us. The taste and smell bring back many good memories.*

Maangchi: *ChaMee, I'm so touched by your story that it makes me cry now! Your mom would be proud of you if she knew you were making your own hotteok and thinking about her.*

Sprout: *The first time I made these, I halved the recipe and used very finely ground whole wheat flour. (I didn't tell my husband that it wasn't white flour. Shh, he still doesn't know!) Then I filled it with a mixture of crushed peanuts, black sesame seeds, and sugar. When my husband finished his, he said, "C'est pas mal (it's not bad)," which is a big compliment for food from a French speaker.*

Maangchi: C'est pas mal. *Nice!*

Facing page: top, filling pancakes with brown sugar mixture; bottom, Sweet Pancake with Brown Sugar Syrup

Above: top row: left, dumpling filling; right, filling mandu skins; center row: left, folding dumplings; right, dumplings ready for frying; bottom, Korean-Style Fried Dumplings

Korean-Style Fried Dumplings *(Gunmandu)*
Makes 50 dumplings

When I go to a Korean restaurant with American friends, chances are good that they will want to start with fried dumplings. The filling for these dumplings is so tasty: a mixture of pork, mung bean sprouts, zucchini, chives, onion, and tofu seasoned with sesame oil and a hint of ginger.

You can find a variety of premade dumplings in Korean grocery stores, but home-made ones always taste better. If you make them yourself, you can be generous with the filling. You can also save some money. (Fifty dumpling skins cost less than $2.)

Fifty dumplings may seem like a lot, but once you form them, you can freeze them and then fry or steam them anytime for a quick snack or lunch. To steam them, bring a few inches of water to a boil in a pot fitted with a steamer basket. Steam the dumplings, covered, until they are cooked through, about 10 minutes. You can also add them to soup; stir them into the simmering broth and cook for 10 minutes or so. *The photos are on page 209.*

for the dipping sauce
2 tablespoons soy sauce
1 tablespoon distilled white vinegar
1 teaspoon sugar
1 green Korean chili pepper (cheong-gochu), stemmed and chopped
¼ cup onion, chopped

for the filling
8 ounces ground pork or beef (or a combination)
1 teaspoon minced peeled ginger
4 garlic cloves, minced
1 tablespoon soy sauce
1 teaspoon freshly ground black pepper
1 tablespoon plus 1 teaspoon toasted sesame oil

2 cups mung bean sprouts, washed and drained
1 small zucchini (about 8 ounces), cut into thin matchsticks
Kosher salt
1 cup chopped Asian chives or scallions
2¼ teaspoons vegetable oil
8 ounces (about 1 cup) medium-soft tofu
1 cup chopped onion

for the dumplings
2 tablespoons all-purpose flour
1 (50-piece) package mandu skins (mandu-pi)
Vegetable oil for panfrying

1. Make the dipping sauce: Combine all the ingredients in a small bowl.

2. Make the filling: Combine the ground meat, ginger, garlic, soy sauce, ½ teaspoon pepper, and 2 teaspoons of the sesame oil in a bowl. Cover and refrigerate while you prepare the other ingredients.

3. Put the mung bean sprouts in a medium heavy saucepan, add ½ cup water, cover, and cook over medium-high heat for 5 minutes. Drain.

4. Meanwhile, mix the zucchini with ½ teaspoon salt in a bowl and let stand for 5 minutes, then squeeze out the excess water with your hands or pat dry with a paper towel.

5. Mix the chives with ¼ teaspoon of the vegetable oil in a small bowl.

6. Wrap the tofu in a piece of cheesecloth or a paper towel and squeeze out the excess water.

7. Heat a large skillet over medium-high heat. Add 1 teaspoon of the vegetable oil and the zucchini and cook, stirring, until slightly softened, 1 minute. Scrape into a large bowl; set the skillet aside.

8. Combine the chopped onion with ½ teaspoon salt in a bowl. Let stand for about 5 minutes, then squeeze out the excess water with your hands or pat dry with a paper towel.

9. Heat the skillet you cooked the zucchini in (no need to wash it) over medium-high heat and add the remaining 1 teaspoon vegetable oil. Add the onion and cook until translucent, 2 to 3 minutes. Scrape into the bowl with the zucchini.

10. Add the meat mixture, mung bean sprouts, chives, and tofu to the zucchini and onion. Add 1 teaspoon salt, ½ teaspoon pepper, and the remaining 2 teaspoons sesame oil and mix well.

11. Make the dumplings: Set out a small bowl of water. Sprinkle the flour over a large cutting board or baking sheet. Remove one dumpling skin from the package and set on the work surface. Dip your index finger into the water and wet the edges of the skin so that it will seal easily. Spoon a heaping tablespoon of the filling into the center, fold the skin over the filling, and press the edges to seal. Place on the floured cutting board. Repeat with the remaining dumpling skins and filling. (At this point, you can place the dumplings on a plastic-wrap-lined baking sheet and freeze them for at least 5 hours, or overnight, then transfer them to zipper-lock bags for longer freezing. Transfer them to a plate, so they don't stick together, and defrost in the refrigerator for a few hours before frying or steaming.)

12. Heat a large nonstick skillet over medium-high heat. Add 2 to 3 tablespoons vegetable oil. Add some of the dumplings, without crowding them, and cook until the bottoms turn golden brown and crisp, 2 to 3 minutes. Turn and cook until the second sides are golden brown, another 2 to 3 minutes. Turn the heat down to low and continue to cook, turning frequently, until the dumplings are evenly browned and the filling is cooked through, a few more minutes. Transfer to a platter. Repeat with the remaining dumplings, adding more oil as necessary.

13. Serve the dumplings hot with the dipping sauce.

Spicy Rice Cakes *(Tteokbokki)*

Serves 2 or 3

For this street snack, rice cakes are cooked in a spicy sauce made from red pepper paste and anchovy stock. As it simmers, the sauce turns creamy and the rice cakes soften and become pleasantly chewy. The fish cakes are optional, but they make the broth more savory and add another texture to the dish.

Rice cakes are sold frozen or refrigerated in Korean grocery stores. If you buy them frozen, you'll need to thaw them at room temperature, then separate them, soak them in cold water for 30 minutes to soften them, and drain. Without this presoak, they will remain hard no matter how long you cook them. Freshly made rice cakes don't need soaking.

If you don't have time to make anchovy stock, you can replace it with canned low-sodium chicken broth.

⅓ cup Korean hot pepper paste (gochujang)

1 tablespoon Korean hot pepper flakes (gochu-garu)

1 tablespoon sugar

4 cups water

7 large dried anchovies (mareun-myeolchi), heads and guts removed

1 (6-x-8-inch) piece dried kelp (dasima; optional)

1 pound cylinder-shaped rice cakes (tteokguk-yong-tteok), soaked and drained if frozen (see headnote)

3 scallions, cut into 3-inch pieces

4 ounces fish cakes (eomuk), cut into bite-size pieces (optional)

2 large hard-boiled eggs, shelled and left whole, (optional)

1. Combine the hot pepper paste, hot pepper flakes, and sugar in a small bowl.

2. Pour the water into a large skillet and add the dried anchovies and dried kelp, if using. Boil over medium-high heat until reduced to about 2½ cups, about 15 minutes. Strain the stock into a bowl; discard the solids.

3. Return the stock to the skillet and reheat over medium heat. Add the hot pepper paste mixture, rice cakes, scallions, and fish cakes and hard-boiled eggs, if using. Cook, stirring occasionally, until the stock bubbles and turns thick and creamy and the rice cakes are soft but still chewy, 10 to 13 minutes.

4. Transfer to a serving plate and serve.

Maangchi and Friends

Hannah: *I am a vegetarian, so I won't be adding the fish cakes. Is there anything I can substitute for the anchovies?*

Maangchi: *Yes! Use dried shiitake mushrooms and add them along with the dried kelp.*

Top, cylinder-shaped rice cakes; bottom, Spicy Rice Cakes

Top row, left, crushed red pepper flakes and liquid smoke; right, combining ingredients; center row, left, beef coated with seasonings; right, beef drying in the food dehydrator; bottom, Beef Jerky

Beef Jerky *(Yukpo)*

Makes 35 to 40 pieces

Beef jerky is an esteemed food in Korea, where it is often given by a bride's mother to the groom's family before a wedding. It is an extravagant gift, because beef has historically been very expensive (even today, beef costs three to five times as much in Korea as in the United States), and it takes careful tending and a long time to dry the beef properly in the sun.

Sun-drying may be traditional, but it isn't convenient. That's why I was so excited when, on my first visit to the U.S. in the 1990s, I saw an ad on TV for an electric food dehydrator. The pitchman demonstrated how the machine could make beef jerky indoors relatively quickly. So I bought the machine and started experimenting. After some trial and error, I came up with a pretty good recipe, but it was lacking something. I realized it was missing the right smoky flavor, so I added a little bit of liquid smoke to the mix. It's not traditionally Korean, but now the recipe's perfect.

3 pounds lean beef, such as flank steak, or bottom round, trimmed of visible fat
½ cup soy sauce
¼ cup sugar
1 tablespoon honey
9 garlic cloves, minced

2 teaspoons liquid smoke
2 tablespoons toasted sesame seeds
2 tablespoons crushed red pepper flakes (American, not Korean)
1 teaspoon freshly ground black pepper

1. Thinly slice the beef along the grain, about ⅛ inch thick. Cut into 5-x-2½-inch pieces.

2. Combine all the remaining ingredients in a large bowl. Add the beef and mix well to coat. Cover and refrigerate for at least for 30 minutes, and up to overnight.

3. Place the slices in the trays of a food dehydrator and set to the jerky, fish, or meat setting (160°F). Dry according to the manufacturer's instructions, about 8 hours, turning once after 4 hours. Remove the slices as they become sufficiently dried.

4. Serve, or store in an airtight container for up to 1 week at room temperature. You can also freeze the jerky in an airtight container for up to 3 months; defrost at room temperature for 5 to 10 minutes before serving.

party and special-occasion food

Koreans are very social. We love to get together with friends and family to celebrate pretty much any occasion: holidays and birthdays, of course, but also Saturday night, or little victories like a high test score or the first paycheck at a new job. And for Koreans, there can be no party without party food.

Where I come from, by the sea, that means seafood, and Spicy Fermented Skate is the biggest party-starter. For many Koreans, a formal celebration calls for something more refined, like the Platter of Nine Delicacies, where the cook displays his or her skill in artful presentation and the intricate balance of color and flavor.

For others, the best way to celebrate is around a table of sizzling Korean barbecue, which has recently become popular in some American cities. It's easy to see why: The Korean style of barbecue, where the meat is cooked on a tabletop grill, is collaborative and fun.

Many of the dishes in this chapter are bold and strongly flavored, but there are subtle, delicate dishes as well. All of them are always enjoyed as part of a larger meal, with rice and soup and side dishes. And each one is a sign to your guests that a party is starting!

Platter of Nine Delicacies (page 245)

Korean Fried Chicken (*Yangnyeom-tongdak*)

Serves 10 to 12 as an appetizer, 4 as a main course

When I started posting recipes on YouTube, one of the most requested recipes was for KFC, otherwise known as Korean Fried Chicken. Coated with a sweet, sour, spicy sauce, yangnyeom-tongdak is a relatively modern dish in Korea: It's take-out food, rarely made at home, so my readers had to wait while I perfected my recipe, which is based on what I saw being made in local fried chicken joints in Gwangju.

When refining the recipe, at first I tried not to use corn syrup or ketchup, replacing them with more wholesome, less sugary ingredients, but I was never satisfied with the result. To get the authentic taste, corn or rice syrup and ketchup are essential. Something else is also necessary: frying the chicken twice. Double-frying makes the batter-coated chicken stay crunchy for hours after cooking, while leaving the inside moist. When I made the chicken for my children and they said, "Mom, this tastes exactly like the chicken place!" I knew that the recipe was finally just right.

You can use a whole chicken; use a cleaver to cut the breast, thighs, and legs into smaller pieces.

for the chicken

2 pounds chicken wings or chunks of chicken, rinsed in cold water and patted dry, tips removed, drumettes and flats separated
½ cup potato starch or cornstarch
⅓ cup all-purpose flour
½ teaspoon kosher salt
½ teaspoon freshly ground black pepper
½ teaspoon baking soda
1 large egg, lightly beaten
Corn oil for deep-frying

for the sauce

2 teaspoons corn oil
3 garlic cloves, minced
⅓ cup ketchup
⅓ cup brown rice syrup (ssal-yeot), corn syrup, or sugar
¼ cup Korean hot pepper paste (gochujang)
2 teaspoons distilled white or apple cider vinegar
1 tablespoon toasted sesame seeds

1. Make the wings: Combine the chicken, potato starch, flour, salt, pepper, baking soda, and egg in a large bowl and mix with a wooden spoon or your hand until the chicken is well coated.

2. Heat about 4 inches of corn oil in a deep pot over high heat until it reaches 350°F. If you don't have a thermometer, test it by dipping one piece of chicken in the oil. If it bubbles, it is ready. One by one, carefully add the chicken to the pot, in batches if necessary to avoid crowding, and fry, turning a few times, until crunchy, 10 to 12 minutes. Transfer to a strainer and shake to drain, then transfer the chicken to a large bowl. Return the oil to 350°F and fry a second batch, if necessary. As it sits, the chicken will become less crunchy.

3. Meanwhile, make the sauce: While the chicken is frying, heat a large heavy pan over medium-high heat. Add the corn oil and garlic and cook, stirring, for 30 seconds. Add the ketchup, brown rice syrup, hot pepper paste, and vinegar. Turn the heat down to low and cook, stirring with a wooden spoon, until the sauce bubbles and becomes shiny, about 7 minutes.

4. Fry the wings again: Fry in batches, turning a few times, until the wings are golden brown and very crunchy on the outside, 10 to 12 minutes. Transfer the wings to a strainer and shake to drain, then add them to the pan with the sauce and stir until the chicken is coated.

5. Arrange the chicken on a serving platter, sprinkle with the sesame seeds, and serve.

> There is a yangnyeom-tongdak place on every corner in Korea. Each one claims its own secret coating and batter mixture, but generally the chicken all tastes very similar. I love the funny names of some of the fried chicken chains: Very Large Chicken (Ahju-keo Chicken), Mother-in-Law's Chicken (Jangmonim Chicken), Son-in-Law Mr. Lee's Chicken (Lee Seobang Chicken), Wife's Mother's House Chicken (Jangmonimjip Chicken).
>
> The dominance of mother-in-law names is a nod to the long tradition of a woman serving chicken to her son-in-law as a sign of respect and celebration. When a son-in-law came to visit his wife's family in the countryside, they always expressed their appreciation by killing the best chicken and serving it for dinner, usually as chicken soup.

Clockwise from top left: pear marinade; steak in the marinade; Bulgogi

Bulgogi

Serves 4

To make bulgogi—classic Korean grilled beef—you marinate sliced steak, then grill it on top of the stove or a tabletop burner, or on an outdoor grill. The marinade has a secret ingredient: Asian pear, which tenderizes the meat. Asian pears are round like apples, with yellow-brown skin. Ripe ones have a sweet aroma.

It's important to slice the steak thin and across the grain, so it won't be tough. You can buy presliced bulgogi meat at a Korean market, but I prefer to choose my own meat and slice it myself. Put the beef in the freezer for 30 minutes to 1 hour before slicing—partially frozen meat is easier to slice thin.

You eat this dish in the traditional ssam style, placing a piece of cooked meat on a lettuce leaf, adding a dollop of Soybean Paste Dipping Sauce, and then wrapping the leaf around the meat to create a package that you can pop into your mouth in one shot. Serve with rice and the side dishes of your choice.

4 large garlic cloves
1 cup peeled, cored, and coarsely
    chopped Asian or Bosc pear
¾ cup chopped onion
1 teaspoon finely chopped peeled ginger
1 pound boneless sirloin, tenderloin,
    or skirt steak, partially frozen and cut
    across the grain into ⅛-inch-thick
    slices

1 scallion, chopped
2 tablespoons soy sauce
1 tablespoon toasted sesame oil
1 tablespoon light brown sugar or honey
½ teaspoon freshly ground black pepper
¼ teaspoon toasted sesame seeds
Lettuce leaves for serving
Soybean Paste Dipping Sauce (page
    272)

1. Combine the garlic, pear, onion, and ginger in a food processor or blender and process until pale and creamy.

2. Put the steak in a large bowl and pour the pear mixture over it. Add the scallion, soy sauce, sesame oil, brown sugar, and pepper and mix well. Cover with plastic wrap and refrigerate for at least 30 minutes, and up to several hours.

3. Heat a cast-iron grill pan or large skillet over high heat. Alternatively, build a charcoal fire or preheat a gas grill to high.

4. Cook the meat, turning or stirring occasionally, 2 minutes for medium or 3 minutes for well done. Sprinkle with the sesame seeds. Serve with lettuce leaves and the dipping sauce.

Top row, left, peeling Asian pear; right, cutting pear into matchsticks;
center row, left, combining garlic-sesame mixture; right, coating meat in sauce; bottom, Seasoned Raw Beef

Seasoned Raw Beef (Yukhoe)

Serves 4

The first time I ever tasted yukhoe was when I was a university student in Seoul. I went with my classmates to a student pub that was well known for its rice liquor and seasoned raw beef. There it was seasoned with a more than generous amount of garlic and had a sweetness from slivers of Asian pear. I went home to try to duplicate it right away, and ever since it's been one of my signature dishes.

When I was older and had my own family, my local butcher used to call me whenever high-quality beef came into her shop. She knew that I would buy her choicest cuts to make yukhoe, because it's best when made with the leanest, freshest beef you can find. I serve yukhoe as a snack or as a side dish with rice.

Many Koreans put a raw egg on top when they prepare it, but I think the egg distracts from the cool spiciness of the raw beef. If you'd like an even spicier version, reduce the amount of soy sauce to 1 teaspoon and add 2 tablespoons of Korean hot pepper paste (gochujang) to the dressing.

8 ounces best-quality flank steak,
    frozen for 1 hour
2 cups cold water
1 teaspoon sugar
1 medium Asian pear, or 2 Bosc pears
6 garlic cloves, minced

1 tablespoon soy sauce
1 tablespoon honey
2 tablespoons toasted sesame oil
¼ teaspoon freshly ground black pepper
2 teaspoons toasted sesame seeds
1 tablespoon pine nuts

1. Remove the flank steak from the freezer and slice into thin matchsticks. Cover with plastic wrap and refrigerate.

2. Combine the water and sugar in a medium bowl, stirring to dissolve the sugar. Peel and core the pear and cut into matchsticks. (You should have about 2 cups.) Put the pear pieces in the sugar water as you work to keep them from discoloring.

3. Combine the garlic, soy sauce, honey, sesame oil, and pepper in a bowl. Add the beef and mix with a spoon to coat.

4. Drain the pear and pat dry with a paper towel. Arrange on a serving platter and arrange the beef over it. Sprinkle with the sesame seeds and pine nuts. Serve immediately.

Maangchi and Friends

Soko2: *Does the beef keep? When you make it, can you save any for later, or will the beef go bad? It's hard to buy small amounts of flank steak at my market.*

Maangchi: *Yes, it's better to eat it right after mixing it with the seasoning sauce, but if you have leftovers, keep it in the refrigerator and panfry it later. Then serve it as bulgogi.*

L.A.–Style Beef Short Ribs *(L.A. Galbi)*
Serves 3 or 4

Galbi means "ribs" in Korean, and when Americans talk about Korean barbecue, they are often thinking of L.A. galbi, the dish served in so many Korean barbecue restaurants here.

L.A. galbi is made not with conventional short ribs but with ribs cut very thinly (⅛ to ¼ inch) across the bone. This style is sometimes called "flanken" and it is easy to recognize because each piece has three or four visible bones. Because they are thin and flat, the ribs absorb marinade quickly and cook in minutes on the grill, making them a great choice for cookouts and picnics. Some say the cut was discovered by Korean immigrants at Mexican markets in southern California, who adapted it for use with a traditional Korean marinade. Others say that the dish originated with Korean immigrants in Hawaii, where these were called Maui ribs.

Pears make the marinade special in two ways: Koreans love the subtle sweetness and flavor they give the meat, and the pears contain enzymes that break down collagen in muscle tissue, tenderizing the ribs.

2 pounds L.A.–style beef short ribs
(⅛- to ¼-inch-thick flanken-style
short ribs; see above)
6 garlic cloves
½ teaspoon minced peeled ginger
½ medium onion
1 medium Asian pear, or 2 small Bosc
pears, peeled, cored, and cut into
chunks

¼ cup soy sauce
2 tablespoons honey
½ teaspoon freshly ground black pepper
2 teaspoons toasted sesame oil
Lettuce leaves for serving
Soybean Paste Dipping Sauce
(page 272)
Cucumber and carrot sticks for serving

1. Rinse the ribs under cold running water to remove blood and any bone fragments. Drain and pat dry.

2. Combine the garlic, ginger, onion, pear, soy sauce, and honey in a food processor and process until smooth and creamy. Transfer to a large bowl.

3. Add the short ribs and toss to coat well. Add the pepper and sesame oil. Toss well. Cover with plastic wrap and refrigerate for at least 30 minutes, or as long as overnight.

4. Build a charcoal fire or preheat a gas grill to high. Grill the ribs, turning them a few times, until cooked through, about 5 minutes. (Alternatively, you can cook the ribs in a large cast-iron grill pan or broil them, turning a few times, until done.)

5. Wrap a piece of meat in a lettuce leaf, top with a small spoonful of dipping sauce, and enjoy, taking bites of the cucumber and carrot sticks in between.

Above, L.A.–Style Beef Short Ribs

Top row: left, cooked mung bean jelly; right, sliced solid mung bean jelly; bottom row: left, mung bean jelly cut into matchsticks; right, Mung Bean Jelly with Vegetables and Beef (page 228)

Mung Bean Jelly with Vegetables and Beef (Tangpyeongchae)

Serves 6

If you've eaten at a Korean restaurant, you may have been served a dish of gelatinous little cubes in a spicy seasoning sauce as an appetizer. Slippery and cold, mung bean jelly is great for whetting the appetite.

But there are other ways to use the jelly, including this traditional dish, which makes a great light meal. It's a throwback to Korean Royal Court cuisine, dishes more subtly seasoned and elaborately presented than today's food.

The name comes from eighteenth-century King Yeongjo's policy, called *tang-pyeong*, of employing officials with a variety of political beliefs. The various ingredients represent that diversity and illustrate how different textures and flavors can harmonize.

If you can't get water dropwort, increase the amount of cucumber matchsticks to 1½ cups. For a simpler dish, cut the mung bean jelly into bite-size pieces and mix with Spicy Soy Seasoning Sauce (page 272) and whatever leftover vegetables you have in the fridge. In minutes, you'll have an exotic, low-calorie lunch. *The photos are on page 227.*

½ cup mung bean starch (cheongpomuk-garu)

3 cups water

Kosher salt

4 ounces beef brisket, cut along the grain into 5-inch-long matchsticks

1 teaspoon soy sauce

½ teaspoon sugar

1 garlic clove, minced

1 teaspoon toasted sesame oil

Pinch of freshly ground black pepper

2½ cups mung bean sprouts, washed and drained

1 cup water dropwort (minari; see above)

2 large egg yolks

½ teaspoon vegetable oil

½ English cucumber, cut into 5-inch-long matchsticks

1 medium red bell pepper, cored, seeded, and sliced into thin matchsticks

½ sheet dried seaweed paper (gim, aka nori), toasted (see page 53) and shredded

Mustard and Garlic Sauce (page 275)

1. Combine the mung bean starch, water, and ½ teaspoon salt in a small heavy pot. Mix well, bring to a boil over medium heat, and boil, stirring constantly, until the mixture becomes translucent and shiny, about 10 minutes.

2. Pour the hot starch mixture into an airtight rectangular container and let cool for 1 hour at room temperature, then cover and refrigerate until solid (test by poking it with a finger), 4 to 5 hours. (The jelly will keep in the refrigerator, covered, for up to 1 week. If you refrigerate the jelly for more than a day, it will turn milky, and it may shrink a little. Soak the jelly in very hot water for a few minutes, and it will regain its translucency and chewiness.)

3. Remove the jelly from the container and cut into matchsticks about 3 inches long. Refrigerate while you prepare the other ingredients.

4. Combine the beef, soy sauce, sugar, garlic, ½ teaspoon of the sesame oil, and the black pepper in a medium bowl. Heat a large skillet over medium-high heat. Add the beef mixture and stir-fry until the beef loses its pink color and all the liquid has evaporated, 3 to 5 minutes. Transfer to one side of a large plate.

5. Put the mung bean sprouts in a small pot, add ¼ cup water and a pinch of salt, cover, and boil over medium heat for 5 minutes. Drain and add to the plate, next to the beef.

6. Bring a medium saucepan of water to a boil. Add the water dropwort and blanch for 1 minute. Drain in a colander and rinse under cold water. Drain again and squeeze out the excess water.

7. Cut the dropwort into 3- to 4-inch-long strips. Toss the strips in a bowl with ½ teaspoon salt and the remaining ½ teaspoon sesame oil. Add to the plate, side by side with the beef.

8. Lightly beat the egg yolks with a pinch of salt. Heat a large nonstick skillet over medium-high heat. Add the vegetable oil and swirl the pan, then remove the skillet from the heat and wipe the inside with a paper towel to coat the cooking surface with a thin film of oil. Add the beaten yolks, tilting the pan so they coat the bottom in a thin layer with the pan still off the heat. Let stand for a minute to set. If the egg does not set, cook over very low heat; do not brown. Turn the eggs with a spatula and let cook in the residual heat of the pan for a few minutes. Slide the egg onto a cutting board and let cool, then cut into matchsticks. Add to the plate with the beef, next to the other ingredients.

9. Add the mung bean jelly, cucumber, and bell pepper to the plate with the beef, side by side. It will be a colorful arrangement with everything next to each other. Sprinkle the shredded seaweed paper over the top. Put the plate on the table, drizzle the mustard garlic sauce over the top, toss in front of your guests, and serve.

Sweet Potato Starch Noodles with Stir-Fried Vegetables and Beef *(Japchae)*

Serves 6 to 8

This dish of clear sweet potato noodles (which are very similar to cellophane or glass noodles), stir-fried vegetables, and beef is more than the sum of its parts. The interplay of the chewy noodles, tender-crisp vegetables, and meaty beef and mushrooms makes japchae a number-one choice at potluck parties. It's a good dish to share with a big group and is a must for special occasions.

3 dried shiitake mushrooms, soaked in water for 3 to 4 hours, drained, and stemmed

8 ounces beef brisket, cut into 2½-inch-long matchsticks

¼ cup plus 1 tablespoon soy sauce

4 garlic cloves, minced

2 tablespoons toasted sesame oil

8 ounces sweet potato starch noodles (dangmyeon)

8 ounces spinach, washed and dried

Kosher salt

2 tablespoons vegetable oil

1 large carrot, peeled and cut into 2½-inch-long matchsticks

1 medium onion, sliced

1 (10-ounce) package white button mushrooms, sliced ¼ inch thick

3 scallions, cut into 2½-inch pieces

3 tablespoons light brown sugar

1 tablespoon toasted sesame seeds

1 teaspoon freshly ground black pepper

Korean Egg Garnish (page 273; optional)

1. Thinly slice the shiitake mushrooms. Put them in a bowl, add the beef, 2 teaspoons of the soy sauce, one quarter of the garlic, and 1 teaspoon of the sesame oil, and mix well.

2. Bring a large pot of water to a boil over medium-high heat. Add the noodles, stirring with a wooden spoon so they won't stick together. Cover and boil until the noodles are tender but still chewy, 7 to 8 minutes. Taste one; if it is still hard, cook for an additional 1 to 2 minutes.

3. Turn off the heat and, using tongs, transfer the noodles to a colander to drain. Transfer to a large shallow bowl. Cut the noodles a few times in the bowl with scissors. Mix them with 1 teaspoon of the soy sauce and 1 teaspoon of the sesame oil.

4. Bring the water back to a boil and blanch the spinach for 30 seconds. Drain the spinach in the colander and rinse under cold running water. Drain and squeeze out excess water.

5. Transfer the spinach to a small bowl and mix with ½ teaspoon salt and 1 teaspoon of the sesame oil. Add the spinach to the bowl with the noodles.

6. Heat a large skillet over medium-high heat. Add 2 teaspoons of the vegetable oil and the carrot and stir-fry for 2 minutes, then add to the bowl with the noodles. Add another teaspoon of vegetable oil to the skillet, then add the onion slices and ¼ teaspoon salt and stir-fry until the onion is translucent, about 3 minutes. Add to the bowl with the noodles.

7. Add 2 teaspoons of the vegetable oil to the skillet. Add the white mushrooms, scallions, and ¼ teaspoon salt and stir-fry until the mushrooms are tender and the scallions are softened, 4 to 5 minutes. Add to the bowl with the noodles.

8. Add the remaining 1 teaspoon vegetable oil to the skillet, then add the marinated beef and shiitake mushrooms and stir-fry until the beef is no longer pink, 3 to 4 minutes. Add to the bowl with the noodles.

9. Add the remaining minced garlic, 1 tablespoon sesame oil, and ¼ cup soy sauce, along with the brown sugar, sesame seeds, and pepper to the noodles. Mix well and transfer to a serving platter. Garnish with the egg strips, if desired, and serve.

Grilled Pork Belly *(Samgyeopsal-gui)*
Serves 3 or 4

Korean-style grilled pork belly starts with a steel or stone grill that is placed right in the middle of the table. It's surrounded by plates of the pork belly, green chili peppers, onions, garlic, mushrooms, carrots, cucumber, lettuce, and fresh shredded scallion salad. You cook the dish at the table in front of your guests, and everyone chooses their own bites, wrapping their choices in a lettuce leaf with some dipping sauce and scallion salad. It's a prime example of Korea's inherently social style of cooking and eating, and it is a great choice for get-togethers. Soju, a distilled liquor often made from sweet potato starch, is often served with pork belly, which makes the meal even more festive.

There's a special grill pan for cooking this dish, and a portable burner too; see Equipment for Korean Cooking, page 28. Both are available in the cookware section of Korean or Asian grocery stores and are relatively inexpensive.

You can substitute pork shoulder or pork tenderloin or even beef tenderloin for the pork belly, but the dish is tastiest when the meat has some fat on it. Most of the fat will melt away as you grill it, but not before it has infused the meat with its rich taste.

2 green Korean chili peppers (cheong-gochu), stemmed and cut into ¼-inch slices

7 large garlic cloves, thinly sliced

7 or 8 white button mushrooms, sliced

1 onion, cut into ⅓-inch rounds

1 small cucumber, cut into 3-x-¼-inch sticks

1 medium carrot, peeled and cut into 3-x-¼-inch sticks

1 head red or green leaf lettuce, leaves separated, washed, and drained

Soybean Paste Dipping Sauce (page 272)

Scallion Salad (page 133)

1½ pounds pork belly, sliced into 1½-x-1½-x-⅛-inch strips

1 teaspoon toasted sesame oil

1. Set a grill pan over a portable burner (see above) and place it in the center of the table.

2. Put the chili peppers and garlic on a small plate, the mushrooms and onion on another small plate, and the cucumber and carrot on a third small plate. Pile the lettuce leaves onto another plate or in a shallow basket. Put all the plates, along with the dipping sauce and the just-dressed scallion salad, on the table.

3. Bring out the pork belly on a large platter. Heat the grill pan over medium-high heat. Spread the sesame oil all over the grill pan for flavor.

4. Place several pieces of the pork belly, some garlic, some mushroom slices, and some onions on the grill and cook until the bottom of the pork belly is crisp. Flip the meat over with tongs and continue cooking until cooked through and both sides are crisp and light golden brown. Turn the garlic, onion, and mushrooms too. If the heat is too high, lower it. Transfer the cooked meat and vegetables to a serving plate and place more ingredients on the grill pan to cook.

5. Have your guests make their own packets, putting some cooked pork belly, a little dipping sauce, a bit of scallion salad, a piece of chili pepper, a piece of raw or cooked garlic, some cooked onion, and some mushrooms into a lettuce leaf, wrapping it up, and eating it in one bite. The carrots and cucumber are for dipping in the sauce.

Top, ready to cook pork belly in grill pan over a portable burner in the center of the table; bottom: left, grilling pork belly, onions, and mushrooms; right, Grilled Pork Belly with dipping sauce, scallion salad, chili pepper, garlic, onion, mushrooms, on a lettuce leaf

Crispy Pork with Sweet-and-Sour Sauce
(Tangsuyuk)

Serves 4 to 6

This dish is very popular in Chinese restaurants in Korea, but it's been so adapted over the years that it would be unrecognizable to diners in China. My family used to feast on it for special occasions when I was little, and I loved the combination of mushrooms and carrots, vinegar and sugar, and apple and pineapple in the sauce.

I learned how to make a light, super crispy coating for the pork from a friend. She mixed potato starch with water in a bowl and then let the starch settle to the bottom. After draining away the water on top, she mixed the clay-like starch with an egg white to loosen it and then coated the pork with this mixture. But the best coating in the world will not get you crispy pork if you fry it only once. As with crispy fried chicken, double-frying is essential.

This isn't a difficult recipe, but timing is everything. Make the sauce first, so it's ready when the pork is. Then reheat it just as the pork comes out of the oil for the second time. And make sure to serve this dish as soon you have combined the pork and sauce so the pork is still crisp when you sit down to eat. *The photos are on page 236.*

1 pound boneless pork shoulder, cut into small strips (1½ x ½ x ¼ inch)
½ teaspoon minced peeled ginger
Kosher salt
¼ teaspoon freshly ground black pepper
2 dried wood ear or shiitake mushrooms
1¼ cups potato starch
6 cups plus 2 tablespoons water
1 large egg white
1 teaspoon vegetable oil
⅓ cup sliced onion
1 medium carrot, peeled and cut into ½-inch rounds

¼ cup packed light brown sugar or turbinado sugar
2 tablespoons plus ½ teaspoon soy sauce
3 tablespoons distilled white or apple cider vinegar
1 red apple, cored and cut lengthwise into ¼-inch slices
3 canned pineapple rings, halved
Corn oil for deep-frying
¾ cup sliced English cucumber
1 teaspoon toasted sesame oil

1. Combine the pork, ginger, ½ teaspoon salt, and pepper in a small bowl. Mix well, cover, and refrigerate while you prepare the other ingredients.

2. Cover the mushrooms with cold water in a bowl. Soak wood ears for 1½ hours, shiitakes for 3 to 4 hours, until softened.

3. Meanwhile, combine 1 cup of the potato starch and 3 cups of the water in a bowl. Stir well, then let sit until the starch settles at the bottom of the bowl, about 1½ hours.

4. Drain the mushrooms and trim off and discard the tough stems. Cut the mushrooms into bite-size pieces and pat dry.

5. Combine 2 tablespoons of the potato starch with 2 tablespoons of the water in a small bowl.

6. Pour off the water from the larger bowl of potato starch, so you are left with the thick layer of starch at the bottom of the bowl. Add the egg white and stir until smooth.

7. Heat the vegetable oil in a large saucepan over medium-high heat. Add the onion and mushrooms and stir-fry for 1 minute. Add the carrot and stir-fry for 1 minute. Add the remaining 3 cups water, the sugar, 1 teaspoon salt, ½ teaspoon of the soy sauce, and 2 tablespoons of the vinegar and bring to a boil. Turn the heat down to medium and add the apple and pineapple. Stir the small bowl of potato starch and water and then stir into the sauce. Cook, stirring, until the sauce thickens and becomes shiny, 2 to 3 minutes. Remove the pan from the heat.

8. Remove the pork from the refrigerator and toss with the remaining 2 tablespoons potato starch.

9. Combine the soy sauce and vinegar in small bowl, for the dipping sauce.

10. Heat about 4 inches of corn oil in a deep pot to 330°F. Turn the heat down to medium-high. Toss the pork with the batter, mixing well to coat each piece. Working in batches, carefully drop the pork pieces into the oil. They will puff up and float to the surface. Stir them occasionally until they begin to turn light golden brown and look crisp, 5 to 7 minutes. Use a slotted spoon to transfer them to a colander set over a bowl to drain.

11. Fry the pork again, in batches, until very crisp and golden brown, 3 to 4 minutes. Transfer to a colander to drain, then arrange on a large platter.

12. Reheat the pineapple sauce. When it's hot, stir in the cucumber and sesame oil and stir for 10 seconds.

13. Pour the sauce over the pork and serve immediately, with the soy-vinegar dipping sauce on the side.

Above: top row: left, pork cut into strips; right, mixing drained potato starch with egg white; center row: left, pork tossed in the batter; right, frying battered pork; bottom, Crispy Pork with Sweet-and-Sour Sauce (page 234)

Facing page: top, trimming Napa cabbage leaves; bottom, Pork Wraps (page 238)

Pork Wraps *(Bo-ssam)*

Serves 8 to 10

Bo-ssam, one of the most popular wraps, consists of braised pork topped with a bit of spicy oyster-radish salad and shrimp sauce and wrapped in a pickled cabbage leaf. My special ingredient may surprise you—hazelnut-flavored instant coffee! I can't take credit for this innovation: I learned it from an expat Korean woman I met at a Missouri potluck party. There was something irresistible about her bo-ssam that I couldn't place, and I had to know what it was. It's certainly not traditional, but it gives the pork a wonderful fragrance, color, and flavor. *The photos are on page 237.*

for the cabbage

¼ cup sugar

1 tablespoon kosher salt

¼ cup distilled white vinegar

¾ cup water

1 pound Napa cabbage leaves, washed and drained

for the pork

1 (3-pound) pork belly or 3 pounds boneless pork shoulder

10 cups water

1 large onion, cut into quarters

12 garlic cloves

2 tablespoons sliced peeled ginger

2 tablespoons fermented soybean paste (doenjang)

1 tablespoon light brown sugar

1 tablespoon hazelnut-flavored instant coffee powder

for the oyster and radish salad

1 pound Korean radishes (mu) or daikon, peeled and cut into matchsticks

2 teaspoons kosher salt

2 tablespoons fish sauce

2 teaspoons sugar

3 garlic cloves, minced

¼ cup plus 2 tablespoons Korean hot pepper flakes (gochu-garu)

8 ounces shucked fresh or frozen oysters, thawed in the refrigerator if frozen

1 tablespoon toasted sesame seeds

for the shrimp sauce

1 tablespoon salted fermented shrimp (saeujeot)

1 scallion, chopped

1 garlic clove, minced

1 teaspoon Korean hot pepper flakes (gochu-garu)

1 teaspoon sugar

2 tablespoons water

1. Make the cabbage: Combine the sugar, salt, vinegar, and water in a wide bowl and stir with a wooden spoon until the sugar and salt are dissolved. Add the cabbage leaves and mix well. Let sit, turning every 15 minutes, until wilted and soft, 1 to 2 hours.

2. Drain the cabbage leaves and squeeze out the excess water. Refrigerate until ready to use. (The leaves can be refrigerated for up to 2 days.)

3. Make the pork: Put the pork into a large pot, add the remaining ingredients, cover, and cook over medium-high heat for 1 hour. Turn the heat down to low and cook for another 15 minutes, or until the pork is tender and fully cooked. Remove the pork from the broth and let cool.

4. Meanwhile, make the oyster and radish salad: Mix the radishes and salt in a bowl. Let stand for 10 minutes, then drain and squeeze out the excess water.

5. Transfer the radishes to a medium bowl, add the fish sauce, sugar, garlic, and hot pepper flakes, and mix well. Add the oysters and mix again. Sprinkle with the sesame seeds.

6. Make the shrimp sauce: Combine the fermented shrimp, scallion, garlic, hot pepper flakes, and sugar in a small bowl. Mix well. Add the water and mix again.

7. To serve: Slice the pork ⅛ inch thick and arrange on one side of a large platter. Put the pickled cabbage and oyster-radish salad on the other side. Put the shrimp sauce in a small serving bowl on the side. Let your guests make their own wraps by placing a piece of pork on the center of a cabbage leaf, topping with some oyster-radish salad and shrimp sauce, and rolling up.

Ssam

The Korean word *ssam* means "wrapped" and refers to a style of dining where small amounts of ingredients are enfolded in a larger ingredient to create a single delicious morsel. Ingredients for the wraps and the fillings are laid out on the table, and the wraps are made one by one on the spot by the diner.

The most well-known example is barbecued meat wrapped in raw, leafy vegetables. It's part of what makes Korean barbecue so unique: Every bite of meat includes a bit of fresh vegetables. On your palm, lay out a lettuce leaf, maybe with a perilla leaf. Add a juicy piece of grilled beef, a sliver of chopped garlic, a thin slice of chili pepper, and a dab of Soybean Paste Dipping Sauce (page 272). I often add an herb leaf like basil or parsley. Fold the whole thing into itself and pop it into your mouth in one shot. Then do it again.

To make some quintessential Korean barbecue wraps, see Grilled Pork Belly (page 232), L.A.–Style Beef Short Ribs (page 226), and Bulgogi (page 223).

Ssam is not just for barbecue. In this book, I introduce you to other varieties of ssam: the ever-popular Pork Wraps (facing page), as well as the refined Royal Court classic Platter of Nine Delicacies (page 245). Thick Soybean Paste Stew (page 152) paired with Steamed Cabbage (page 152) makes for a hot, hearty choice, while Vegetable Leaf Wraps with Rice and Apple Dipping Sauce (page 148) is my go-to for a light meal in a hurry.

Mung Bean Starch Sheet Noodles with Pork, Seafood, and Vegetables

(Yangjangpi-japchae)

Serves 8

Surrounded by a variety of artfully arranged ingredients and topped off with a spicy mustard-garlic sauce, this platter of pork and noodles is easy to make but takes some time to prepare—most of it chopping. It's a good one to serve at a party when you want to impress. Bring out your gorgeous platter and let your guests admire it, then dress and toss the ingredients to mingle their flavors.

A special type of mung bean starch noodles, yangjangpi noodles come in large sheets. When cooked, they become clear and shiny and have a slightly chewy, gelatinous texture. You tear them into pieces once they're cooked so they'll be easy to eat.

Have a baking sheet handy, so you can make piles of the elements for this dish as you prepare them. You can prepare all of the ingredients hours ahead of time and refrigerate if you need to, with the exception of the noodles.

5 ounces pork tenderloin, cut into 3-inch-long matchsticks (about 1½ cups)

1 garlic clove, minced

½ teaspoon minced peeled ginger

2 teaspoons soy sauce

Pinch of freshly ground black pepper

1 tablespoon potato starch or cornstarch

8 large shrimp, in the shell

8 ounces fresh or frozen cleaned squid bodies, thawed if frozen, skinned

3 ounces (3 or 4 sheets) yangjangpi noodles

1 teaspoon kosher salt

2 teaspoons sugar

2 tablespoons distilled white vinegar

1 tablespoon toasted sesame oil

1 tablespoon vegetable oil

7 white button mushrooms, sliced

½ medium onion, thinly sliced

2 teaspoons oyster sauce

1 English cucumber, cut into very thin (¹⁄₁₆-inch) 3-inch-long matchsticks

1 red bell pepper, cored, seeded, and cut into thin matchsticks

1 yellow bell pepper, cored, seeded, and cut into thin matchsticks

Korean Egg Garnish (page 273), thinly sliced

1 teaspoon toasted sesame seeds

Mustard and Garlic Sauce (page 275)

1. Combine the pork strips, garlic, ginger, 1 teaspoon of the soy sauce, and the black pepper in a small bowl. Mix well, add the potato starch, and mix again. Cover and refrigerate while you prepare the remaining ingredients.

2. Bring a large pot of water to a boil. Cook the shrimp in the boiling water until pink and opaque throughout, about 5 minutes. Remove with a slotted spoon; keep the water hot. Shell the shrimp, then cut them lengthwise in half down the back. Remove the vein with your fingers. Transfer to a bowl.

3. Slice open the squid bodies so they lie flat on a cutting board and use a sharp knife to score each piece of squid diagonally from right to left. Turn the bodies around and then score again, to create a diamond pattern. Cut the squid into 2½-x-½-inch strips.

4. Bring the water back to a boil and cook the squid just until it turns opaque, a few minutes; do not overcook. Remove with a slotted spoon and transfer to a bowl. Keep the water at a boil.

5. Add the noodles to the boiling water, stirring with a wooden spoon so they don't stick to each other. Cover and cook over medium-high heat until soft and translucent, about 5 minutes. Drain in a colander.

6. Tear the noodles into strips that will be easy to eat and put them in a bowl. Stir in the remaining 1 teaspoon soy sauce, the salt, sugar, vinegar, and sesame oil.

7. Heat 1 teaspoon of the vegetable oil in a large skillet over high heat. Add the mushrooms and cook, stirring, until tender, a few minutes. Transfer to a bowl.

8. Heat the remaining 2 teaspoons vegetable oil in the skillet over medium-high heat. Add the pork and onion and cook, stirring, until the pork is fully cooked, about 5 minutes. Add the oyster sauce and cook, stirring, for another 2 minutes. Remove from the heat.

9. Arrange the shrimp, squid, cucumber, mushrooms, bell peppers, and egg garnish on a large platter, leaving a space in the center. Place the noodles in the center and top with the pork mixture. Sprinkle with the sesame seeds.

10. Immediately bring the platter to the table. In front of your guests, pour on the Mustard and Garlic sauce and mix with tongs or a large spoon, then serve. Prepare small plates for each of your guests.

Left, cooked yangjangpi noodles; right, Mung Bean Sheet Starch Noodles with Pork, Seafood, and Vegetables

Cold Jellyfish Salad *(Haepari-naengchae)*

Serves 6

This cold, garlicky, sweet-and-sour delicacy is a Korean-style Chinese dish. I always make it when I'm celebrating something special. It's one of the most popular dishes at Korean buffets, and whenever I go to one, I reserve a large corner of my plate for it.

Shredded salted jellyfish is easy to work with. Just soak it, blanch, and then soak again to plump it up and remove excess salt. At Chinese markets, you can buy salted jellyfish that hasn't been preshredded. It looks like a folded sheet of thin, light brown paper. This type of jellyfish will take longer to soften, but it is much cheaper and crispier than presoaked and shredded jellyfish. After rinsing, soaking, and blanching, soak it in cold water for several hours to 1 day, changing the water occasionally. When it is soft and no longer salty, cut it into matchsticks and it is ready to use.

1 (2.2-pound) package shredded salted jellyfish (haepari)
2 tablespoons sugar
1 teaspoon kosher salt
1 tablespoon distilled white or apple cider vinegar
Vegetable oil
5 ounces crab sticks (ge-massal)

3 cups water
1 large Asian pear, or 2 Bosc pears
1 English cucumber, cut into 3-inch-long matchsticks
Korean Egg Garnish (page 273)
Mustard and Garlic Sauce (page 275)
Pine nuts for garnish (optional)

1. Rinse the salted jellyfish strips under cold running water to remove some of the salt. Soak in a large bowl of cold water for 1 hour. Drain.

2. Bring 7 cups water to a boil in a large pot. Remove from the heat and add 2 cups cold water to the pot to lower the water temperature slightly. Add the jellyfish and stir for 10 seconds. Drain. Soak the jellyfish in a fresh bowl of cold water for another hour to plump it up.

3. Drain the jellyfish again and squeeze out excess water. Put it in a clean bowl, add 1 tablespoon of the sugar, the salt, and vinegar, and mix well. Cover and refrigerate.

4. Heat a large skillet over medium heat. Add a few drops of vegetable oil and then the crab sticks and cook, turning once, for 1 minute. (Alternatively, you can microwave the crab sticks on high for 1 minute, or steam them for a few minutes to heat them through.) Let cool slightly and then pull each crab stick into thin strips.

5. Dissolve the remaining 1 tablespoon sugar in the 3 cups water. Peel and core the pear and cut into matchsticks, adding them to the sugar water as you go (this will prevent the pear from turning brown). Drain.

6. Arrange the crab sticks, pear, cucumber, and egg garnish on a large platter, leaving a space in the center for the jellyfish. Pile the jellyfish in the center like a mountain. Just before serving, pour the sauce over the salad. Sprinkle with pine nuts, if desired, and serve.

Quick Variations

If you can't find jellyfish or you want to substitute, use steamed and peeled shrimp, which are tasty with the crab sticks, cucumber, pear, and mustard-garlic sauce. For a vegetarian version, skip the jellyfish and crab sticks and use carrot matchsticks and some extra cucumber and pear instead.

Clockwise from top left: soaking salted jellyfish; Korean egg garnish; Cold Jellyfish Salad

Top row: left, crepe batter; right, cooking crepes;
center row: left, crepes; right, filled rolled-up crepe; bottom, Platter of Nine Delicacies

Platter of Nine Delicacies *(Gujeolpan)*
Serves 6

The Platter of Nine Delicacies consists of bite-size crepes, called *miljeonbyung*, served with a variety of fillings and a spicy mustard sauce. The traditional platter on which the dish is served is shaped like an octagon, with nine compartments. The middle one holds the stack of crepes and the surrounding eight sections hold the fillings. In fact, the literal translation of *gujeolpan* is "nine-section plate." If you don't have such a platter, you can use any large platter.

The real skill in preparing this dish is in the artful arrangement and balance of the items in accordance with the Five Elements (see page 7). Traditional versions of this dish include dark manna lichen mushrooms to represent the black of the elements, but these mushrooms are not easy to find outside of Korea. I replace them with extra cucumber, since its crunchiness is a welcome contrast to the chewier shiitake mushrooms, shrimp, and beef.

4 dried shiitake mushrooms, soaked in water for 2 to 3 hours, until softened
4 teaspoons soy sauce
1 tablespoon honey
2 teaspoons toasted sesame oil
Freshly ground black pepper
4 ounces beef brisket, cut into 2½-inch-long matchsticks
1 garlic clove, minced
1 medium carrot, peeled and cut into 2½-inch-long matchsticks
Kosher salt
1 large English cucumber, cut into 2½-inch-long matchsticks

4 ounces large shrimp, shelled and deveined
About 1 tablespoon vegetable oil
½ cup all-purpose flour
¾ cup water
1 tablespoon chopped pine nuts, plus 5 whole nuts
Korean Egg Garnish (page 273), cut into 2½-inch-long matchsticks
Mustard and Garlic Sauce (page 275)
Short wooden skewers

1. Drain the mushrooms and squeeze out the excess water. Remove the stems and reserve for another use, such as stock, if desired. Thinly slice the mushrooms. Mix with 2 teaspoons of the soy sauce, 1 teaspoon of the honey, 1 teaspoon of the sesame oil, and a pinch of pepper in a small bowl.

2. Mix the beef with the garlic, the remaining 2 teaspoons soy sauce, 2 teaspoons honey, 1 teaspoon sesame oil, and a pinch of pepper in a small bowl.

3. Mix the carrot with a pinch of salt in a bowl. Let stand for 5 minutes, then pat dry with paper towels.

continued

4. Meanwhile, mix the cucumber with a pinch of salt in another bowl. Let stand for 5 minutes, then squeeze gently to remove excess water.

5. Thread each shrimp lengthwise onto a wooden skewer (this will prevent them from curling as they cook).

6. Heat a large skillet over medium-high heat, then turn the heat down to medium. Add ½ teaspoon of the vegetable oil and the carrot and stir-fry for 30 seconds. Transfer to a large platter.

7. Add another ½ teaspoon vegetable oil and the cucumber to the skillet and stir-fry for 20 seconds. Transfer to the platter.

8. Add 1 teaspoon vegetable oil and the shrimp skewers to the skillet and cook until the undersides of the shrimp turn pink, about 1 minute. Turn and cook for another minute. Turn the heat down to low and cook until the shrimp are cooked through but not browned, another minute or so. Transfer to the platter.

9. Turn up the heat to medium-high. Add 1 teaspoon vegetable oil and the mushrooms to the skillet and stir-fry until tender, a few minutes. Transfer to the platter.

10. Add the marinated beef to the skillet and cook, stirring, until most of the moisture has evaporated and the beef is cooked, 3 to 4 minutes. Transfer to the platter. Cover the platter with plastic wrap to prevent the ingredients from drying out.

11. Combine the flour, ¼ teaspoon salt, and the water in a bowl and stir well. Strain the batter into another bowl, pressing down on any lumps with the back of a spoon. Stir again.

12. Heat a large nonstick skillet over medium-high heat. Add a few drops of vegetable oil and swirl to coat the pan. Turn the heat down to low. Add 1 tablespoon of the batter to the pan and spread it with the back of the spoon into a circle about 2½ inches in diameter. Repeat to fill the pan, without overcrowding. Let the crepes cook until they are slightly translucent and the edges are a little dry, 1 to 2 minutes. Turn and cook for another minute. Transfer the cooked crepes to a large plate or a large baking sheet. Repeat with the remaining batter. You will have about 30 crepes.

13. Stack the crepes in the center section of a gujeolpan (or other large platter). As you stack, sprinkle a few chopped pine nuts between each layer so the crepes won't stick to each other. Arrange the 5 whole pine nuts in a flower shape on the top crepe.

14. Fill the remaining compartments with the carrot, egg white matchsticks, egg yolk matchsticks, beef, shrimp, mushrooms, and cucumber, filling the extra two sections with some of the mushrooms and cucumber (or arrange on the large platter). Put the mustard-garlic sauce in a bowl.

15. To eat, each guest should place a crepe on an individual plate, add a little of the fillings as desired, drizzle with the sauce, and wrap up.

Spicy Fermented Skate *(Hong-eo-hoe)*
Serves 10 to 12

In the Korean province of South Jeolla, where I come from, no large family gathering happens without this special dish. Now that I live in New York City, I find myself craving it. Luckily, I can always find fermented skate at a Korean grocery store. I bring it home, season it, and eat it, or I let it ferment in the fridge for 1 to 2 weeks, which makes it even more flavorful. Fermentation is a kind of cooking, and the texture of this dish is somewhere in the realm between raw and cooked. I've experimented a lot to come up with just the right ratio of water to vinegar.

If you are developing a passion for authentic Korean food, you will want to add this to your list of recipes to try. You can't say you are a real Korean food expert until you've eaten it, and the best will come from your own kitchen.

1 pound fermented skate (hong-eo)
½ cup distilled white vinegar
1 pound Korean radishes (mu) or daikon, peeled and cut into matchsticks
Kosher salt
½ cup mild Korean hot pepper flakes (gochu-garu)

½ cup Korean hot pepper paste (gochujang)
5 garlic cloves, minced
2 scallions, chopped
2 tablespoons sugar
¼ cup brown rice syrup (ssal-yeot)
1 tablespoon toasted sesame seeds

1. Rinse the skate under cold running water and pat dry with a paper towel. Slice across the grain into 1-x-3-inch pieces.

2. Combine 6 cups water and ¼ cup of the vinegar in a large bowl. Add the skate and soak for 1 hour. Drain and squeeze to remove excess water.

3. Meanwhile, combine the radishes and 1 teaspoon salt in a bowl and let stand for 30 minutes. Drain and squeeze to remove excess water.

4. Combine the hot pepper flakes, hot pepper paste, garlic, scallions, sugar, rice syrup, the remaining ¼ cup vinegar, the sesame seeds, and 1 teaspoon salt in a large bowl. Mix well. Add the radishes and skate and mix again. Transfer to a platter.

5. Serve immediately, or refrigerate in an airtight container for up to 2 weeks.

Left, mixing ingredients together; right, Spicy Fermented Skate

traditional
fermented
foods

The Korean art of fermentation represents the essence of our cuisine and culture.

When I was young, I watched my grandmother making fermented dishes, but by the time I was an adult and cooking for my own family, I had forgotten much of what I had learned from her. It has been a challenge and a joy to rediscover my cooking roots as I've relearned how to make such traditional recipes as soy sauce, hot pepper paste, soybean paste, fish sauce, and rice liquor and adapted them for today's cooks.

None of these is particularly difficult—the basic techniques were developed by my ancestors millennia ago—but they require patience and a watchful eye. By making them, you're taking an active part in an ancient practice. In time, you'll develop a sophisticated sense of fermentation, which is the first step to becoming a true expert.

Yes, you can buy any of these in Korean grocery stores. But if you want to experience real Korean cooking on a new level, the recipes in this chapter will enable you to do so.

Korean Hot Pepper Paste (page 258)

Fermented Soybean Paste *(Doenjang)*
Makes about 5 quarts

Doenjang is an essential ingredient in Korean cuisine. Salty, earthy, and hearty, it's very versatile and used in many recipes in this book. It adds its distinctive flavor to countless soups, stews, side dishes, and marinades.

It is not a "quick and easy" recipe, to say the least—the batch you start this year won't be ready for almost a year. Traditionally Koreans start it in the winter, so the freshly made soybean blocks can dry and ferment in a cool place in the house without spoiling, as they would in warmer weather. Making doenjang in my apartment is a different story; I can control the temperature, so I can make soybean paste anytime, although starting in the winter seems most natural to me. Depending on the climate in your area and your kitchen, you will need to plan your doenjang making accordingly.

When you taste homemade doenjang, you will be amazed by how delicious it is, especially compared to the commercial product. Even the simplest bean paste soup made with it is irresistible. In addition, Korean Soup Soy Sauce (page 264) is a by-product of doenjang. So let's get started!

You'll need some special equipment:

An electric blanket

Cotton flour sacking or cheesecloth

Cotton butcher's twine

A large shallow bamboo basket about 17 inches in diameter or a large baking pan lined with waxed paper

Dried rice straw or hay (check your farmers' market; optional)

A cardboard box (an 18-x-10-x-7-inch box will hold 3 bean blocks)

A 4- to 5-gallon earthenware crock with a lid

A 5-quart earthenware crock with a lid

---

5 pounds dried yellow soybeans (meju-kong), picked over, rinsed, and soaked in cold water for 24 hours

3½ gallons water

5 quarts plus ¼ cup kosher salt

2 tablespoons honey

3 dried jujubes (daechu)

3 large dried hot chili red peppers (any variety; about 4 inches long)

3 (4-x-1½-x-1-inch) pieces hardwood charcoal

1. Drain the beans and put them in a large heavy pot. Add water that is three times as deep as the beans, cover, and cook over medium-high heat for 1 hour.

2. Turn the heat down to medium and continue cooking until the beans are soft enough mash easily, 4½ to 5 hours, checking to make sure the beans remain covered with water, and replenishing as necessary. Drain the beans in a colander.

continued

Facing page: top row: left, cooked yellow soybeans; right, kneading soybean paste; second row: left, divided paste; right, paste formed into blocks; third row: left, fermented blocks; right, hanging blocks to dry; bottom row: left, soaking blocks with charcoal, jujubes, and chilies; right, Fermented Soybean Paste

3. Mash the drained beans to a paste in batches with a large mortar and pestle or in a food processor. Divide the mashed beans into 3 portions. Knead each portion with both hands and shape into a firm rectangular block measuring 6 x 3 x 4 inches.

4. Traditionally Koreans dry the bean blocks on the heated floor of their homes, but I use an electric blanket. Line the blanket with a clean cotton cloth or waxed paper and set the blocks on top. Set the heat to low. Dry the blocks, rotating them occasionally, until they are solid enough to hang, 3 to 4 days.

5. Tie each block up in cotton twine and hang them from the ceiling with hooks— all sides of the blocks should be exposed to air. Let the blocks hang for 6 weeks.

6. Now it's time to ferment the bean blocks. Place a layer of dried rice straw or hay in the bottom of a cardboard box that's just big enough to hold the blocks with a little space between them; the straw will insulate the blocks and attract good bacteria like *Bacillus subtilis* in the air. (Don't worry if you can't find straw or hay; the blocks will still attract good bacteria.) Cover the box and wrap the entire box with the electric blanket. Set the heat to low and let the bean blocks ferment for 2 weeks. At this point, the well-fermented bean blocks will smell a little earthy and pungent and will be covered with white, brownish-yellow, or sometimes greenish fungi. (These fungi change the bean proteins to peptides and amino acids, which will give the bean paste its delicious nutty flavor.)

7. Tie the fermented bean blocks up in cotton twine and hang from the ceiling, as before, for 1 month.

8. Wash the blocks in cold water to remove the fungi. Place the blocks in a shallow basket or on a baking sheet lined with waxed paper and let them dry in the sunlight for 1 day, turning them until every side of each block is dried.

9. Combine the 3½ gallons water and 5 quarts of the kosher salt in a large bowl. Stir with a wooden spoon until the salt is thoroughly dissolved.

10. Set out a 4- to 5-gallon earthenware crock. Set 2 pieces of the charcoal on a gas burner; turn on the flame, and heat until they are glowing red. (If you don't have a gas burner, use the broiler: Put the charcoal pieces under the broiler and turn it on; remove the charcoal when it is red.) Use tongs to transfer the charcoal to the earthenware crock. Drizzle the honey over the burning charcoal. Cover the crock and wait for 5 minutes. Remove the lid. You will see lots of smoke and smell a good caramel aroma. This process sterilizes the inside of the crock and will give the sauce good flavor.

11. Remove the charcoal and wipe the inside of the crock with paper towels. Add the bean blocks and salted water to the crock. Add the remaining piece of charcoal, the jujubes, and dried hot peppers; they will float on the surface of the water. (The charcoal will attract and absorb any dust. The jujubes add sweetness and the dried red peppers help prevent the blocks from going bad.) Cover the crock with flour sacking or cheesecloth and put on the lid. Let the blocks soak in the salty water until well fermented, 2 to 3 months. On clear days during the fermentation period, it's best to remove the lid and let the crock sit in the sunlight during the day and close it at night—be sure to keep the crock covered with the cloth so bugs and dust can't get in. As time passes, the salty water will turn brown and smell like deeply fermented soy sauce.

12. Discard the charcoal, jujubes, and peppers. Transfer the soaked bean blocks to a large bowl. The blocks may have broken up during the soak, so use a bowl to scoop the soy sauce out of the crock and into a sieve set over another large bowl. Add any pieces of bean block to the bean block bowl. Save the liquid for making Korean Soup Soy Sauce (page 264).

13. Mix the doenjang with both hands, breaking it up into a paste, and transfer it to a 5-quart earthenware crock. Pack it down and sprinkle with the remaining ¼ cup salt. Cover with the cotton cloth, secure it with a rubber band, and put on the lid.

14. Put the doenjang crock in a sunny spot for its final fermentation. About twice a week on sunny days, remove the lid and let the sunlight shine into the crock through the cotton cloth. When it's well fermented, the doenjang will smell sweet and taste salty and earthy, with a deep flavor. This will take 5 to 6 months.

15. Store the doenjang in the crock at room temperature. Whenever you take some out, press the rest down with a spoon to keep out the air. Once in a while, take the lid off, cover with a cotton cloth, and let the sun hit it again.

Doenjang Timeline

Here's the timeline for my most recent batch of soybean paste, made in New York City, to give you an idea of how long each step in the process takes. I boiled my soy sauce 1 week after I separated the doenjang from the soy sauce, but you can boil it on the same day.

January 4—Soaked the beans.

January 5—Made the bean blocks.

April 6—Started soaking the bean blocks in salty water.

June 15—Took the bean blocks out of the salty water and packed them in the crock for the final ferment.

June 22—Boiled the salty water for Korean Soup Soy Sauce (page 264).

December—Fermented soybean paste was ready to eat.

Extra-Strong Fermented Soybean Paste
(Cheonggukjang)

Make 6 cups

This extra-strong soybean paste is made by fermenting boiled soybeans with the healthy bacteria that float around in the air. It has a much stronger flavor than Fermented Soybean Paste (page 253), almost like aged cheese, but it takes a lot less time to make: 2 to 3 days instead of almost a year. Pungent and earthy, cheonggukjang has a slippery texture; it is also much less salty than doenjang. Koreans make a stew with it (see page 99).

Koreans have long believed that cheonggukjang is good for your stomach and recent science suggests that *Bacillus subtilis*, the bacteria proliferating in the mixture, has probiotic properties that can contribute to digestive health. Researchers are also exploring its possible role in lowering the risk of stroke or staving off dementia (as well as giving a smooth complexion).

But there's no getting around the fact that when the soybeans ferment, they have a very strong smell. I love it, but others call it stinky. I hope you will grow to love it the way we Koreans do, associating the aroma with the soulful fermented soybean paste stew so integral to our cuisine. In the meantime, know that once you place your cheonggukjang in the freezer for later use, its smell will be muted.

You'll need some special equipment:

A shallow 12-inch bamboo basket, about 12 inches in diamaeter

An electric blanket

Cotton cloth or a few layers of cheesecloth

An instant-read thermometer

---

1 pound dried yellow soybeans (meju-kong), picked over, rinsed, and soaked in cold water for 24 hours

1 cup water

Sliced green and red Korean chili pepper (cheong-gochu or hong-gochu, page 19)

1. Drain the beans and rinse a couple of times in fresh water in a large bowl; remove the floating skins and any brownish beans. Drain and transfer to a large heavy pot. Cover the beans with 10 cups water. Bring to a boil over low heat, covered, and cook over low until the beans are soft, about 4 hours.

2. Line a large shallow bamboo basket with cotton cloth or cheesecloth. Drain the beans and put them in the basket. Set a small cup filled with 1 cup water in the center of the beans to maintain humidity during fermentation. Cover the basket with moistened paper towels or a few layers of cheesecloth.

Facing page: clockwise from top left: cooked yellow soybeans set up to begin fermentation; stirring fermented yellow soybeans; balls of Extra-Strong Fermented Bean Paste

3. Wrap the whole basket in an electric blanket. Set the temperature to low and let the beans ferment for 48 hours at a temperature between 110° and 130°F—don't let them get warmer than 140°F. Use an instant-read thermometer to check them during fermentation, adjusting the temperature as necessary. Check the temperature with a thermometer often; if it's more than 130°F, unplug the blanket to lower the heat.

4. After 48 hours, uncover the beans. (If they ferment longer, they will smell too strong and may turn sour.) Remove the cup of water and stir the beans well with a wooden spoon. You should see thin, translucent threads when you stir the beans. If you don't see these, continue to ferment, checking every few hours, until you do.

5. Working in batches, pound the beans using a mortar and pestle or process in a food processor until the mixture is partially smooth with a few chunky beans. Divide the paste into 8 portions (about ¾ cup each). Place some chili peppers on each of the balls. Wrap each portion in plastic wrap and roll into a ball. Put the balls in a zipper-lock bag. Use immediately, or freeze for up to 3 months. Defrost overnight in the refrigerator before using.

Korean Hot Pepper Paste (Gochujang)
Makes 8 quarts

A red, thick, shiny paste, gochujang is one of the cornerstones of Korean cuisine, adding spiciness to many dishes.

It's readily available in all Korean markets, but homemade gochujang has a much deeper, more complex flavor and a richer color and consistency. It takes about 3 months to ferment, and during that time, you need to look after it and care for it the same way Koreans have been doing it for hundreds of years. This will put you in touch with what you're making and give you a sense of anticipation for all the delicious things you're going to do with it when it's done. *The photos are on page 260.*

2 cups barley malt powder (yeotgireum)
4½ quarts water
5 cups glutinous rice flour (chapssal-garu)
2 cups fermented soybean flour (meju-garu)

8 cups (1½ pounds) Korean hot pepper powder (gochujang-yong-gochu-garu; not hot pepper flakes)
4 cups brown rice syrup (ssal-yeot)
2 cups kosher salt

1. Combine the barley malt powder and water in a large bowl. Mix well, then strain the liquid into a large heavy pot. Heat over medium heat until the water reaches about 100°F, about 15 minutes. When you dip your finger into it, it should feel warm, not hot. Make sure it doesn't come to a boil.

2. Remove from the heat, add the rice flour, and mix well. Cover and let stand for 2 hours. The liquid will become sweet.

3. Return the pot to medium heat and cook, stirring occasionally with a wooden spoon, until reduced to about 4 quarts, 1½ to 2 hours. Let cool completely.

4. Add the fermented soybean flour, hot pepper powder, rice syrup, and salt to the liquid and mix well with a wooden spoon until shiny and creamy.

Maangchi and Friends

Strawberry: *I'm worried about my gochujang. The weather has changed here, and almost every day has been very cold and cloudy. My gochujang is not fully fermented yet. Will it still ferment properly without sun? Should I move it to a warmer location, like the kitchen? Perhaps I made the gochujang too late in the season.*

Maangchi: *Don't worry too much about it. It will ferment in a few months. It needs sunlight, so when the weather is sunny, remove the lid, leaving the crock covered with the cheesecloth, and let sit in the sun. When the sun goes down, stir the gochujang with a wooden spoon and replace the lid. When the weather is not good, just keep it closed. Good luck!*

5. To ferment the pepper paste, transfer it to an earthenware crock or glass jar. Cover with a few layers of cheesecloth, secured with a rubber band. Place the lid on the crock. Let stand at room temperature, removing the lid on sunny days and letting some sunlight penetrate the cheesecloth to help the fermentation along, for about 3 months.

6. Well-fermented hot pepper paste tastes sweet, salty, and spicy, with a deep aftertaste. There's no need to refrigerate it. Store it at cool room temperature or in a cool place outside.

In the old days, every Korean housewife made her own hot pepper paste, and today many still do. Traditional houses have a small area in the corner of the backyard where earthenware crocks containing pastes, sauces, fermented fish, kimchis, and other pickles ferment and are then stored. But you don't need an outdoor spot dedicated to fermented foods.

In my New York City apartment, I ferment my hot pepper paste in the sunniest corner of my home, next to a closed window; I make sure the sunlight hits the paste directly. It turns out wonderfully. If you leave your paste outdoors, cover it at night to protect it from the dew and rain, since that would ruin it.

The best time to start making gochujang is either February or March or the fall. It's better to avoid the hot summer months, because the gochujang would ferment too fast then, bubbling up and exploding from its container. If you live in a warm climate, put it in the sun in the morning when it's cooler and bring it into an air-conditioned part of your house during the hot afternoon and evening hours to avoid this messy outcome.

Facing page: top row: left, barley malt powder; right, mixing barley malt powder and water; second row: left, straining; right, adding rice flour; third row: left, adding Korean hot pepper powder; right, stirring in fermented soybean flour; bottom row: left, fermenting in earthenware crock; right, Korean Hot Pepper Paste (page 258)

Above: top row: left, rice and nuruk in an earthenware pot; right, earthenware crock; center row: left, bubbles on the surface; right, clear liquid; bottom, straining the rice liquor

Korean Rice Liquor *(Makgeolli)*
Makes 4 quarts

A traditional Korean alcoholic beverage, makgeolli is made by combining rice, yeast, and water with a starter culture called *nuruk* (a mixture of wheat flour, water, and micro-organisms that encourage fermentation). The result is a milky-white, slightly fizzy drink that is about 7.4 percent alcohol by volume. Drink it as you would beer, out of cups. It goes great with Kimchi Pancakes (page 182) and Pollock Pancakes (page 192), and with Dried Anchovies and Nuts (page 157).

Because it's invigorating and has a lot of carbohydrates, makgeolli was tradition-ally served to farmers as part of a midmorning snack or with lunch. It gave them the strength to work hard for the rest of the day. I remember going with my grandmother when she took lunch out to the farmers during the rice harvest. They savored their bowls of makgeolli, and I can still picture them using their pinky fingers to give it a stir before it went down the hatch.

Buy nuruk at a Korean market and mix it with the rice, yeast, and water. Sugar is optional. My grandmother didn't use a sweetener, but these days, Koreans like a sweeter style of rice liquor. Be patient. If you drink your makgeolli too soon, it won't have enough alcohol. Once it has stopped producing any bubbles—after 8 or 9 days—it is ready. *The photos are on page 263.*

You'll need some special equipment:

Food dehydrator or a 12-inch shallow bamboo basket	A 7-quart earthenware crock with a lid
	4 (1-quart) glass jars
Cheesecloth if you're using a basket to dry the rice	

---

5 cups short-grain white rice, rinsed well and soaked in cold water for 2 hours
5 quarts water

1 package active dry yeast
1½ cups starter culture (nuruk)
¼ cup sugar (optional)

1. Drain the rice and put it in a heavy pot. Add 4 cups of the water, cover, and cook over medium-high heat for 15 minutes. Stir and turn the rice over a few times with a rice scoop or wooden spoon. Turn the heat down to low, cover, and simmer until the rice is cooked, another 15 minutes. Fluff the rice with the scoop or spoon.

2. Transfer the rice to the trays of a food dehydrator or a wide shallow basket and spread it in an even layer. Dry the rice in the dehydrator set to 160°F until it is hard on the outside but still chewy and moist on the inside, 2 to 3 hours. Or, if you are using a basket, cover it with cheesecloth to protect the rice from dust and bugs and place it in a sunny, breezy place outside until dried as above, at least 7 hours or up to 1 day.

3. Transfer the rice to a 7-quart earthenware pot. (You can also use a glass jar, but be sure not to screw the top on tightly; the mixture needs to breathe.) Add the yeast, nuruk, and 8 cups of the water and mix well with a wooden spoon. Cover with cotton cloth or a piece of folded cheesecloth and place the lid on top. Let stand for 6 to 7 hours.

4. Stir the mixture with the wooden spoon. The rice will have absorbed some of the water and the mixture will be thick. Cover and leave the crock on the counter at cool room temperature (about 68°F). A few times every day, take off the lid and the cotton cloth and stir the mixture, mixing it well. After 1 or 2 days, bubbles will come to the surface. On day 5 or 6, you will see clear liquid on top, separated from the milky mixture below. Mix well with the wooden spoon.

5. On day 8 or 9, when there are no more bubbles on the surface (though the liquid will be tingly in the mouth), the makgeolli will be well fermented. Transfer it to a large bowl. Add the remaining 8 cups cold water and the sugar, if using. Stir to dissolve the sugar. Strain into a large bowl, pressing on the solids with the back of a wooden spoon to extract as much liquid as possible. Discard the solids.

6. Wash the strainer and strain the rice liquor into large glass jars. Refrigerate the makgeolli until chilled, or for up to 2 to 3 weeks. Shake or stir before pouring into cups and serving.

Korean Soup Soy Sauce

(Joseon-ganjang or Guk-ganjang)

Makes about 7½ quarts

Very salty and strong, Korean soup soy sauce is not just for soup, as the name might suggest; it's also good for seasoning stews, meat, seafood, and vegetables. It's very different from the commercial soy sauce you're used to. That darker and sweeter soy sauce was invented in China and introduced to Korea through Japan (Koreans call it *jin-ganjang*). It is good as a dipping sauce or a light flavoring agent, but it's not robust enough to flavor a whole pot of soup—and it's too dark for that anyway. Korean soup soy sauce has a richer, more savory flavor. It is light in color, and it doesn't change the color of a broth much.

I've never found a commercially made version that satisfied me, so I don't use it: I substitute fish sauce if I don't have homemade.

This recipe is a by-product of Fermented Soybean Paste (page 253). All you have to do is boil the liquid left in the jar after the bean blocks have fermented. It's a simple step, but it does require attentiveness: Do it wrong, and the soy sauce will have an off flavor and eventually attract mold.

Strained liquid from Fermented Soybean
   Paste (page 253)

1. Fill two 4-quart glass jars or one 8-quart jar (or use any number of jars as long as the total will hold 8 quarts) with boiling water and let sit for 10 minutes. Pour the water out and let containers air-dry.

2. Place a folded piece of cheesecloth in a strainer set over a large bowl. Strain the liquid, leaving any solids behind. Transfer the clear soy sauce to a large heavy pot, cover, and heat over medium-high heat until it begins to boil, 15 to 20 minutes. Turn the heat down to medium and boil for 15 to 20 minutes to sterilize the sauce without boiling too much of it away. Remove the lid and cool the sauce thoroughly.

3. Transfer the sauce to the sterilized glass jars. The soup soy sauce will keep indefinitely at room temperature.

Facing page: clockwise from top left: straining liquid; cooling cooked sauce; Korean Soup Soy Sauce

When I was young and my neighbors boiled their soy sauce, it used to perfume the whole town! Who said that it's stinky? I love that smell! But not everyone does, not even all Koreans. I remember boiling my Korean soup soy sauce when I lived in Missouri, and my apartment manager knocked on my door. "What's that smell? I got a complaint from your neighbor." I was so embarrassed that I didn't make soup soy sauce again for a long time, even after I moved back to Korea.

Now that I live in New York City, I make my own, but when the time comes to boil it, I pack it in my handcart along with a picnic lunch and a portable gas burner and take it to Spuyten Duyvil Creek, at the base of the Henry Hudson Bridge at the northernmost point of the island of Manhattan. I boil it there, where no one will complain.

Fermented Sardines *(Jeong-eo-ri jeotgal)*
Makes about 2 pounds

Fermented fish lend complex flavor to a variety of Korean dishes. Filleted, chopped, and seasoned, the fish is also a popular side dish with rice. And if you make Home-made Fish Sauce for Making Kimchi (facing page) with your own fermented fish, your kimchi will be laden with flavor.

Making fermented fish takes time and some patience. Salt the fish, pack it into a jar, and let it stand at room temperature for a few weeks and then in the refrigerator for 6 months to 1 year. After the long, slow fermentation, the fish becomes pinkish in color and very soft, with the flesh separating easily from the bones. Its powerful aroma reminds me of aged cheese—assertive in a good way.

In Korea, many kinds of seafood are given this treatment, including squid, clams, oysters, octopus, cod gills, and tiny shrimp, but the most popular seafood for fermenting is anchovies. It's hard to get the anchovies I need in New York, but I've found that fresh sardines make a good substitute. You can also use this to make Seasoned Fermented Sardine Side Dish (page 176).

2 pounds whole sardines, washed and patted dry

1 cup kosher salt

1. Combine the sardines and ¾ cup of the salt in a bowl. Toss to coat the fish. Transfer them to a glass jar or earthenware crock that will just hold them with 1 inch of space at the top. Spread the remaining ¼ cup salt on top and press down on the salted fish with a spoon.

2. Cover and leave the salted fish on the counter at room temperature for 3 weeks.

3. Put the jar in the refrigerator and let ferment for at least 6 months before eating. As time passes, the fermented fish will liquefy (except for the bones), which makes a great fish sauce. Store in the refrigerator until it runs out; it won't go bad.

Left, salting sardines; right Fermented Sardines

Homemade Fish Sauce for Making Kimchi

(Aekjeot-kimchiyong)

Makes about 1½ cups

Store-bought fish sauce is fine, and I used it to develop all of my kimchi recipes. But homemade fish sauce will make your kimchi even more tasty and deeply flavored. If you've made your own fermented sardines, it is very easy to make homemade fish sauce.

1 cup Fermented Sardines (facing page), with their liquid

1 cup water

1. Put the fermented fish and liquid in a small saucepan, add the water, and bring to a boil over medium heat. Boil until reduced to a little more than 1½ cups, 10 to 15 minutes.

2. Pour through a fine strainer set over a bowl to remove the bones and solids. Let the fish sauce cool completely.

3. Use the fish sauce right away to make kimchi or put it in an airtight glass jar and refrigerate for up to 1 week.

Local market in Korea

sauces and garnishes

Most Korean dishes need no extra seasoning, relying, as they do, on soy sauce, hot pepper paste, soybean paste, hot pepper flakes, fish sauce, garlic, and other flavorful ingredients. But some call for a little something to give them a bit of a boost or to pull their ingredients together.

Mustard and Garlic Sauce lends subtle heat to cold salads, and sauces like Creamy Pine Nut Sauce and Sesame Lemon Dipping Sauce can also make quick dips for raw vegetables. Spicy Soy Seasoning Sauce enlivens other dishes.

Since attractive presentation is an essential element of Korean cooking, I've also included a recipe for a traditional egg garnish. Whites and yolks, cooked separately into thin sheets and finely sliced, add a graphic touch to a variety of dishes.

Korean Egg Garnish (page 273)

Spicy Soy Seasoning Sauce
(Maeun-yangnyeom-ganjang)
Makes about ⅓ cup

This seasoning sauce adds flavor to a number of dishes in this book, including Bibim-bap (page 48), Soybean Sprout Rice (page 40), Steamed Oysters with Rice (page 47), and Roasted Porgy (page 175).

For a mild version, omit the hot pepper flakes. *The photo is on page 274.*

¼ cup soy sauce
2 or 3 scallions, chopped
1 garlic clove, minced
1 teaspoon sugar

2 teaspoons Korean hot pepper flakes (gochu-garu; optional)
2 teaspoons toasted sesame seeds
2 teaspoons toasted sesame oil

Combine the soy sauce, scallions, garlic, sugar, hot pepper flakes (if using), sesame seeds, and sesame oil in a bowl. Use immediately, or cover and refrigerate for up to 1 week.

Soybean Paste Dipping Sauce *(Ssamjang)*
Makes about ⅓ cup

This all-purpose dipping sauce with umami flavor is especially good wrapped inside lettuce leaves with Bulgogi (page 223), Grilled Pork Belly (page 232), or L.A.–Style Beef Short Ribs (page 226). Or use it as a dip for cucumber or carrot sticks or whole green Korean chili peppers. *The photo is on page 274.*

¼ cup fermented soybean paste (doenjang)
1 to 2 teaspoons Korean hot pepper paste (gochujang)
1 garlic clove, minced

1 scallion, chopped
1 teaspoon sugar or honey
2 teaspoons toasted sesame oil
1 teaspoon toasted sesame seeds

Combine the soybean paste, hot pepper paste (to taste), garlic, scallion, sugar, sesame oil, and sesame seeds in a small bowl. Use immediately, or cover and refrigerate for up to 1 week.

Sesame Lemon Dipping Sauce *(Kkae-sauce)*

Makes ⅓ cup

This creamy dipping sauce is great with fried foods such as Potato Croquettes (page 204). It also works well as a dip for raw vegetables like carrot, cucumber, and celery sticks.

1 tablespoon toasted sesame seeds   2 tablespoons fresh lemon juice
3 tablespoons mayonnaise   1 teaspoon honey

1. Put the sesame seeds in a spice or coffee grinder and grind to a powder.

2. Transfer the ground seeds to a small bowl. Add the mayonnaise, lemon juice, and honey and mix well. Use immediately, or cover and refrigerate for up to 3 days before using.

Korean Egg Garnish *(Gyeran-jidan)*

Makes about ½ cup

This classic garnish of egg yolks and whites cooked separately into thin sheets and then thinly sliced is added to many dishes to make them attractive and give them an additional touch of flavor. You need to cook the eggs without letting them brown—you want the strips to be as bright white or yellow as possible. *The photo is on page 271.*

3 large eggs   2 teaspoons vegetable oil
Kosher salt

1. Separate the eggs, putting the yolks in one bowl and the whites in another one. Remove the stringy bits from the whites. Add a pinch of salt to each bowl and beat with a fork. If some foam floats to the surface, remove it with a spoon.

2. Heat a 10- to 12-inch nonstick skillet over medium-high heat. Add 1 teaspoon of the oil and swirl to coat the bottom of the skillet. Wipe off the excess with a paper towel so only a thin coating remains in the skillet and remove from the heat. Pour the yolks into the skillet and tilt so they coat the bottom of the skillet in a thin, even layer. Let sit just until the yolks are set, a few minutes. Lift the edge of the yolks with a spatula and flip over. Set over low heat and cook until just set, 30 seconds to 1 minute. Don't let the yolks brown. Slide onto a cutting board.

3. Wipe out the skillet and repeat the process with the remaining 1 teaspoon oil and the egg whites.

4. Cut the yolks and whites into thin matchsticks. Use immediately, or roll up in plastic wrap to prevent the eggs from drying out and refrigerate for up to 4 days.

Creamy Pine Nut Sauce (*Jat-jang*)

Makes about ⅓ cup

This rich, traditional sauce goes well with all kinds of Korean panfried vegetables, seafood, and meat. Its creamy texture makes it great for dipping. You can use Mediterranean pine nuts here, but if you have the opportunity, buy Korean pine nuts, which are smaller, thinner, and, to my taste, nuttier and more delicious.

¼ cup pine nuts (see above)

1 garlic clove, chopped

½ teaspoon kosher salt

1 tablespoon honey or sugar

1 tablespoon distilled white vinegar

1 tablespoon water

Combine all the ingredients in a food processor or blender and process until creamy, scraping down the sides of the bowl as necessary, about 1 minute. Scrape into a small bowl and serve, or cover and refrigerate for up to 2 days.

Mustard and Garlic Sauce (*Gyeoja-maneul-jang*)

Makes about ½ cup

This sauce accompanies many Korean salads, including Cold Jellyfish Salad (page 242) and the Platter of Nine Delicacies (page 245). Traditionally the sauce isn't made with garlic, but I like the pungent flavor that it adds.

Korean mustard seed powder is available at any Korean grocery store. It is similar to regular mustard powder (which you can substitute), but it has a brighter yellow color, which gives the sauce greater vibrancy.

1 tablespoon Korean mustard seed powder (gyeoja-garu)

1 tablespoon warm water

1 tablespoon minced garlic

1 tablespoon kosher salt

1 tablespoon plus 1 teaspoon sugar

1 teaspoon honey

3 tablespoons distilled white vinegar

1 teaspoon toasted sesame oil

½ teaspoon soy sauce

5 pine nuts

1. Stir the mustard powder and warm water together in a small bowl. Let stand for 10 minutes to allow the flavors to develop.

2. Stir in the garlic, salt, sugar, honey, vinegar, sesame oil, and soy sauce. Sprinkle the pine nuts on top and serve immediately, or cover and refrigerate for up to 1 week, and add the pine nuts before serving.

Facing page: clockwise from top left: Spicy Soy Seasoning Sauce (page 272); Soybean Paste Dipping Sauce (page 272); Creamy Pine Nut Sauce; Mustard and Garlic Sauce

desserts

A Korean meal isn't presented as a parade of courses like a Western one, but we do have a wide range of sweet cakes, drinks, and candies that would be welcome at the end of any meal. Our desserts rely less on refined sugar than Western sweets do, and instead use rice, cinnamon, seasonal fruits, honey, nuts, and ginger.

This chapter contains a few recipes that use rice in ways you might not be used to: Panfried Sweet Rice Cakes with Edible Flowers, Rice Cake Balls Coated with Black Sesame Seed Powder, and refreshing, sweet Rice Punch.

Healthful punches have long been offered to aid digestion after a meal, boost the energy and health of the diner, and clear the mind. Pear Punch, with a spicy kick from ginger and peppercorns, satisfies my sweet tooth and wakes me up after a big meal.

Ginseng Candy, made with fresh ginseng, is a great example of traditional Korean confectionery and a bracing, tingly refresher after any meal.

Panfried Sweet Rice Cakes with Edible Flowers (page 286)

Dessert Punch with Persimmons, Cinnamon, and Ginger *(Sujeonggwa)*

Serves 6

This drink is a great way to cap off a meal. The dried persimmons become plump and soft after macerating in the sweet, spicy tea overnight. Usually the cinnamon and ginger are cooked separately and then combined, but to save time, I cook them together, and I don't think you can tell the difference. Korean restaurants often serve a ginger and cinnamon tea that they call sujeonggwa, but without the persimmons, it's just not the real thing.

For an elegant presentation, you can freeze some of the sweet punch in a shallow pan or dish, scraping it with a fork or a spoon every 30 minutes until it freezes into granita. Float a spoonful of granita in each serving of punch.

10 cups water

1 (3-ounce) piece ginger, peeled and thinly sliced

5 cinnamon sticks

1 cup sugar

6 dried persimmons (got-gam), stems removed and washed

Pine nuts for sprinkling

1. Combine the water, ginger, and cinnamon sticks in a medium heavy pot, cover, and cook over high heat for 25 minutes, or until the ginger and cinnamon flavors are infused and the water has turned light brown. Turn the heat to low and simmer for another 25 minutes.

2. Remove from the heat and strain into a heatproof bowl. Add the sugar and stir to dissolve. Let cool to room temperature.

3. Pour the punch into a large glass jar. Add the dried persimmons, cover, and refrigerate overnight.

4. Place 1 persimmon in each of six dessert bowls. Pour 1½ cups cold punch into each bowl. Sprinkle each bowl with a few pine nuts and serve immediately. (The leftover sujeonggwa can be kept in the fridge for up to 1 week.)

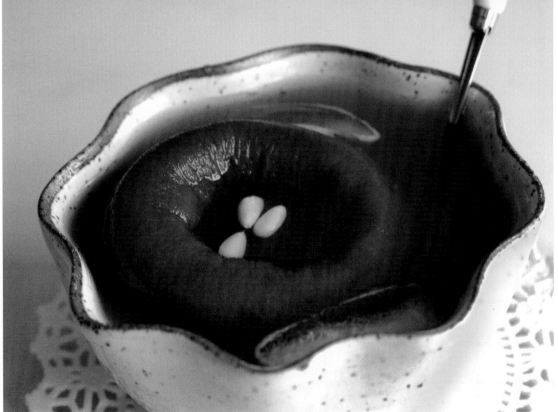

Top, infusing the punch; bottom, Dessert Punch with Persimmons, Cinnamon, and Ginger

Pear Punch *(Baesuk)*

Serves 4

Baesuk is a variety of *hwachae*, or Korean fruit punch, that's sweet and flavorful, with ginger and peppercorns giving it an unexpected spicy kick. Koreans enjoy this invigorating punch as a snack or dessert throughout the year, but especially during the Korean harvest festival day of Chuseok, when pears are in season and at their peak. These days Asian (Korean) pears are available all year round in Korean grocery stores, so you can enjoy this punch anytime.

If you can't find Asian pears, you can substitute Anjou, and the result will be just as delicious as the traditional version. You can make this ahead and store it in the fridge. Here's a tip: Put some of the punch in a shallow pan and freeze it. When it's showtime, shave the frozen punch into the chilled punch to make it bracingly cold and refreshing.

7 cups plus ¼ cup water
½ cup sugar
1 large Asian pear or 2 large Anjou
   pears (about 1⅓ pounds)

24 black peppercorns
1 (1-inch) piece ginger, peeled and thinly
   sliced
Pine nuts for sprinkling

1. Combine ¼ cup of the water and ¼ cup of the sugar in a medium pot and stir with a wooden spoon to dissolve the sugar.

2. Peel the Asian pear and cut lengthwise in half, then cut each half lengthwise into quarters, so that you have 8 pieces; or peel and quarter each Anjou pear. Remove the core and seeds. Push 3 black peppercorns into each piece of pear— be sure to push them in deeply so they won't come out.

3. Add the 7 cups water, the pear pieces, and ginger to the pot, cover, and cook over low heat until the pears are translucent and tender, about 1½ hours. Remove from the heat and stir in the remaining ¼ cup sugar. Let cool.

4. Transfer the punch to a glass pitcher or jar. Cover and refrigerate for at least 6 hours, and up to 1 week.

5. Ladle the cold punch into small ceramic or glass bowls, adding 2 pieces of pear per bowl. Sprinkle with pine nuts and serve with spoons.

Rice Punch (Sikhye)

Makes about 5 quarts

A traditional sweet drink made of fermented malt and rice, sikhye has a pleasantly malty aftertaste. As the rice ferments, the grains turn white and become spongy, releasing their starch into the liquid, which turns light amber. The punch is never fermented long enough to become alcoholic, and it's often served as a dessert in Korean restaurants. It's also sold in cans at Korean grocery stores, but the homemade version has a more powerful malt flavor than anything you can get in a can. Sikhye is usually served cold, but when you make it at home, you can enjoy it right after boiling it.

For proper fermentation, you must steep the rice grains in the malt for about 4 hours at a constant temperature. You can use a rice cooker for small batches (if you have a 10-cup rice cooker, it will hold a half recipe), but be sure to set it on "warm," not "cook," or your rice will cook and overflow. The timing will be the same.

In this recipe, though, I show you how to make sikhye the old-fashioned way: as a big batch in a large pot, keeping a watchful eye on it to make sure the temperature remains steady.

1 pound (3 cups) barley malt powder (yeotgireum garu)
6 quarts water
2 cups short-grain white rice, soaked in cold water for 2 to 3 hours

Sugar (optional)
Pine nuts for sprinkling

1. Combine the malt powder and water in a large bowl and stir with a wooden spoon to mix well. Set aside until the malt solids have settled on the bottom and the liquid is clear; it will take 2 to 3 hours to separate completely. Pour the clear liquid into a large heavy pot and discard the dregs.

2. Meanwhile, drain the rice and put it in a steamer basket lined with cheesecloth. Put the steamer in a pot filled with about 5 cups water. Cover and cook over medium-high heat for 30 minutes. Check the rice to see if it's fully cooked: Each grain should be a little translucent and tender. If the rice is still a little hard, continue to cook, adding more water to the pot if necessary, until it is soft.

Maangchi and Friends
Kathy: *Is it OK to store the rice and the punch together in the same container?*
Maangchi: *Yes, if you serve it in a few days. However, be aware that the rice will continue to ferment in the liquid, so the rice may turn a little gray and start to break up, and the punch may become grayish and a little cloudy. And after more than a week, the punch will start to taste sour if stored this way, so drink it before that.*

3. Transfer the cooked rice to the pot of liquid. Stir with a wooden spoon to separate the grains. To ferment the rice, you will have to keep the temperature of the liquid at between 122°F and 140°F. To do so, cover the pot and heat over low heat until the temperature reaches about 140°F on an instant-read thermometer, about 20 minutes. (If you don't have a thermometer, dip your finger into the liquid: If it feels warm but not hot, it should be at the proper temperature.) Turn off the heat and let sit until the temperature falls to 122°F, about 30 minutes. Then reheat to 140°F. Repeat the heating and cooling process until several rice grains float to the surface, signaling that the rice is fermented. This will take about 4 hours.

4. Bring the punch to a full boil over high heat. Skim the bubbles from the surface with a skimmer. Remove the pot from the heat and let cool.

5. Set a strainer over a large bowl and pour the contents of the pot into the strainer. Rinse the rice under cold water, drain, and transfer to an airtight container. Add cold water to cover the rice, cover, and refrigerate for up to 2 weeks.

6. Line the strainer with cheesecloth, set it over a large glass jar, and strain the liquid again. The brownish foam will collect in the cheesecloth, and the liquid will be a clear light amber. Cover and refrigerate for up to 2 weeks.

7. To serve, ladle about 1½ cups of the liquid per serving into a serving bowl and add 2 to 3 tablespoons rice per serving. The punch will be mildly sweet; if you'd like, you can add a teaspoon or two of sugar to each serving. The beautiful white rice will float to the surface. Sprinkle with pine nuts and serve.

Panfried Sweet Rice Cakes with Edible Flowers *(Hwajeon)*

Serves 2 or 3; makes 5 pancakes

These small, thin rice cakes are panfried and then seasonal, edible flowers are pressed into them and they are drizzled with a sweet syrup (or honey, if you prefer). They brighten the day of anyone who eats them, and they're great with warm tea.

Traditionally, in the springtime, women would go on picnics to celebrate and enjoy the beauty of nature in the mountains. They would take sweet rice flour and a pan with them and would pick some Korean mountain azaleas. Then they'd set up their picnic and make hwajeon with the petals of the azaleas that they had just picked.

Azaleas available in the United States are not edible, but you can make hwajeon with flowers such as roses or nasturtiums in the summer or chrysanthemums in the fall. If your flowers are small, use 2 or 3 for each cake. If they are large, use just a few petals. I get snapdragons and Gem marigolds from my local farmers' market and use them. Do be careful, though, because not all flowers are edible, and only flowers grown without pesticides are safe to eat.

for the syrup
3 tablespoons sugar
3 tablespoons water

for the pancakes
½ cup glutinous rice flour (chapssal-garu)

Pinch of kosher salt
¼ cup boiling water
About 1 tablespoon vegetable oil
Edible flowers, such as roses, snapdragons, Gem marigolds, chrysanthemums, or nasturtiums

1. **Make the syrup:** Combine the sugar and water in a small heavy saucepan and cook over low heat for 5 minutes, without stirring. Tilt and swirl the pan to dissolve any remaining sugar granules. Remove from the heat. Transfer to a small bowl.

2. **Make the pancakes:** Combine the rice flour, salt, and boiling water in a medium bowl. Mix with a wooden spoon until the dough comes together and is no longer too hot to handle. Knead it in the bowl until smooth, a few minutes.

3. Divide the dough into 5 equal pieces and roll the pieces into balls. Cover with a sheet of plastic wrap. Press each one into a 2½-inch disk; keep the disks covered.

4. Heat a large nonstick skillet over medium heat for a few minutes, then turn the heat down to very low. Add a few drops of vegetable oil. Add 2 or 3 of the cakes to the pan and cook until the bottoms become a little crisp but haven't yet begun to brown, 3 to 4 minutes. Turn them over and press down with a spatula to keep them thin and round. Cook until the second sides are a little crispy but still white, another 3 to 4 minutes. (Sometimes these will puff up a little bit.) Place a flower or a few flowers, or a few petals, depending on their size, on top of each pancake and turn them flower side down. Press down with the spatula for 1 second to seal the flowers into the cakes. Transfer to a serving plate, flower side up. Repeat with the remaining cakes.

5. Drizzle the syrup over the cakes and serve.

Sweetened Rice with Dried Fruits and Nuts *(Yaksik)*

Makes 9 pieces

Yak means "medicine" in Korean, and *sik* means "food." Koreans have long associated honey, jujubes, pine nuts, chestnuts, and cinnamon with good health. Made by steaming rice with nuts, dried fruits, sugar, and honey, yaksik is most often eaten as a snack, but it can also be served as a dessert. It is chewy like rice cakes but sweeter, and the twice-steamed rice glistens and sticks together nicely.

Jujubes are less well known in the United States than in Korea, where they are prized for their medicinal properties and enjoyed for their sweetness. If you have trouble finding them, you can substitute an additional 1½ cups raisins or dried cranberries (which have a similarly brilliant color).

Yaksik is not difficult to make, but it does take some time. I like to make a large batch, portion it out, and keep it in the freezer, ready to defrost and serve when needed.

¼ cup granulated sugar

¼ cup water

2 cups glutinous rice (chap-ssal), rinsed and soaked in cold water for 4 to 6 hours

¼ cup packed light brown sugar

2 tablespoons soy sauce

2 tablespoons vegetable oil

1 tablespoon toasted sesame oil

½ teaspoon ground cinnamon

15 to 20 dried jujubes (daechu), washed and patted dry

1 (13-ounce) can chestnuts in syrup, drained and left whole

¼ cup raisins or dried cranberries

2 tablespoons pine nuts

¼ cup honey

1. Combine the granulated sugar and 2 tablespoons of the water in a small heavy saucepan and cook over medium heat, without stirring, until the syrup bubbles and begins to turn golden, about 6 minutes. Turn the heat down to low, swirl the pan, and cook until the caramel is uniformly deep amber. Remove from the heat, add the remaining 2 tablespoons water, and swirl again; do not stir. Let the caramel sauce cool in the pan.

2. Drain the rice. Put about 5 cups water in a large pot and bring to a boil over medium-high heat. Line a steamer basket with cheesecloth or a clean cotton kitchen towel and spread the rice evenly in the basket. Steam the rice, covered, for 40 minutes. Turn the rice over with a wooden spoon, cover, turn the heat down to medium, and cook until the rice is tender, about 20 minutes more.

3. Meanwhile, combine the brown sugar, soy sauce, vegetable oil, sesame oil, and cinnamon in a bowl and mix well to make the seasoning sauce.

4. Cut the jujubes in half and remove the pits with a knife.

Facing page: clockwise from top left: chestnuts and dried fruits; cooling sweetened rice in plastic-wrap-lined pan; Sweetened Rice with Dried Fruit and Nuts

5. Transfer the cooked rice to a large bowl. Add the chestnuts, raisins, pine nuts, jujubes, caramel sauce, seasoning sauce, and honey. Mix well with a wooden spoon.

6. Add more water to the steamer and bring to a boil over medium heat. Put the rice mixture in the lined steamer basket, cover, and cook over medium heat for 30 minutes until the rice is chewy and sticks together.

7. Line an 8-x-10-inch square baking dish with plastic wrap so the ends extend over the sides of the dish. Transfer the rice to the baking dish, pressing it down with a spatula to get the grains to stick together. Let cool completely.

8. Use the plastic wrap to lift the yaksik out of the dish. Cut into 9 rectangles. Serve immediately, or wrap the pieces in plastic and freeze for up to 1 month. Thaw on the countertop for 30 minutes before serving, or reheat each piece in the microwave for about a minute and serve warm.

Rice Cake Balls Coated with Black Sesame Seed Powder (Heukimja-gyeongdan)

Makes about 75 rice cake balls

Chewy confections made with glutinous rice flour, these rice cake balls are filled with red bean paste, then coated with toasted black sesame seed powder. I love the powder's nutty taste and beautiful black color, but if you'd like to make some of your rice cake balls a striking contrasting color, pick up yellow castella (a bright-colored pound cake) from a Korean or Japanese bakery, make crumbs from it, and coat some of your rice cake balls with the crumbs.

½ cup azuki beans, picked over, rinsed, and drained
3 cups water
½ cup packed light brown sugar
Kosher salt

3 cups glutinous rice flour (chapssal-garu)
3 cups boiling water
1 cup toasted black sesame seeds
All-purpose flour for dusting

1. Put the beans in a medium heavy saucepan, add the 3 cups water, cover, and cook over medium-high heat for 30 minutes.

2. Turn the heat down to low and simmer until the beans are very soft and easy to mash, about 1½ hours longer. There should be just a little bit of liquid left in the pot. If the beans are still hard, add more water and continue cooking over low heat until soft.

3. Remove the pan from the heat and mash the beans with the remaining liquid, using a wooden spoon. (The consistency should be like that of canned refried beans.) Add the brown sugar and ½ teaspoon salt. Cook over medium-high heat, stirring with the wooden spoon, until the paste thickens and turns dark and shiny, about 5 minutes. Scrape the paste into a bowl.

4. Combine the rice flour and 1 teaspoon salt in a large bowl. Add the boiling water and mix with a wooden spoon until the dough is cool enough to handle. Then knead in the bowl until the dough is soft and smooth, about 5 minutes. Put the dough in a plastic bag and let sit on the kitchen counter for 30 minutes.

5. Grind the sesame seeds in a spice or coffee grinder until fine and powdery.

6. Dust a cutting board or a baking sheet with flour. Pull a little piece of dough out of the plastic bag and roll it between your hands into a ½-inch ball. Make a hole in the middle of the ball with your thumb to turn the ball into a cup. Put about ½ teaspoon bean paste into the middle of it, pinch together to seal, and roll again into a smooth ball. Place on the floured board. Repeat with the remaining dough and filling. You should have about 75 rice cake balls.

7. Bring a large pot of water to a boil over high heat. Add all the rice cake balls and stir with a wooden spoon to prevent them from sticking to the bottom of the pot and to each other. Boil until the balls float, 3 to 5 minutes. Drain the rice cake balls in a colander, transfer them to a large bowl, and cover with cold water to rinse and cool them. Drain again.

8. Put the sesame seed powder in a shallow bowl. Roll the cooked rice cake balls in the powder to coat. Transfer to a serving plate and serve, or freeze the rice cake balls in an airtight container for up to 1 month. Defrost on the countertop before serving.

Clockwise from top left: filling the rice cake balls with mashed azuki beans; rolled rice cake balls; Rice Cake Balls Coated with Yellow Castella and Black Sesame powder

Top row: left, ginseng roots; right, cutting off the root tips;
center row: left, cooking ginseng in bubbling sugar-honey syrup; right, ginseng tea;
bottom, Ginseng Candy

Ginseng Candy *(Susam-jeonggwa)*

Makes about 25 pieces

For thousands of years, ginseng roots have been highly prized in Korea for their medicinal benefits. This candy is the most delicious supplement I can imagine. It's a little crunchy on the outside with a jelly-like interior. It's probably not like any other candy you've ever eaten: The flavor is sweet with herbaceous and bitter notes.

Ginseng roots can be cultivated, but the best grow wild in the mountains. Recently a wild 120-year-old root sold at auction for $300,000! But don't worry. The 4 to 5 ounces that you will need for this recipe will cost you only about $15 at a Korean market.

After making the candy, don't wash the skillet right away. It'll be coated with a flavorful syrup. To make delicious ginseng tea, add 2 to 3 cups of water to the pan and bring to a boil. Add a few pine nuts to each cup before serving.

5 or 6 fresh ginseng roots (4 to 5 ounces)

2 cups water

1½ cups sugar

2 tablespoons honey

1. Wash the ginseng. Cut off and discard the tip of each root. Trim off and reserve the tiny roots. Cut the ginseng into thin lengthwise slices and then cut crosswise into 2-inch pieces.

2. Put the ginseng pieces and roots in a large heavy skillet and add the water and 1 cup of the sugar. Cover and cook over low heat, stirring with a wooden spoon a few times, until the ginseng is softened, about 1 hour.

3. Uncover the skillet and stir in the honey. Cook, uncovered, until the syrup is vigorously bubbling, 10 to 20 minutes, stirring frequently so the syrup doesn't burn.

4. Spread the remaining ½ cup sugar on a piece of parchment paper set on a cutting board. Remove the ginseng pieces and small roots from the skillet one by one and, using a fork or chopsticks, roll them in the sugar to coat, then transfer to a parchment-lined plate or baking sheet. Let cool completely before serving. Store leftovers in an airtight container in the freezer for up to 3 months.

MENUS FOR KOREAN MEALS

Korean breakfasts, lunches, and dinners are less distinct from each other than their American counterparts. No matter what the time of day, rice is the center of almost every meal, with the possible substitution of porridge or noodles. Kimchi and soup are almost always served at every meal too, along with banchan, the side dishes.

Below are some typical menu combinations, to give you an idea of authentic ways of serving the recipes in this book.

Breakfast

Though Western-style breakfasts of toast, milk, coffee, and a few pieces of fruit are gaining in popularity, Koreans traditionally eat a light breakfast of rice, soup, and kimchi, with a few side dishes. Porridge is also a classic choice and is still a go-to breakfast for busy people. Because kimchi and mitbanchan are usually on hand, preparing the meal usually requires little more than making the rice and soup.

Here are breakfasts I make for my own family. All these menus are also suitable for lunch or dinner.

STEAMED EGG BREAKFAST
Multigrain Rice (page 38)
Soybean Sprout Soup (page 93)
Diced Radish Kimchi (page 120)
Panfried Tofu with Spicy Seasoning Sauce (page 155)
Steamed Eggs in an Earthenware Bowl (page 156)
Seasoned Oysters (page 167)

PORRIDGE BREAKFAST
Shrimp Porridge (page 76)
Vegetable-and-Fruit-Water Kimchi (page 124)

SOUP BREAKFAST
Multigrain Rice (page 38)
Napa Cabbage Kimchi (page 114)
Soybean Paste Soup with Chard (page 98)
Blanched Spinach with Scallions and Sesame (page 137)
Meat and Tofu Patties (page 191)
Dried Anchovies and Nuts (page 157)

Lunch

At home, Koreans eat rice, soup, kimchi, and side dishes. Working people or students pack lunch boxes of rice, kimchi, and side dishes. These side dishes are chosen for their ability to stay fresh and dry all morning until they're ready to eat. These items include Braised Black Beans (page 153), Seasoned Dried Filefish (page 166), Kimchi Pancake (page 182), Meat and Tofu Patties (page 191), and Braised Beef in Soy Sauce (page 158).

On the weekends, when everyone is home, Korean housewives might make a special treat such as Soybean Sprout Rice (page 40), Steamed Oysters with Rice (page 47), Bibimbap (page 48), Knife-Cut Noodles with Clams (page 70), or Hand-Torn Noodle Soup (page 66), or even dishes like Bulgogi (page 223), Grilled Pork Belly (page 232), or Crispy Pork with Sweet-and-Sour Sauce (page 234). These are meals that the whole family can enjoy together. Here are some of the weekend lunches my family likes best.

KIMCHI STEW LUNCH
Fluffy White Rice (page 36)
Kimchi Stew with Tuna (page 104)
Cooked and Seasoned Soybean Sprouts (page 140)
Braised Beef in Soy Sauce (page 158)
Spicy Stuffed Cucumber Kimchi (page 123)
Braised Black Beans (page 153)

HAND-TORN NOODLE SOUP LUNCH
Hand-Torn Noodle Soup (page 66)
Napa Cabbage Kimchi (page 114)
Braised Black Beans (page 153)
Sautéed Zucchini and Shrimp (page 176)
Seaweed Salad (page 134)
Stir-Fried Fish Cakes with Soy Sauce (page 170)

STEAMED CABBAGE WRAP LUNCH
Fluffy White Rice (page 36) or Multigrain Rice (page 38)
Napa Cabbage Kimchi (page 114)
Thick Soybean Paste Stew with Steamed Cabbage (page 152)
Cold Cucumber Soup (page 136)
Stir-Fried Bellflower Root (page 150)
Steamed Eggplant (page 141)

Dinner

Dinner is the most important meal, and Korean housewives take it seriously, often discussing it throughout the course of the day, right up to the dinner itself. It's typically a meal when the whole family eats together, and on special occasions, moms plan ahead and are sure to inform the whole family of the food they can look forward to that night: "Grilled pork for dinner tonight; don't be late!"

Rice and kimchi are always served with all of these menus.

NUTRITIOUS DINNER EVERYDAY
Fluffy White Rice (page 36) or Multigrain Rice (page 38)
Napa Cabbage Kimchi (page 114)
Spicy Beef and Vegetable Soup (page 96)
Korean-Style Zucchini Pancakes (page 190)
Braised Beltfish (page 168)
Braised Dried Sweet Potato Stems (page 142)
Green Chili Peppers Seasoned with Soybean Paste (page 132)
Dried Anchovies and Nuts (page 157)

SOYBEAN PASTE STEW AND SPICY STIR-FRIED PORK DINNER
Fluffy White Rice (page 36) or Multigrain Rice (page 38)
Napa Cabbage Kimchi (page 114)
Perilla Leaf Kimchi (page 119)
Soybean Paste Stew with Dried Anchovies (page 108)
Spicy Stir-Fried Pork (page 161)
Blanched Spinach with Scallions and Sesame (page 137)
Fernbrake with Garlic and Soy (page 146)
Stir-Fried Fish Cakes with Soy Sauce (page 170)

SPECIAL BARBECUE DINNER
Fluffy White Rice (page 36) or Multigrain Rice (page 38)
Soybean Paste Soup with Chard (page 98), or Dried Pollock Soup (page 94),
   or Soybean Sprout Soup (page 93), or Beef Radish Soup (page 95)
Diced Radish Kimchi (page 120)
Kimchi Pancake (page 182)
Bulgogi (page 223) or L.A.–Style Beef Short Ribs (page 226)
Cooked and Seasoned Soybean Sprouts (page 140)
Stir-Fried Kale with Soybean Paste (page 138)
Braised Lotus Root (page 145) or Braised Burdock Root (page 151)

New Year's Day Feast

Traditionally Koreans celebrate the lunar New Year (aka Chinese New Year). Rice cake soup is the essential dish to eat on New Year's Day, but many other side dishes are prepared to celebrate the occasion. You can choose your favorites from the Side Dishes and Party and Special Occasion Food chapters, but don't skip the soup!

Fluffy White Rice (page 36)
Rice Cake Soup (page 72)
Napa Cabbage Kimchi (page 114)
Diced Radish Kimchi (page 120)
L.A.–Style Beef Short Ribs (page 226) or Bulgogi (page 223)
Fernbrake with Garlic and Soy (page 146)
Cooked and Seasoned Soybean Sprouts (page 140)
Blanched Spinach with Scallions and Sesame (page 137)
Stir-Fried Bellflower Root (page 150)
Braised Dried Sweet Potato Stems (page 142)
Spicy Fermented Skate (page 247)
Cold Jellyfish Salad (page 242)
Sweet Potato Starch Noodles with Stir-Fried Vegetables and Beef (page 230)
Chili Pepper Pancakes (page 194)
Perilla Leaf Pancakes (page 196)
Pollock Pancakes (page 192)
Sweetened Rice with Dried Fruits and Nuts (page 288)
Rice Punch (page 284) and/or Dessert Punch with Persimmons, Cinnamon, and
    Ginger (page 280)
Rice Cake Balls Coated with Black Sesame Seed Powder (page 290)

Birthday Celebration Breakfast

Koreans celebrate birthdays at breakfast, and the meal must always include seaweed soup (miyeokguk). I usually buy a beautiful birthday cake at a Korean bakery and put it in the center of the table. We start the celebration by singing "Happy Birthday," and the birthday person blows out the candles. Then I remove the cake from the table and we eat an elaborate breakfast; the cake is served as dessert later.

Fluffy White Rice (page 36) or Multigrain Rice (page 38)
Seaweed Soup (page 89)
Napa Cabbage Kimchi (page 114)
Bulgogi (page 223)
Roasted Porgy with Spicy Seasoning Sauce (page 175)
Sweet Potato Starch Noodles with Stir-Fried Vegetables and Beef (page 230)
Pollock Pancakes (page 192)

Cooked and Seasoned Soybean Sprouts (page 140)
Blanched Spinach with Scallions and Sesame (page 137)
Fernbrake with Garlic and Soy (page 146)
Panfried Tofu with Spicy Seasoning Sauce (page 155)
Sweetened Rice with Dried Fruits and Nuts (page 288)

Parties and Other Special Occasions

Koreans love to get together and celebrate with family, friends, and coworkers. Preparing something special is a way to express your love, respect, and gratitude toward the important people in your life.

BARBECUE PARTY

Korean barbecue is a popular party food that takes a lot less work than you might think. For best results, marinate the beef ribs overnight; if you're doing pork belly, you don't have to marinate it at all. Make rice if you have Koreans coming, because they will always expect it, even at a barbecue.

Fluffy White Rice (page 36)
Egg Soup (page 87) or Potato–Soybean Paste Soup (page 88)—if you are cooking
    outdoors, skip this
Napa Cabbage Kimchi (page 114) or Spicy Stuffed Cucumber Kimchi (page 123)
L.A.–Style Beef Short Ribs (page 226) or Grilled Pork Belly (page 232)
Soybean Paste Dipping Sauce (page 272) and assorted raw vegetables
Scallion Salad (page 133)
Fresh fruit

MIX-AND-MATCH PARTY

Of course you can simply choose a few dishes from the Party and Special-Occasion Food chapter, add a few from the Side Dishes chapter, and serve with rice, soup, and kimchi, but here is one of my favorite menus for entertaining.

Platter of Nine Delicacies (page 245)
Pork Wraps (page 238)
Sweet Potato Starch Noodles with Stir-Fried Vegetables and Beef (page 230)
Korean Fried Chicken (page 220)
Fluffy White Rice (page 36)
Napa Cabbage Kimchi (page 114)
Seafood Stew (page 102)
Pear Punch (page 283)
Fresh fruit

PARTIES ON A BUDGET

These quick and inexpensive crowd-pleasers will ensure that everyone has a good time and eats well.

Tangsuyuk Party
Crispy Pork with Sweet-and-Sour Sauce (page 234)
Fluffy White Rice (page 36)
Napa Cabbage Kimchi (page 114)
Fresh fruit

Yangnyeom-tongdak Party
Korean Fried Chicken (page 220)
Radish Pickles (page 127)
Fluffy White Rice (page 36)
Napa Cabbage Kimchi (page 114)
Fresh fruit

Bo-ssam Party
Pork Wraps (page 238)
Fluffy White Rice (page 36)
Napa Cabbage Kimchi (page 114)
Fresh fruit

ONLINE SOURCES

Korean grocery stores exist in all major metropolitan areas in the United States, as well as in many smaller cities and towns. A directory of Korean grocery stores around the world on my website is constantly being added to and updated by readers. Check it out at www.maangchi.com/shopping.

Shopping online for Korean ingredients in English, though, is still in its infancy. It can be difficult to find what you need in the quantity you desire for a good price, and Korean fruits and vegetables are often nearly impossible to find. The websites can be difficult to navigate and full of broken English, and the online checkout process can be confusing. Many of my readers will drive for hours to shop at a physical store rather than shop online.

However, since I started my website, the online stores have improved, and they will continue to do so, I'm sure. If you're in the United States, you'll find a lot of what you need on the websites below, but keep checking the directory on my website for updates and new sources.

H Mart (www.hmart.com): The H Mart chain of Korean grocery stores in the Northeast is well known for being comprehensive and well stocked, but if there's not one near you, you can shop a limited range of their inventory online. They sell rice, pastes, sauces, and dry and canned goods, as well as small appliances like rice cookers and electric grills, on their website.

H&Y Marketplace (www.hy1004.com): Based in New York and New Jersey, this Korean grocery store offers only a limited selection on its website. However, in addition to shipping nonperishables (such as Korean curry powder and dried bellflower root), H&Y will ship refrigerated and frozen foods, including rice cakes and fried tofu, to seventeen states and the District of Columbia.

KOAMart (www.koamart.com): A good source for a variety of ingredients, including Korean hot pepper flakes and paste, dried noodles, dried squid, dried shrimp, dried anchovies, and dried filefish, KOAMart also stocks a small selection of earthenware bowls, rice scoops, chopsticks, and soupspoons.

Amazon (www.amazon.com): More and more independent suppliers are selling Korean ingredients on Amazon, and the site is convenient to use, with hassle-free checkout. However, some of the prices can be eye-popping compared to those in an actual Korean grocery store. Be sure to double-check prices and products to ensure you're getting the items you need, because there are no returns on grocery items. The selection at Amazon depends on what the vendors are offering, but it's been expanding rapidly as more vendors come on board. Amazon is experimenting with selling fresh vegetables too.

index

F

fermented foods, 248–67
   containers for, 28, 30–31
   fish sauce for making kimchi, 267
   hot pepper paste, Korean, 258–59
   rice liquor, Korean, 262–63
   sardines, 266
   skate, spicy, 247
   soup soy sauce, Korean, 264–65
   soybean paste, 253–55
   soybean paste, extra-strong, 256–57
   see also kimchi
fernbrake, 10, 17
   bibimbap, 48–51
   with garlic and soy, 146
   mung bean pancakes, 186–87
filefish, dried, 14
   seasoned, 166
fish:
   raw, mixed rice with, 52–53
   see also seafood; *specific fish*
fish cakes, 17
   stir-fried, with soy sauce, 170
fish sauce, 17
   for making kimchi, homemade, 267
five elements, 7, 8
flowers, edible, 16
   panfried sweet rice cakes with, 286
food processors, 28
fruit-and-vegetable-water kimchi,
   124–25

G

gaji-namul, 141
galbi, L.A., 226
galchi-jorim, 168
gamja-croquettes, 204–5
gamja-doenjangguk, 88
gamjajeon, 183
gang-doenjang, 152
ganjang-eomuk-bokkeum, 170
garlic and mustard sauce, 275
gas burners, portable, 29
geomeunkong-jorim, 153
geundae-doenjangguk, 98
gimbap, 44–46
ginger, dessert punch with persimmons,
   cinnamon and, 280

ginseng (root), 18
   candy, 293
gochujang, 258–59
gochujeon, 194–95
gosari-namul, 146
gujeolpan, 245–46
guk-ganjang, 264
guksu, 64
gulbap, 47
gulmuchim, 167
gunmandu, 210–11
gyeoja-maneul-jang, 275
gyeran-guk, 87
gyeran-jidan, 273

H

haemul-jeongol, 102–3
haemul-pajeon, 189
haepari-naengchae, 242–43
health considerations, 7, 8
heukimja-gyeongdan, 290–91
hobakjeon, 190
hobakjuk, 79–81
hobak-saeu-bokkeum, 176–77
hoe-deop-bap, 52–53
hong-eo-hoe, 247
hot pepper flakes, Korean, 19–20
hot pepper paste, Korean, 20, 258–59
hot pepper powder, Korean, 20
hot peppers, *see* chili pepper(s)
hotteok, 206–7
hwajeon, 286–87

J

jangjorim, 158
janmyeolchi-ttangkong-bokkeum, 157
japchae, 230–31
japgokbap, 38
jat-jang, 275
jellyfish:
   salad, cold, 242–43
   shredded salted, 24
jeong-eo-ri jeotgal, 266
jeong-eo-ri jeotgal-muchim, 176
jerky, beef, 215
jjajangbap, 63
jjajangmyeon noodles, 10, 22
   noodles with black bean paste, 62–63